It's So You

it's so you

EDITED BY
MICHELLE TEA

35
WOMEN WRITE ABOUT
PERSONAL EXPRESSION
THROUGH FASHION & STYLE

SEAL PRESS

It's So You
35 Women Write About Personal Expression Through Fashion and Style
Copyright © 2007 by Michelle Tea

Published by
Seal Press
A Member of the Perseus Books Group
1400 65th Street, Suite 250
Emeryville, CA 94608

Library of Congress Cataloging-in-Publication Data

It's so you : 35 women write about personal expression through fashion and style / edited by Michelle Tea.
p. cm.
ISBN-13: 978-1-58005-215-3
ISBN-10: 1-58005-215-0
1. Women's clothing–Social aspects. 2. Fashion–Social aspects. 3. Lesbians–Clothing. 4. Feminism–Social aspects. I. Tea, Michelle.

GT1720.I88 2007
391'.2—dc22
2007016661

Cover design by Kate Basart/Union Pageworks
Interior design by Megan Cooney
Printed in the United States of America by Edwards Brothers
Distributed by Publishers Group West

For those who've given me clothes,
for the girls who have a hard time dressing themselves,
and in memory of the perfect leopard-print vintage half-slip,
lost somewhere in the U.S.A. while traveling, 1999.

contents

Introduction

MICHELLE TEA

LAST NIGHT I HAD a reading at a local bookstore. I was getting dressed in my room, a safe space for fantasy perhaps made even safer by the broken light on the ceiling that keeps the place swaddled in shadows. I put on a floor-length, lightly flowered skirt I'd found at a thrift store in Tucson, with a sort of crappy, thin sweater I got years ago at Forever 21 at the Mall of America, and a pair of tall black strappy shoes that a friend who worked for a magazine tossed my way following a photo shoot. I pulled fingerless knit gloves over my wrists because, despite the pastel explosion frothing down my legs, it's winter still, and cold. I needed a coat, so I grabbed a beat-up leopard one from my closet. The pockets are torn jokes, the lining is shredded, and it doesn't button, so I belted it around the waist with a gold lamé belt I found at a secondhand shop in Florida. I loved how dramatic the outfit felt, how I had to kick out when I walked to shoo the long hem of the skirt out from under my feet. I wore a locket with a pastoral scene around my neck and some junky fake-gold hoops in my ears. I left my house, and that's when it all fell apart.

Once in the real world, waiting at the corner to catch a bus, I realized my outfit looked insane. The edges of the skirt scraped along the filthy ground, sweeping a tide of grime behind me. Walking through a space larger than my cramped apartment was a challenge; the heels were so high, they required the high-legged pony trot of an over-eager *America's Next Top Model* aspirant, and with each step I risked tripping on the skirt and wiping out. Walking onto the bus, I had to gather the garment into my hands like some grand Edwardian dame ascending a staircase. Folks looked at me curiously, though *that* I am used to.

I have never been able to dress appropriately. Not ever. Not appropriate for the weather, not appropriate for age, not appropriate for the situation. Growing up in a broke family in a run-down town and attending Catholic school, I learned straightaway that clothes—fashion—were the key to everything. They transmitted your economic class, your social class, the state of your home life (a doting mother? a broken family? neglect? care?), probably your race, defiantly your subcultural affiliations, whether you were uptight or sluttish, whether you were smart or slovenly. As a kid, my clothes came from long-gone East Coast department stores like Bradlees or Zayre, but the good stuff came from Auntie Ella, who was so tight with the local Salvation Army that they called her whenever a fresh load of clothes came in. She'd get stuff that was often donated from the big, fancy stores in Boston: Filene's, Jordan Marsh. Sometimes the tags still dangled from the garments. Still, I learned to not let anyone know the clothes had such ignoble provenance. I learned that lesson while dashing through a cousin's house at a birthday party. *"What a pretty outfit!"* Someone complimented my getup, my most favorite to date—a blue velvet skirt and vest set with a creamy satin blouse that bowed at the neck. "Thank You, Auntie Ella Got It For Me At

The Salvation Army!" I crowed. Auntie Ella, sixty years old in leather pants, a turtleneck sweater, and tons of turquoise jewelry, choked on her Benson & Hedges 100. *"You tell 'em you got it at Filene's!"* she instructed. A few years later, in junior high, I found the best shirt ever at that same Salvation Army, a purple mesh football jersey with some boy's name on the back. I wore it all the time and told everyone it came from a made-up boutique in Boston. By the end of junior high, I refused to step foot in the thrift store at all, feeling retroactive shame for all I'd ever worn from the place. I'd stubbornly hang around outside while Auntie Ella and my grandmother gleefully shopped.

In Catholic school we wore uniforms, I was told, to squash the class jockeying and competition that fashion provokes. Uniforms were the great equalizer: Identical in our plaid skirts and button-up blouses, there was no way to tell whose parents could afford stuff from the mall and whose family was clothed in worn hand-me-downs. But, of course, there was. There were the girls who came to school with tight Jordaches under their skirts in the winter months, girls who wore coveted leather high-top Nikes on gym day. Gym day threw a huge wrench into the school's communist uniform intentions, and gym days, as I got older, increasingly became days when my inappropriateness was on parade. Black sweat suits with fuschia new wave stripes; black-and-white checkered shirts with asymmetrical snaps up the collar; leopard earrings; and spiked belts. My classmates called me "punk rock" like it was a bad thing, and I was stung. I'd always gotten along with them, the same kids for the past seven years, and I assumed that we'd all continue to like the same things.

I thought, naively, that they'd be excited by my new look, bought by my freshly divorced dad in an effort to show up my mom. He'd succeeded; the clothes were from Tello's, a heavily mirrored shop in East Boston that blared dance music and sold clothes I'd never seen before: miniskirts, clothes with slashing zippers, striped everything. My mother couldn't afford to buy us things from Tello's on her single-mom paycheck, but bachelor Dad could. His generosity was short lived, but the items he bought me that winter of 1984 have shaped my entire aesthetic since.

On a uniform-free school day that year—the Christmas holiday party—the nun who ran Our Lady of Assumption phoned my mother, asking her to bring a more "appropriate" outfit for me to wear to the school-wide party. I'd arrived in a purple striped miniskirt made of soft sweatshirt material; purple tights; a lighter-purple set of leg warmers; actual ballet shoes; a thin purple braid tied around my forehead, dangling purple feathers into my hair. Last, a Jordache pleather purse was slung across my body by its skinny purple cord. I have never again looked so awesome. In fact, every outfit I put together is a weak attempt to replicate that perfect, unappreciated look. Before my class assembled in the main hall, where I would debut the best outfit ever before the entire school, my mother showed up with a dress for me to change into—a prairie dress with an empire waist, tiers of navy blue gingham with a velvet bib. I looked like a giant baby, and the bothered principal was happy.

The power struggle between the head nun and me went on for the rest of my Catholic-school career. She called my mother on my junior high graduation day to bring me a dress to replace the strapless polka-dotted one I'd worn; amazingly, my mother refused. I felt a pissed-off triumph when I left that school, strangely proud of how they'd changed the school handbook to deal with girls who followed in my footsteps: no costume jewelry allowed, and the forbidden hairdos section had crappy illustrations of my own barely punk hair.

All this policing of my appearance helped shape my young understanding of the world as a place that punishes what it perceives as different. It helped me conceptualize the world—my world—as a land where those who dressed, thought, and acted ugly ruled, and anyone attempting to insert a bit of imagination got branded a troublemaker and punished accordingly. I entered a Catholic high school that asked me to leave when I dyed my hair black and began teasing it into a spidery snarl. Fights sprang up at home, became a permanent installation as my clothing got more wild and my mother more bewildered. Lots and lots of teary screaming as I began to realize I could say no to Mom and walk out of the house in my bondage-strap skirt, my shredded vintage dress, white clown makeup, and black lipstick. My stance made me an unsympathetic character, one who brought on her own doom. When some jocks beat up some of my friends and me in a Boston park—because the boy looked like a "fag," and the other girl and I like "freaks"—the basic feeling was that we'd asked for it, soliciting the violence with our big weird hair and pointy boots.

I understood deeply, instinctively, that there was a political dimension to all this. I knew that the people who spat at me in the street for wearing the big gold crucifix I'd found at the Salvation Army—I'd given up my protest and returned to the treasure trove, finding mounds of black lace dresses and Catholic accessories—didn't start trouble only with oddly dressed teenagers, but picked fights with gay people, black people, Puerto Rican people, Cambodian people. They were guys who thought certain girls were sluts and therefore fair game for their intentions. They messed with anyone they perceived to be weak or different. In Boston in the '80s, the streets were filled with these types of guys. I understood that their impulse to hurt or humiliate me and my friends was inseparable from their urge to beat up any one of their targets. It made me feel, years before I realized I was queer, an allegiance with gay people, with people of color, with homeless people. Fashion is a powerful thing, capable of provoking strong reactions. Fashion displays your cultural allegiances, or where you dissent. Where the larger culture is invested in keeping people in line, the punishment for dressing like a weirdo is real. People hurled projectiles out car windows. The head of the cosmetology shop at the lousy vocational high school I wound up at wouldn't allow me into her class, despite my good grades and earnest interest, because my blue hair disgusted her. I had gone to the voke specifically with the hope of getting into the cosmo shop and becoming a hairdresser. I spent my years there hiding out in the graphic arts shop, where I was allowed to slack off reading V. C. Andrews novels all day. I graduated from the trade school without a trade. Fashion determines everything.

Later, I had my own struggle with fashion, marking the era of my Lesbian-Feminist Nervous Breakdown. After learning that my stepfather had been spying sexually on my sister and me, I became obsessed with how women's clothing frames their bodies as vulnerable things to be looked at. I became painfully sensitive toward feeling vulnerable, being looked at. I sold trash bags full of the best girlie clothes ever to Buffalo Exchange (a Mode Merr hot-pink satin girdle with a matching bra encrusted with rhinestones, swagged with fake pearls, and dangling with fringe particularly breaks my heart) and began wearing neutered ensembles, lots of baggy denim, roomy T-shirts. Some hippie-esque skirts and dresses survived the cut, because they were comfortable and weren't trying to make me look sexy. I cut my hair short and stopped wearing makeup. I wore overalls, often with no shirt underneath, my scrawny boobs visible.

I had understood that women's objectification through clothing hinged on not only what we were encouraged to flaunt, but what we were forbidden to show. Why were my tits sexual? I was earnestly working to desexualize my entire body, and I resented the larger culture that had been trying to control my appearance for years, the larger culture that decided that my breasts were sexual and to be revealed only in strip bars, while men were free to walk around topless, grossing everyone out as they pleased. So I started going topless myself, and, with a gang of similarly pissed-off girls, got arrested for not wearing shirts in a calculated attempt to overthrow the law. The judge threw the case out; apparently, our toplessness was covered under freedom of speech.

Is fashion speech? What we wear or don't wear says a lot.

This period of policing my own wardrobe, driving any hint of femininity from it—as if I could control male creepiness by whittling myself down to a gender-neutral ball of anger draped in natural fabrics—faded out when I moved to San Francisco and discovered a community of queer girls who were managing to work out their issues with abuse, misogyny, feminism, men, and gender while looking totally hot. This was the '90s, so that hotness took the form of leather pants, leather boots, the occasional leather cap or vest borrowed cheekily from the leather fags we sometimes shared space with. I know it sounds bad, but trust me, it worked. Especially if the leather was ironically mixed with ripped-up concert T-shirts. There were also political T-shirts, denim vests covered with silk-screened patches and pins, dog collars as jewelry. There were lots of trucker hats, and wallet chains swung from many an ass. Everyone looked excellent and ready to fight. I started wearing dresses again, but the femininity was checked by spikes and tears and big clunky boots. If I wore dresses too often, I'd have to go on a spree of wearing ripped-up jeans and a shrunken flannel. In San Francisco in the '90s it was painfully clear that people communicated with each other through fashion; you had to carry a guide to what hanky color equaled what sexual proclivity as you cruised the bars, straining your eyes in the dark to see what color hanky was stuffed into the back pocket of whichever girl you liked. Which pocket, right or left, was crucial, too. I was ambivalent about being feminine, and when everyone was reading so deeply into each other's clothes, it seemed important to keep people guessing, though I'm sure it didn't help my love life any.

Another thing about that fashion moment was that it was cool to look broke. Mostly this was an authentic thing; there were a lot of broke people with great style. This meant I could run the streets in a layer of slips I bought from a homeless person selling stuff on the street. (Another thing: After being traumatized for years in Boston, it took me a while to not respond with a hostile "Fuck you!" every time a stranger said, "Nice hair." In San Francisco, they meant it.) Eventually, this working-class look got annoying, with many not-broke people adopting the style and the larger culture eventually appropriating the look on a grand scale, selling ironic netted baseball hats at Urban Outfitters. But San Francisco in the '90s was a great place to get my fashion back, taking cues from the girls dancing in bars beside me, standing on stages reading their poetry, marching in the street against something oppressive, always looking great in brutal-looking boots and prom dresses or assless leather chaps or mechanics' jumpsuits.

Now I'm at the tip of another fashion ship. I recently realized that I am thirty-whatever years old and my wardrobe consists mainly of outfits that make me look like a child, a slut, or both. It definitely leaves no questions about my economic status. But my economic status has changed. I am, amazingly, no longer broke, managing to make a comfy living doing my writing, something that occasionally makes me burst into tears, usually while taking a shower and marveling at my good fortune. It's hard to have money after you've spent your life judging and feeling superior to people who aren't broke. Now I'm one of them. What does this mean when it comes to how I should dress myself? At some point I realized I could buy *new* clothing, something I hadn't done in a long, long time. This realization that I maybe needed some new-new clothing hit me after I didn't get a job I wanted at the library. I almost certainly didn't get the job because I simply wasn't qualified—patching up broken books, fixing their cracked spines, not my forte—but in my depressed mind, I didn't get the job because I'd gone to the interview in a hand-me-down leather jacket with a permanent kink in the wide collar; a thrifted polyester skirt with a hole in the seam; a cast-off mock turtleneck a friend had given me when I realized that I was still at her party at 6 AM, had to be at work in an hour, and was still in slutty party clothes; and secondhand purple suede go-go boots. And this was my conservative outfit. A similar fashion meltdown occurred when I had to find a place to live and was being interviewed by landlords. Nothing I had looked like the clothing of a person who could indeed afford to live in these places. Something about my age nagged at me, too. Running around looking like a tore-up wreck was glamorous in my twenties, but ten years later it had begun to feel creepingly pathetic.

When I finally decided to buy some new-new clothes, I freaked out when I found out how much things cost. *Forty dollars! For a skirt?! Do you know what I could get at Thrift Town for forty dollars?* Walking around the giant department store full of clothing I *loved*, I felt a burst of anxiety that grew to the size of my environment, where all around me females shopped, not hyperventilating, just buying or not buying their $40 skirts. I ran out of there, caught my breath on the escalator to Muni, calmed down. Thank god I had been recently poor enough to get free therapy from the City of San Francisco and could process my inability to purchase a $40 skirt—which I could absolutely afford—without having a major meltdown. My therapist suggested that buying new clothes felt like a betrayal to my mom, since my last real memory of having new clothes were those great outfits my jerky dad bought me. Oh, therapy. I did worry about betraying—someone. Was it okay for me to buy a new skirt? Would people—who?—judge me? Was I selling out? My head was a mess. The passing of time helped fix it, as I simply adjusted to my new situation, my new desires. I fucking *wanted* a $40 skirt.

The way life moves, and moves me along with it, has brought me to a place where I can deal with having some money just as well as I could deal with having none at all; where I can have a variety of clothes to pick from, some put together, like the *suit* I just bought for important business meetings I swear I'm going to have any day now, some my beloved and familiar thrift-store-disaster fashions, like the metallic polyester gown with the broken snap I just bought for five bucks at Goodwill. Don't think it didn't hurt me to spend five bucks on it; with that broken snap, it should have been three. It was actually easier to spend a hundred and fifty bucks on the suit, which was probably worth $800 new, than to spend five bucks on a broken dress that was only worth three. But I bought it anyway, because it's blue and green and looks like the gown of a space-age mermaid queen. I no longer take it personally that people will judge me based on my appearance, nor do I feel torn up inside at the very real injustice of it. Instead, I work on having a vast enough wardrobe to manipulate the judgment I *want*. Sometimes I want to look like I just stepped out of a fantasy, and sometimes I want to look like I grew up with a trust fund. *Money goes to money,* my mother would often mutter ruefully, and she was right; looking like one of the moneyed classes is invaluable if you're trying to work with and get money from them. The fucked-up reality is, if you walk into a joint looking like you've got money to blow on clothes, people assume you're successful, which means capable, and they're more likely to entrust you with whatever you're trying to be entrusted with. After the '90s, when so many in my sphere bitched about the upper classes appropriating working-class fashion, I've decided to return to favor by appropriating rich-girl fashion, complete with a fake Louis Vuitton bag that is a total *trip* to carry around, as it makes rich people and high-end salespeople nicer to me, and broke people and low-end salespeople hostile.

You don't need to take my word that fashion—so often maligned in females as proof of our shallowness, our vanity, our childish simplemindedness—is a key that opens issues of class, safety, opportunity, politics. Keep reading and you'll find a whole mess of essays— hilarious, touching, bitchy, sweet, blissed-out, and angry—on how fashion has impacted the lives of the contributors to this book. How does any woman figure out what she wants to look like when so many cultural and subcultural forces are invested in what she should and should not wear?

Frances Varian reveals how, as a working-class woman, fashion hasn't failed her any more than feminism has, and that the two can come together in a way that is truly empowering. Felicia Luna Lemus takes a Proustian trip into the past on a wave of stinky Christian Dior lipstick, recalling past loves and her first glimpse at badass females. Jill Soloway struggles with how she wants the world to see her and with our complicity in crafting our visages. Parisa Parnian shows us how a genderqueer fashion line of clothing for female-born people who don't dress female was born. Adele Bertei takes us back to the birth of punk style in the East Village, tracing the safety pin as cultural icon to one broke artist's ripped shirt. Ali Liebegott merges fashion fantasy and fashion utility in the search for the perfect pair of bedroom slippers—the sort a cartoon bear might wear. Mary Woronov rants caustically about how American's once-glamorous fashion has slid *way* down into glorified underwear. Nicole Georges dips her toes into the dark thrill of scary fashion and scary sex. Debbie Rasmussen shows us how her politically motivated fashions took her away from and back to an outrageously dressed grandma. Chelsea Starr testifies to how shabbily dressed kids (and adults) get treated. Trina Robbins brings us into a temporary community of rabid thrifters. Diane di Prima runs through her own fashion epiphanies, from the Depression to today. Cintra Wilson pulls us with her out onto her wild fashion limbs. Sherilyn Connelly demonstrates how high the stakes are for a trans woman trying to find clothes that fit. Meghan Ward gives us a behind-the-scenes look at the runway. Laurie Stone navigates the feminist fallout from her face-lift. Laura Fraser details a lifetime of figuring out how to dress, and getting it right. Beth Lisick sees in a humble coat all she would like to see in herself. Cookie Woolner rails against the fashion industry's fat phobia. Jewelle Gomez explores how fashion interacts with economics, race, and girls' bodies. Samara Halperin shares her ingenious strategy for embracing and defying a trend. Kat Marie Yoas investigates the limits of using fashion to pass as a higher class. Kate Bornstein traces her fashion evolution from hippie to Scientology skipper to SM dyke to Betsey girl. Jenny Shimizu reflects on her fashion education, aging, and motorcycles. Dexter Flowers details the horror a teen feels when her mom's hippie boyfriend starts wearing the same clothes as her. Sandra Tsing Loh free-associates laser surgery, the pressure to work out, and receiving another author's mail. Eileen Myles speaks in praise of shades of gray and adopting the casual elegance of the upper class. Silja J. A. Talvi shares her adventures in front of and behind the makeup counter. Cindy Emch offers a shoe-lover's manifesto. Tara Jepsen takes her boobs into her own hands. Kim Gordon ruminates on the trend of celebutante crotch-flashing. Mary Christmas explains how a model finds punk rock and feminism. Jennifer Blowdryer takes us on her personal fashion carousel. Rhiannon Argo finds fashion in the street and offers suggestions on spontaneous fashion creation. Ellen Forney invites you to help dress a butch girl named Pony.

These essays show the real possibilities of fashion, as both a delight and an escape in its own right, and as a springboard for talking about, oh, everything worth talking about. I hope you dig them as much as I do.

My Body (Yawn!), My Self: A Wee Rant

SANDRA TSING LOH

SOMEWHERE PAST THE isle of forty, I realized I had become very, very tired . . . of looking at myself in the mirror. I was so bored of it! Good grief, I'd been looking at this Self for decades now. When would the tedium end? Note that I say "tired," not "upset." The upset part—lying spread-eagle, facedown on the covers, the body racked with hysterical, gutteral sobs because, as I aged, I realized I was rapidly turning into Abe Lincoln— had occurred several years earlier, during my conveniently scheduled Early Midlife Crisis.

Yeah, that meltdown occurred at age thirty-six, a year, for me, of mirage-like TV-writing deals. I live in Los Angeles, a city whose Hollywood horrors have already been more thoroughly covered than a running-fence Christo installation. From the point of view of my face, suffice it to say that during that television pilot–heavy year, I found myself many mornings at ten o'clock riding glass-walled elevators to a lot of frightening meetings with a lot of fresh-faced young people wearing a lot of pale colors off which daylight reflectively bounced and binged and boomeranged. In multiple funhouse reflections, I could see I looked not just like Abe Lincoln, but like a hound dog, Leonard Nimoy–esque, the veritable twin of Bert Lahr (a.k.a. the Cowardly Lion in *The Wizard of Oz*). Those eye bags haunted me day and night.

So I took $3,000 of the mirage-like, now-long-gone television money and had the bags lasered right out. What with the Valium (and Vicodin?), one of the most truly euphoric days of my life. I remember much helpless giggling behind my ice pack.

But now here comes the strange part: The lunchtime outpatient procedure was so quick, so simple, so painless, and so effective—I suddenly looked effortlessly well rested, no one could deny it—that my outer appearance began not to improve, but to literally unravel. Not just the bags, but the scales, fell from my eyes. For a decade I had cosseted my eye bags like royal invalids, creaming them, lotioning them—after reading a tip in a beauty magazine, I even tried smearing them with Preparation H. For years, I had believed my outer appearance depended on my own painstaking, self-lacerating efforts, my own magical, secret, pseudoscientific rituals. But no. So now that I was free of the baggage, both fleshy and mental . . . there, there, there on the bathroom counter! That busy, self-important cityscape of skin revitalizers, moisturizers, scrubs, washes, lifters, exfoliators. I suddenly saw that drab, dusty shantytown for what it was—an utter sham! With one sweep of my arm I razed it down. I threw those Clinique and Nivea jars and tubes away, every single one!

When I was the servant of the eye bags (and they my master), oh, I used to be so caved over in apology for my hideous presence. I wouldn't dare leave the house without my hair meticulously styled, makeup labored over, wearing what I hoped (prayed!) were my hippest outfits. But now, with the eye bags gone, it was like my female debt was finally, suddenly paid in full. And the pendulum was swinging wildly the other way. With the flotilla of worthless cosmetics gone, what else could I do away with? Ideas were flying to me—why wear earrings, why put on lipstick, why even (the sloth that dare not speak its name) . . . *change out of the clothes you slept in?* I have this pair of $10 black drawstring Target pants that balance perilously on culture's very mother-who-works-from-home fulcrum. Are they running pants? Exercise pants? Pajamas? Who knows? This is what we citizens ponder, in the new Target clearance rack Isaac Mizrahcracy.

And so I have developed a sliding scale for wearing outside the house the clothes I slept in. I believe it is acceptable to drop my kid off at preschool in these pants. And to grocery shop in said pants. It is definitely *not* okay to go on television with them . . . well, not unless one is appearing on the panel of some poorly rated news show on some MSNBC 2 or 3 channel and they're shooting just from the waist up. No one expects style from haggard political pundits!

Although, luck of the draw, sometimes one might surprise oneself into style anyway. Check out this Ann Taylor striped T-shirt I'm wearing—Goodwill, $1! That's right—$1! Don't mean to brag, but I paid for it in quarters! I'll admit my giant Costco painter's pants were a bit of a Waterloo. The price was okay—$12—but the waist was so big, it called to mind female prison guards, and then you're walking around with the big red KIRKLAND label stamped across your buttocks like they're massive twin hamhocks of Costco-brand chuck. I'm still wearing them, sure, but . . . on the upside, look at my fabulous shoes. They are these very compli-cated leather walking shoes with conspicuous stitching and ribbing and important-looking, almost bossy, ventilating holes all over them. They are probably German and expensive, but for me? Free! Because, like all my shoes, they're castoffs! That's the upside of having Los Angeles girl-friends of a certain age who are rabid shoe buyers. It's such trouble to go back to Nordstrom to return a color they don't like; it's easier just to give them to me. Thanks! A half size too large, but better too big than too small. And to fill the void, here come the men's sweat socks.

It's not new clothes I hate so much as clothes shopping. Several decades in, it is the mall (a valley girl who herself is in her forty-somethingth year) that has become wearisome to me—depressing, odious, exhausting. Somehow one always ends up at Victoria's Secret in a Sisyphean daze, listening—yet again—to Madonna dance beats (she, too, seems one hundred), pawing through endless piles of not just bras but underpants (high waisted, bikini, Angel, thong, et cetera). Meanwhile, glowering all around are posters not just of ten-foot-tall, eighteen-year-old supervixens, but of men! Men of rock-hard pecs, gelled hair, curled lip! How gay are our Madison Avenue ad executives? I just came to buy underwear!

Speaking of which, even aside from my hair salon's rates having risen over the years from $50 to $90, one day it hit me how much I'd come to physically loathe getting my hair cut. The faux-antiqued walls, the *WWD* magazines, the jumping, club-kid haircutters (who are by now quite middle-aged, just like me, never mind the desperately spiky hair, the papery skin), the sudden, kidney-piercing shrieks of "Oh my *god!*" The owner of the salon is Taz—that's the name of the salon, "Taz"—and it suddenly struck me how sick to death I was of hearing about Taz: Taz was here, Taz was there, Taz was in South Beach, Taz was on a film shoot in Arizona, where he was developing a new line of "product," including some $30 chi-flavored botanical serum I'd have to, as usual, fake interest in. You know what, Taz? They're just split ends. *Fuck off!*

Due to a computer mailing list error, there's a hip Melrose art gallery that mistakenly believes JERRY STAHL (author of *Permanent Midnight*) lives at my house. Hovering before the recycling bin, I sometimes cradle, to my chest, the mail of JERRY STAHL. Every time I see JERRY STAHL in photos—author, party, or otherwise—it seems he's wearing the same black T-shirt and leather jacket. Why can I not also wear just the one Gap tee? Why do *women* writers need to keep changing their look with complicated shoes and belts and jewelry and hats? I suddenly realize I want to be a man, and not just any man, but JERRY STAHL.

Does JERRY STAHL weigh himself every day? I doubt it. Now, I do not either. Talk about egocide. For a woman to not know how much you weigh—who *are* you? Can you believe it took my female brain almost three decades of stepping on the scale before I realized that? It wasn't really panning out for me. I was never going to see a pleasing number. I was never going to jump up, pump my fist in the air, and say, "Mission accomplished!" And anyway, who cares? When I grow so fat I have to butter myself to get out the door, then I'll deal with it. (I know JERRY STAHL would approve—he's probably buttering himself now!)

You think I'm pathetic? Look at my friend Carolyn, who in the last three months has lost twelve and a half pounds. Good for her, you say, but consider what she's spending:

- Jenny Craig: $100 initiation fee, $30 a month for counseling, plus many little tins of food at $400-plus a month

- What with all the deprivation and the sensitized palate, the feel-good sports ion water she deserves: $2 a bottle, several a day

- New gym membership: $40 a month

- New running shoes that really fit, air spring, cushioned heel, plus important new sports leggings, new socks, et cetera: $100

- iPod to entertain her during all that treadmilling: $350

- "Distressed" new jeans recently purchased to celebrate a drop of two sizes: $300

That's right, that's what distressed skinny jeans cost now: $300. Carolyn tried on jeans at the mall for three hours before she finally found the right snug fit. Let's not even count the new high-heeled, strappy shoewear to go with the jeans, the $120 haircut with highlights

(I admit, when she asked, I sent her to Taz!). Carolyn's self-esteem is glowing, she's going out more at night, and what with all the *miles* she's earned, she's contemplating a vacation—maybe a cruise, with salsa dancing, windsurfing, parasailing. There's more confidence, laughter, tossing the head back. At this point in time, in America, I can't think of one person who wouldn't pump the air and say, "You go, girl!" I can't name one female self-help book that urges you, now that you're forty, to simply accept the extra twelve and a half pounds.

If we were all wearing sarongs, no one would know the difference—that's why we need the status of the skinny jeans. When it comes to cultural oppression, jeans are our burqa. We labor for the jeans, we starve for the jeans, we pray to the jeans that they'll close ... and $300 later, we've brought our seventy cents on the dollar down to forty-three. Female emancipation is always defined in terms of expanding our economic footprint. Our personal power is defined by our earning; our cultural power is defined by purchasing—how we vote with our dollars, how we flock (or don't) to movies on opening weekends (where we lose to teen boys, where we fail Susan Sarandon and reward Adam Sandler). In this era of feminism's Condé Nasticization ("I feel, therefore I buy"), there's no desired female identity unrelated to the flow of dollars. (Although recently I saw a comforting PBS show called *The Cheese Nun*. She's just a nun who loves cheese—though probably by now even The Cheese Nun has a booming business. Damn you, Cheese Nun!)

But what this implies, conversely, is that a woman who buys nothing *is* nothing.

And I think this is wrong.

I think we should revolt. I think we should simply *stop buying!* Yeah, I see us women piling into our SUVs, our Volvos, our minivans, our cute little lime green VW bugs, our bikes—no, a bus, we should charter a bus, an old bus, an old municipal transportation–type bus filled with thermoses of yes, damn it all anyway, *tap water*, and driving out to the desert. Grrrls doing it for themselves, all together, we could get off this consumerist, fashion, Taz-ridden grid! We'll dump the cars, change into sarongs . . . go barefoot . . . drop out . . . unplug . . . start our own Burning Woman Festival! At the very least, we could burn our bras! Which would probably take a full month, because by now we have so damn many of them. From Victoria's Secret alone, I have Angel bras, T-shirt bras, Wonderbras, Miracle Bras—I've bought so many bras through the years, I could make my own giant bra ball.

It would make some kind of giant, fabulous, D-cup-size conflagration!

All we need is some beer!

And now that I'm saving so much on moisturizer, for that I will spring.

S.W.A.K.

FELICIA LUNA LEMUS

*I raised to my lips a spoonful of the tea in which I had soaked a morsel of
the cake. An exquisite pleasure had invaded my senses, something isolated,
detached, with no suggestion of its origin. And at once the vicissitudes of life
had become indifferent to me, its disasters innocuous, its brevity illusory—
this new sensation having had on me the effect which love has of filling me
with a precious essence; or rather this essence was not in me it was me. I
had ceased now to feel mediocre, contingent, mortal.*

—Marcel Proust, *Remembrance of Things Past*

*. . . and round the neck of the bottle was a paper label, with the words
DRINK ME BEAUTIFULLY printed on it in large letters. However, this bottle
was NOT marked poison, so Alice ventured to taste it, and finding it
very nice (it had, in fact, a sort of mixed flavour of cherry-tart, custard,
pine-apple, roast turkey, toffee, and hot buttered toast), she very soon
finished it off.*

—Lewis Carroll, *Alice's Adventures in Wonderland*

I.

Exfoliate: Reveal what exists just below the surface.
(And the ritual begins. . . .)

Proust bites into his legendary madeleine cookie, and gulp, Alice downs the contents of a bottle marked DRINK ME. Before they know it, they're wandering a twisting road of recollections and alternate realities. Personally, I don't do dairy, so no buttery madeleine has touched my lips in the recent past. And, unlike Alice, I would most assuredly puke if I drank turkey-flavored liquor. Those differences aside, I did recently partake of an indulgence similar to theirs—a tempting morsel, a mysteriously intoxicating substance . . . a too-expensive tube of red lipstick.

Stuck in a gloomy mood, Bauhaus playing on my iPod, the sky filled with heavy, dark clouds about to unleash a storm, I'd suddenly found myself—how can I say this without sounding like a complete loser?—at Sephora, obsessively searching for the perfect shade of gothy, blood-red lipstick. Christian Dior red lipstick, to be precise—the same brand my friends and I used to lust after in high school. Dressed head to toe in black, witch-boot buckles jangling with each step, we'd troll the mall on weekends and steal tester tubes of Dior off spotlessly shining department store displays. Vampires might not cast reflections in mirrors, but they are damned vain creatures. Our designer lipstick made us untouchably regal, like no matter how fucked-up and out of control our lives were, at least we were impeccably pouted through it all. Action Red #526.

Seeing as I no longer rely on sticky fingers to satisfy my transgressive needs, this time I paid for the lipstick. Unfortunately, as happens so often when I spend more money than I really can afford, buyer's remorse accompanied the receipt. I left the lipstick untouched in its glossy cardboard box for days. When I finally gave in to temptation, I took my time. I slowly wound the lipstick's angled tip up. I admired its shining, smooth, and untouched surface. And I sniffed the lipstick, expecting some expensive, subtle scent of luxury to tickle my senses.

Instead, the lipstick smelled rank, like maybe it'd been sitting on warehouse and retail shelves too long. Any normal person would have taken that as reason to exchange the lipstick or maybe just throw it out, but I'm stubborn. I wanted the lipstick, the exact one I already had in my hands. Besides, corporate retail promises of worry-free returns or not, I feared if I took the lipstick back to the store, the salesperson would be thinking, *You're just not cut out for red lipstick. Maybe you should try a neutral taupe.* This pathetic, I'm-scared-I'm-getting-old-and-boring social anxiety horror film playing in my brain, I told myself to ignore the lipstick's repugnant perfume, to quit being so particular, to just get over it and wear the stuff.

So I scrubbed my lips gently with a toothbrush to smooth my canvas. I hadn't bought a "primer" base coat lip liner or brush, so I just steadied the lipstick in my characteristically caffeine-trembling hand the best I could. And with that one gesture—Proust's cookie-crumb trail and Alice's boozy-woozy looking glass combined—my unexpected adventure began.

II.

Apply first layer: Carefully coat your lips.

I bite lips—the lips of other writers from which words dangle, my lover's lips, my own lips. I'm not talking about some now-and-then nibbles for cutesy emphasis. No, my cannibalism is serious business; I chipped one of my lower teeth just last month because of how much I bite my own lips and pull on dried flakes until they tear free. This habit—one I seemed to have acquired at some unmarked crossroads of adulthood— made itself instantly known as incompatible with the wearing of lipstick, particularly red lipstick, and most especially rancid red lipstick. Within minutes of pristine application, Dior Action Red #526 coated my teeth and tongue and—stranger things have been known to happen, but I can't think of many—snap, my brain was flooded with lucid memories of the first girlfriend I ever fucked with self-confident bravado.

In homage to said long-ago ex's preferred shade of lipstick, let's call her Cherry. Cherry and I were in a relationship—or whatever it is one could call that type-A-personality, processing-laden, fuck-filled mess we tortured each other with—nearly a decade ago. We were both living in the misery of Southern California's neoconservative stronghold, Orange County. The place was my hometown; she was only passing through. Back then I was trying my hand at being boyish, and I liked it. Lots. I had a barbershop haircut and fresh-washed face, and I wore lads' clothes. She, on the other hand, was a lipstick girl: imported lip tints encased in miniature etched glass jars; 99-cent-store lipsticks with faux-tortoise-shell plastic tubes; trendy, matte-black bullet-shaped lipsticks that she traded with her friends—just always lipstick, from the minute she woke until the second she fell asleep, lipstick. Cherry's bathroom drawers were overflowing lipstick treasure chests. When she was getting ready to go out, she'd close her eyes, reach her skinny, nail-bitten hand into the top drawer, randomly select a tube, apply that day's mystery shade, blot with a ragged scrap of toilet paper, reapply, smack her lips together, and tuck the paint into her back pocket. The one thing she never did was check her teeth. More often than not, she wore a healthy smear of color on her crooked front teeth. Usually maraschino-cherry red. On occasion orange. Once purple. Rarely pink. Creamy, glossy, frosted, and sometimes glittery. All of it incredibly hot.

One night we went to see *The Maltese Falcon* at a revival theater. We were killing time at a coffeehouse before the movie. We'd finished our coffees, her mug lined all along its lip with red smeared from her lips, and we were about to leave. She dug into her purse and pulled out a tube of lipstick—also red, but apparently not the same one she was already wearing. She put it on. "Whale ass," she said, and scrunched her face. Whale ass. That's what she called lipstick that had gone bad. Strange girl; no matter how whale ass old they were, she never threw out her lipsticks. We went off to the movie and ate up the Orange County stink-eye we got walking down the street holding hands. Me with my little-boy outfit and her with those damn red lips. We looked dangerously good.

Cherry only wore that particular lipstick once or twice again while we dated, but from that night forward I was filled with anticipatory thrill every time I saw her lips painted red. Polite, distant cousin to scat play, the stagnant petroleum and decomposing floral taste of whale ass left on my mouth after we made out was pure, deviant thrill.

III.

Blot: Using tissue, remove excess.
Whale ass or not, red lipstick is criminal.

I first learned this rule when I was seven years old. My grandma and I were visiting one of her neighborhood friends. While they drank coffee and talked, I snuck off to the bathroom to rifle through whatever treasures I might find. Jackpot—one sink drawer held a trove of items that I'd seen ladies on television use but that didn't exist in my puritanical home. A silver-handled eyelash curler, mascara (black, brown, and blue!), eyeliner pencils, pearly eye shadows, bright rosy blusher, fancy pink cotton swabs . . . and lipsticks. Oh my, the lipsticks! So many colors and scents, and all of them exotic and thrilling and damn, I wanted to steal one so badly. The first I opened smelled like Juicy Fruit, another smelled like baby talc, a third stung my lips when I tried it on. I wiped off that one with toilet paper and resumed my hunt. And that's when I found heaven.

Bright ruby red, like peppermint candies, Dorothy's shoes, and my Radio Flyer wagon all combined, the lipstick shimmered invitingly. I knew there'd be hell to pay for putting it on, but I didn't care. I'd always been good at coloring within the lines, but my expertise included felt-tip markers on paper, not lipstick on chapped lips. The staining, thick red lipstick ended up on the skin around my mouth as much as on my actual lips. Still, I thought I did a good job. I thought I looked glamorous. And I thought I just might be able to pull it off.

No such luck. The second I walked back into the living room, my grandmother had a conniption. "You horrible girl, what have you done?"

"Ay, it's okay," her friend said, laughing. "You were just playing dress-up, weren't you?"

The scowl on my grandma's face made it clear she wanted me to beg for forgiveness, but I didn't. My grandma was so horrified by my behavior—rummaging through her friend's things, failing to apologize— that she abruptly cut her visit short. She didn't even take time to wipe my face clean first; she just picked up her purse and dragged me out the door. My chaos-inducing red lipstick sealing my lips shut, it was as my grandma and I raced toward home that the cops came.

We had just turned the corner and were approaching the house where our block's *cholos* and *cholas* hung out. Same as on most afternoons, they sat clustered together on the front porch, laughing and flirting and drinking beer. For no readily apparent reason, a patrol car pulled onto the block and slowed as it approached the house. A couple of the *cholos* started throwing their empties lazily toward the car, the bottles landing softly on their scraggly dried lawn and nowhere near the patrol car. With this, the officers parked and exited their vehicle, hands on holsters and batons. That's when things got ugly. The bottles turned into well-aimed missiles. As my grandmother pulled me across the street, one bottle hit the patrol car's windshield and shattered on the sidewalk near my feet.

I knew I was supposed to be scared, but I wasn't. I was inspired. Although my grandma taught me to think the gangster kids were bad and we were good, the reality was that my own seemingly goody-two-shoes household harbored a festering mess of secrets and transgressions that no kid should have to deal with. Even though I was usually a very well-behaved kid, right then I wanted to yank myself free of my grandmother's grip and throw some bottles, too, maybe not at the cops, but at the cracked sidewalk at the very least. My arthritic grandma kept whisking me down the block. I could feel the tight mask of red lipstick smeared across my face as I turned and saw the police officers draw their service pistols and aim.

THE LAW:

January 1845: New York State legislature passes "An Act to Prevent Persons Appearing Disguised and Armed," which authorizes the pursuit and arrest of any person who, "having his face painted, discolored, covered, or concealed, or being otherwise disguised, in a manner calculated to prevent him from being identified, shall appear in any road or public highway, or in any field, lot, wood, or enclosure."

1800: Queen Victoria declares the use of makeup to be an impolite and vulgar habit worthy only of prostitutes and actors.

1770: Legislation condemning "lip paint" is introduced to British Parliament. The proposed law states that "women found guilty of seducing men into matrimony by a cosmetic means could be tried for witchcraft." Who founded our country six short years later? Those same sexually repressed, witch-fearing, capital punishment–crazed Pilgrims. But of course.

As two more cop cars, sirens blaring and lights pulsating, pulled onto the block in a suspiciously near-immediate response, I rubbernecked to watch the gangster girls in their high heels, skin-tight black jeans, and tube tops cheering on their boys. Same as I would later in my goth days, those girls wore their hair teased high, powdered their faces geisha pale, and lined their eyes with tons of liquid black eyeliner. Best of all, their bright Chevy-red lips curled into sexy snarls as they screamed at the cops to go fuck themselves.

"Hands above your head, bitch," I heard one cop shout in response. Red lips curled even harder and spat at the cops. Those girls refused to go down without a fight. Their screams echoed down the block. When we finally got home, my grandma triple-locked the front door behind us and pushed me into the bathroom.

"Clean off that junk," she said. She handed me a wad of tissues and left the room.

I stared at myself in the mirror and carefully wiped away only the lipstick that had smeared onto my chin and cheeks. And then I admired my reflection. With my red lipstick, I saw in myself a miniature version of our block's tough gangster girls. I was counting the years until I could join their ranks. I replayed on my lips, over and over, what the cops had called the girls, and I decided then and there that it must be a good thing to be a bitch. This, I later learned, was exactly true.

IV.

Reapply: This will set the desired result.

In contemporary American society, where any girl with DIY chops knows a powder package of Cardinal Red #9 Rit dye can be bought for less than three bucks at her corner drugstore, it's hard to understand how red dye was ever considered sacred, let alone more valuable than actual gold, but it was.

Since prehistoric times, my ancestors have harvested cochineal beetles *(Dactylopius coccus)* from prickly-pear cacti found in what is now Mexico to make red dye. When Montezuma I, the fifth emperor of the Aztec Empire, came to power in 1440, he tyrannically forced his subjects to pay extravagant tributes—including forty bags of cochineal dye—in his honor each year. And when Hernán Cortés "discovered" the Aztec Empire in 1519, he took control of the region's goods, including cochineal dye, and shipped them to Spain. Cochineal was instantly the most sought-after dye in all of Europe.

How was it that a bunch of bug coloring could be so valuable? Well, the ancients may not have known that cochineal beetles produced carminic acid to avoid being attacked by other insects, but the fact remained that, when ground and boiled, the parasitic little bugs made for what was long the world's most wicked, bright, and colorfast carmine dye. Perhaps adding to the appeal, cochineal dye was rare. The labor process was prohibitively intensive: About a million of the tiny insects were needed to produce one pound of water-soluble dye. Considering this, and the cost of maintaining a vicious police-state colony and sixteenth-century shipping, Spanish-traded cochineal dye was truly worth more than its weight in gold.

Something deep in my Chichimecca Mexican-Indian genetic being knows my ancestors didn't freely hand over their bags of cochineal to any of the colonizing jerks who came to power. Ancient Chichimeccas were anarchists; they actively resisted Aztec and Spanish rule alike.

Their name, a Spanish derivation of a Nahuatl word that roughly translates into "barks nonsensically like dogs and bitches," was meant to be the lowest of insults. Fuck that. I have a strong hunch that my ancestors proudly fought like dogs and bitches for their independence and power. Vanity schmanity; like the cochineal-dyed blankets and baskets ancient Chichimeccas carried with them on their nomadic journeys, my red-dyed lips are radical inheritance.

V.
S.W.A.K.

I have a confession to make: After trying to wear the Dior red lipstick for a couple days, I ended up returning it. The rotting-flower stench and perpetually ruby-tinted-teeth gig just weren't my cup of tea. Like Proust's sweets and Alice's bottle of tricks, the magic-potion red dye has passed from my lips. But the trip it took me on will stay with me forever.

My Most Absurd Risks

CINTRA WILSON

A GUY FRIEND once told me, "Cintra, you don't wear outfits, you wear *costumes.*"

He was kind of right. I lack subtlety and dress for theatrical effect. I hit my fashion moods square on the nose with a crowbar—and there are a lot of them. I invariably end up looking like one of the seventeen discrete schizophrenic personalities of Sybil, if they had all been styled by Quentin Crisp.

There are, however, some recurring themes.

I like to dress for power, to inspire lust, awe, and intimidation. It's protective. These days, I settle for pinstripes and sexually hostile footwear, but that's only because therapy has mellowed me out a lot. If I thought I could pull it off without serious controversy, I would wear a high-tech, dominatrixy, rubberized Kevlar Batgirl suit every day, replete with tool belt and stun baton. I've always found a certain amount of dazzle camouflage useful, probably because I was permanently traumatized by my early teen years in the San Francisco Bay Area.

As it is for most weird children, junior high was a largely regrettable and humiliating experience. I had always gone to nurturing, sheltered little schools for the gifted and/or emotionally disturbed, usually with less than forty kids in them. As a result of trying to emulate my personal friend and idol, Matt Kramer—a boy prone to attending all ceremonies of life in an Adidas tracksuit—I had become accidentally androgynous. I had a very short Dorothy Hamill haircut (which was also, coincidentally, the 1950s greaser style known as a "DA," or "duck ass," and therefore redolent of Fonzie) and wore deliberately unisex ensembles. My favorite article of clothing was an ochre T-shirt with a black velveteen decal of Daffy Duck ironed upon it. I felt that friendship with Matt Kramer somehow required me to soft-pedal the whole "girl" thing, because if I were too obviously female, in those heady days of Judy Blume and Farrah Fawcett-Majors, social embarrassment threatened to make our cross-gender friendship wholly impossible. I tried to conceal from Matt that I was any more a potential social liability than his other friend Eric Frampton—therefore, gender was out.

I was successful, in that I pretty much forgot I was a girl. It wasn't really brought to my attention much, except when people in parking lots would say to my mother, "Ma'am? Your boy just hit my Mazda when he opened his car door." My mother apologized but never bothered to correct these people about my sex. I never apologized, because I was annoyed they couldn't tell I was a girl.

My biggest fashion crisis, at that point, was that I never succeeded in getting a coveted Matt Kramer–style Adidas tracksuit. For my birthday, my mom got me an ill-fitting, double-knit polyester warm-up ensemble from JCPenney—in bright fuchsia, with two thick, uncool idiot stripes up the legs and sleeves. Needless to say, it went directly under the bed until I could sneak it into the Hefty bag full of discarded household items that was picked up once a month on the curb in front of our house by a truck that read AID TO RETARDED CITIZENS on the side.

"That tracksuit and an Adidas tracksuit are *not the same thing at all*," I complained. "And those plastic Korean nurse shoes you're wearing aren't fooling anyone, either."

"Everyone thinks they're Reeboks!" my mom squealed, doing something like a small Mexican hat dance to mock me. I didn't point out that anyone with better than 20/100 vision could read the ersatz label on them that said REAKOOR, which for me would have been as mortifying as wearing one of those plastic Queen Anne collars that dogs wear after surgery. I prayed I'd get the Adidas suit for Christmas, two months later—instead, I got the exact same double-knit JCPenney abortion . . . but in *lime green*. Santa Claus really fucked me that time.

"*Only* Retarded Citizens would wear that thing," I sneered.

"Well, then, you're retarded!" my mom said, cheerfully.

This tragic Christmas experience branded a permanent imprint on my mind, the same way that Scarlett O'Hara was forever marked by visions of the burning South. As God was my witness, *someday I would have fashionable clothing, by any means necessary*.

My dream would take a long, long time to realize. Right then, sadly—due to my status as a non-wage-earning child at the mercy of my mother's unintentionally sadistic generosity—it was wholly impossible. For a long time, however, my largest obstacle was my own taste.

I didn't realize that outward androgyny was a problem until I transferred to the local Middle School of the Great Unwashed in the middle of seventh grade. I was oblivious to the fact that girls had complex, Byzantine fashion laws, which would be rigidly enforced by an abusive jury of my peers. "Are you a *lesbian?*" small packs of evil-smiling Lolitas with matching camel toes, visible nipples, and four-inch wedges would ask me. At that point, I was not yet the terrifying verbal gorgon I would later become, so I would say nothing. I would sulk, feeling hurt, angry, and weak. I thought my female classmates looked like whores—real, actual whores—but I wasn't about to get up in their orthodontic grills about it. I tried to be invisible, to simply dress in order to avoid derision, while hiding my body as much as possible.

When I went to high school, I apparently failed to conceal my body well enough, because I got Male Attention. I was fundamentally too weird to do anything with it, but I did get it. This, paired with my natural obnoxiousness, eventually alienated all of the other girls in my class—which was painful, but in truth, I wasn't ever going to successfully work out as "one of the girls" anyway. They were the wealthy daughters of proctologists and ballerinas and knew, more or less, how to behave like civilized people in public. I, on the other hand, was just beginning to really feel the postpubescent effects of attention deficit disorder, which they didn't have a name for yet. Back then it was known by the clinical name of "being a total spaz."

I did, however, realize an instant benefit of being ostracized from the In Crowd and having no friends: I was now at liberty to disregard their penny loafers, 501 jeans, and layered polo shirts (which in my pathetic case were all palsied imitations from JCPenney, anyway) and dress the way I had always secretly yearned to, which was in the style of a new wave supervillain. Overnight, I embraced punk rock as a serviceable day look. Punk was a nice creative outlet, with the distinct advantage of thrift. But, contrary to what I had believed, it was not an inoculation against humiliating fashion disasters.

I tried once, in lieu of actual punk accessories, to wear a rather large industrial boat chain, which hampered my movement considerably and made me look styled not by Vivienne Westwood, but by Ghost of Jacob Marley. Once, before a concert, I rushed to soak some overly new-looking jeans in an entire gallon of bleach, didn't rinse them very well, and wore them soaking wet, since there was no time to dry them.

The smell was overpowering; my legs were wrinkled and itchy. I spent the night at an older Cool Girl's house that night, and she forced my pants to sleep outside.

My real style travesties, however, were yet to come: They mostly took place after the first weeks of a revolutionary new youth corruption known as MTV.

When the Madonna "Borderline" video came out, a latent capsule of brazen sluttiness burst within me. Somehow, in that come-to-Madonna moment, I realized I was born to wear a white men's tank top with a black lace bra underneath. Everything changed and was suddenly better for me. The older female gym teacher even warned other girls against hanging out with me, telling them that I was "bad news." This was a small sort of infamy (read: attention! At last!), the success of which encouraged me greatly to redouble my efforts and go *further*.

Madonna, within what seemed like seconds, became the internationally recognized symbol for high school slut-ism, so instead I went completely bonkers for Grace Jones. I shaved the back of my head, dyed it black, sprayed the rest straight up, bleached it white, and bought some candy-apple-red patent stiletto heels and a boxy gray dress with the most enormous shoulder pads available. Needless to say, being a short white chick, this was a less successful wannabe effort than my homage to Madonna, but when you're fifteen, you believe you can do anything. The architectural angles of Grace Jones inspired my lifelong love affair with severe tailoring. Madonna's cushy navel was teasingly available—even a wee bit daring and avant garde, if you were jailbait. But Grace Jones had real couture menace—elegance, control, savage juju—all the visual earmarks of a *predator*. I was inspired to abandon whatever slim fashion inhibitions I had left.

❁

Delighted by the attention-getting possibilities of 1980s fashion, I became a club kid. My first efforts usually involved long black gowns with big ropes of pearls, an enormous black taffeta bow wrapped around my hair, and a shellacked little spit curl in the middle of my forehead, inspired by the verse "When she was bad, she was horrid." I was extremely rude, always carried a thermos full of espresso to enhance my already intolerable personality, and lied that my last name was Sinatra.

As a result of frequenting nightclubs, my next fashion hero was Leigh Bowery, a British club celebrity whose outfits I scanned obsessively in *The Face* magazine. Leigh Bowery wore red sequined bodysuits he'd constructed with a built-in ski mask that made him look like a hybrid of Jayne Mansfield and an angry manatee. He had cheek piercings and used extra foam padding and corsets to create illusions of bewildering physical deformity similar to that of an overweight fire hydrant. A bald man, Bowery's "hairstyle" was often a sunburst of melted black wax. The advent of Leigh Bowery meant that the outermost reaches of fashion absurdity were ripe, available, and ready to be exploited.

During this phase, a popular brunch restaurant in San Francisco 86ed me because I wore cleated golf shoes and left a number of puncture tracks in their wooden deck. They may have been equally offended by my outfit that day: a number that I called "Clash of the Tartans," which consisted of as many conflicting plaid clothing items as my wardrobe could provide.

I totally would have worn a Queen Anne dog collar at that point. Still, I never would have been caught dead in fake Reeboks.

At my worst, I went out one night wearing a white plastic bathing cap, a white jockstrap over black tights, and swim fins. Friends carried me across the dance floor so I could do an Australian crawl. As a day look, I wore a bright red nylon graduation gown with a kind of homemade pope hat. Friends would kiss the large fake rings that were turning my fingers green. This look also included a necklace made of a large chrome Jesus on a doggy choke chain. The rings at either end of the chain went through the holes in Christ's hands. "Look, I can make him do flips," I once demonstrated to a respectable older man I'd just been introduced to, unaware that the man was a priest.

One day I went out in a white steel pith helmet with earrings made from live goldfish stuck on wires through their back fins. As the fish died in a series of small, terrible metallic thumps against my helmet and finally lay cold and smelly against my neck, I thought, with pangs of terrible guilt, *Perhaps there are limits to fashion.* I still half expect PETA to Extraordinary Rendition me to a salmon farm in Romania for that one.

Anyway, I finally went to rehab and back to school. Nightclubs had become less interesting the closer I got to being legally able to visit them.

For several years, I embraced a fairly standard, all-black goth look and saved the bulk of my costumes for the actual theater. There were still a couple of regrettable moments when I actually thought I was "trendsetting."

I once saw a Betsey Johnson runway show that featured thongs and "ass cleavage," and I thought, *This is the future.* I immediately pulled my thong over my hipbones, pulled my baggy hip-hop jeans down a little too low, and went to the movies with a friend who didn't tell me, until years later, how mortified he was to be seen with me.

I went through a very unfortunate period almost exclusively in Lycra bicycle shorts as the result of finding sporadic employment as a physical trainer at a gym. I confess that there was also a deplorable summer when I returned to shamelessness in L.A. by complementing my 1976 convertible Cadillac El Dorado with Daisy Duke cutoff short-shorts, a cowboy hat, and a white bikini.

These days, since I've started spending time in Washington, D.C., I try to look wealthy and deceptively conservative. I like the idea that truly strange people keep their strange on the inside and try to "blend." My friend Nancy calls my present wardrobe "Fifth Avenue Ironic." I call it "Stewardess of Human Evil," particularly when I'm wearing a sarcastic American flag lapel pin and big ten-millimeter fuck-you pearls. I do like the luxury trimmings of this current phase, although someday some PETA zealot like Brigitte Bardot will probably make pan flutes out of my femurs.

This is my philosophy: I don't like to condone the fur industry, but to not enjoy outerwear that has already been dead for twenty years is, in my opinion, just overly rigid and wasteful. That goes double for crocodiles. I think it's *especially* okay to wear fur if it is a *pest*. A raccoon, after all, is not a lynx. If antifur people get their chinchillas in a ringer over my winter warmth, I tell them, "Look, it's a *rodent*. Eight less garbage cans got knocked over in Connecticut that year. Big deal."

My secret to obtaining these long-deceased items is better consignment stores. There was a real gem in Brooklyn that obtained most of my income. It was run by a Polish woman with shaved eyebrows who got all of her stuff "from de synagogk."

I walked in one day and she grabbed my arm, wild eyed, and said, "You *muss* buy these boot. Dey are mayde of *kink cobra*." Her thumb was boring painfully into my arm. "De *beeg snayke*."

She was absolutely right, of course. King cobra ankle boots, I hate to admit, are a necessity, not a luxury. I would never buy them new, of course, because that would condone the making of deadly cobras into shoes. But if I could buy a king cobra tracksuit . . . oh my *god*. The only thing that could make it even better would be a matching ski mask.

One may dream.

Look at Me

- -

JILL SOLOWAY

I WAS READY to make out with someone new.

I'd been in a relationship for five years, with a manly man who made me feel like a lady, a real lady. He was older than me and white trashier than me and more of a Vietnam vet than me (I am not a Vietnam vet at all). It's not like he wanted me to dress all girlie. In fact, when I did dress up, he hated makeup and anything that made me look like I was trying as hard as any of the other women out there in the world. But the dynamic—big man and little lady—was there.

I never cheated, and even during the time that we were breaking up, I stayed true. While I was waiting for the relationship to end, I spent a lot of time in my mind, imagining what it would feel like to make out with someone new.

That's one of the things about marriage that freaks me out—not that I can't sleep with someone new, but that I don't ever get to make out with someone new. All those movie actors who say how awkward and truly uncomfortable it is to shoot a kissing scene with another actor are complete liars. That, I think, is the greatest reward of being a movie and TV star—not the scads of money or the Oscars gift bags, but the right to come home from a day at the office where you ever so ever so gently hovered your lips around Johnny Depp's lips, and were not only not lying nor cheating, but were actually supporting your brood.

Dreaming About Making Out With Someone New. If I'm not in love, I'm in longing mode. It's got to be one or the other. A rare day or week has passed in my life when I am not either trying to figure out how to get out of being in love, or trying to fall into it.

But when this relationship ended and I got to legally long out loud for a new person, a new soul, a run up the hill, this longing was different. This story in my mind—my daydreaming-myself-to-sleep story—was different.

That was not Jill in those scenes.

I froze the action and stepped closer and closer, then walked right up to the Jill who was making out with the mysterious guy—who, by the way, was much shorter than my ex and was, in fact, nearly my same height.

In the movie of my mind, I had short hair.

I was kissing a guy. Damn. Still not a lesbian. But the me being kissed, the me kissing back, was a me with short hair. I have always, my whole life, had long hair. This Jill was someone else. I couldn't wait to make out with someone new. But I would have to get my hair cut short first.

I tapped myself on the shoulder and got to know her from all angles. As she turned around for me, I could see how this kiss would be different from all other kisses and, perhaps, what would be different about all future relationships: This girl with the short hair, she is kissing back, instead of just being kissed.

The girl is kissing back, because.

Although this has been a long, long, long-ass way to get to my story about fashion, there's a point: I want the way I look to be not so much about being seen, but instead, to be a story about who is seeing.

I didn't want to have long hair anymore because I didn't want to be the girl to the man. That has always been my go-to shortcut: I am girl, he is man, and it is in this way that I am sexy.

Days after I cut my hair, I had to have a new outfit. I was in New York when I cut my hair short, and it was the zenith of that moment—hell, the moment may still be going on when this book comes out—the moment when you *had to get a skinny jean* and a tunic. The world was being cleaved in half. If you were still wearing your old ass crack–showing, boot-cut True Religions, they might as well have been high-waisted Lee mom jeans.

I haven't had a lot of looks in my life, but I was sick and tired of my old fallback: long-haired Jewish lady with a center part, an ironic T-shirt, and a long skirt. Then there's the closely related Northern Cal hippie-hoppie (that's a hip-hop–influenced hippie) and the Long Island real estate agent (this one happens to me out of nowhere). It can strike at any time—one weird day without humidity, and my hair straightens out and helmets itself in a way that makes me look like I should be selling real estate with my own bus-bench ads. I used to call that look Debby Goldberg. I was also Rasta Girl for a few years, with real food in my three real dreadlocks. And Jeans and T-Shirt Girl, of course—that's me always, my Production Assistant look.

I have no idea how to dress like a lady. Every outfit I have ever had is the outfit of a boy or a tomboy or a camp counselor, but a girl camp counselor with a sweaty T-shirt and a wide leather belt I crafted myself in the craft corner.

A couple of days ago I got an email update to an old invite to my friend Jessica's birthday dinner—she said, "Oh yeah, tonight, ladies, please wear cocktail dresses."

"Cocktail" and "dress" are two words that, placed next to each other, strike fear in my heart. To go out for an entire evening and carry around "hotness" or "sexiness" is like asking me to leave the house with a log for a purse. I can't do it. I won't do it. I get mad when there's an occasion that people would ask me to do it for.

It was sometime in my early twenties that I thought I was the first to come up with the word "fascion," a vision of fashion as fascist. I have always had this awful relationship with fashion. In the past, it felt like an agreement: If I am going to put thought into putting on clothes, then I am agreeing to be looked at. If I am agreeing to be looked at, then I am agreeing to being wanted, courted, chased, whistled at, looked at, and, I guess, the opposite: I am agreeing to being disappointed if no one does so.

I am black and white, the icy-cold, slippery slope of an arguer. I have no shades of gray. Let's say, for the sake of the argument, that college sorority girls in sweet tight sweaters and headbands and flatironed hair look askance at community college girls in tank tops and leggings and superhigh stilettos. Do these college girls know that the straight-girl journalism students look askance at the sorority girls? And that the butch, severe women's studies majors look askance at the straight-girl journalism students for their earrings and shaved armpits? In other words, I am unable to accept any woman's argument that her amount of makeup/jewelry/underwire/contact lenses/hair product/hair dye/you could go on and on/but I won't . . . is the right amount. As I see it, any amount of grooming, dressing, or pomading is an entry into an agreement—*I know that when I leave the house today, I will be* looked *at, and* this *is what I would like people to see.*

All of this is why that new short-haired girl making out in my mind-movie was so interesting to me. She wasn't the unmade-up, just-woke-up version of me who refuses to enter into the agreement that I'd like to be looked at.

And she wasn't the in-drag caricature of "hot" that I feel like I am when I have to put on feminine clothing. She was some new, integrated (fashion-wise, anyway) version of a girl/woman/lezzie-influenced/ straight chick who likes guys who are the same size as she.

Who wants to be in a relationship with an equal.

My boyfriend just walked in here and asked me what I was writing about, and I said fashion. "But you don't know anything about fashion," he said.

"That's what I'm writing about," I said back.

I picked him because I got tired of imagining people to make out with and wanted to actually try making out again. He is much, much taller than me, but he fell in love with the short-haired, boy-girl, lesbian-ish, side-parted, camp-counselor me.

Lately I want to let my hair be long again. I am letting it grow. And when I went to that cocktail party, I wore my sea foam–green leggings under my miniskirt, because I am starting to feel something that feels like I don't want to wear mostly black or brown anymore; I want to wear pink and light green and sky blue. I want my outfits to be sillier and happier.

I don't know anything about fashion. Every day as I invent myself—the night before a meeting, the hour before a party—when I have my boots and leggings on and nothing else yet, I am trying to see myself being seen, seeing what I look like. I am wearing my current interior emotional state, as a signal to those around me to treat me more like myself.

I was at a big feminist event where Gloria Steinem spoke a few months ago. There was a woman there who is well known in the Hollywood powerwoman scene. She was pretty overweight and was having difficulty walking, so she was using a cane. But she was so beautiful, her hair blown full and long and honey colored, with highlights and lashes, a face full of makeup, and a startling red dress, that it occurred to me that she was actually signaling all of us who interacted with her that night to say, "Wow, You Look Great." Her outfit was a cue and a clue that, though she may not be at a nightclub dancing with a line of suitors, she wanted to be told she was beautiful over and over again that night. Her outfit was a clue that she didn't want anyone to ask her about her health.

I may not know anything about fashion, but I know that this latest boyfriend was imagineered into existence by a longing. Upon closer inspection, that longing was dressed in something new because she was ready for something new. The clothes were my clue. Maybe fashion is our way of marking our evolution. I am wearing what I am wearing to help you know who I am and who you are looking at and, most of all, who is looking back.

How to Dress like a Cowgirl

LAURA FRASER

I REMEMBER WHAT I was wearing when I went to visit an East Coast college my senior year in high school, because it made an impression. I showed up in a beige cotton blouse with a pink-flowered Western yoke and a self-tie at the neck that I had made in home ec. I wore the top tucked into brown corduroys, with a wide, hand-tooled leather belt that curled in the back at the waist.

Amy, my host—a second cousin from New York City whom I'd never met—opened the door with a squinty smile and said hello. The next thing she said was, "Would you like to borrow a sweater?" It wasn't particularly cold out, but I realized I ought to put on her light brown turtleneck before anyone else had a chance to see me. Amy is tall and thin, with an innate grace and aesthetic sensibility that I instantly grasped as superior to my own. She went to Miss Porter's School in Farmington, Connecticut; I went to Heritage High School in Littleton, Colorado.

45

The sweater was tight; on top of being dressed like a suburban cowgirl, I was chubby, back when being chubby was unusual. But dressed in Amy's sweater, with the hair I had curled à la Farrah that morning pulled back into a more collegiate ponytail, I was ready to meet her friends without fearing ridicule.

We went to a dive bar near campus that smelled like stale beer and had peeling red vinyl stools and a surly bartender. When he asked me what I wanted, I automatically ordered a margarita, because I was seventeen and from Denver, where the only time anyone I knew drank was on a special occasion at a Mexican restaurant. "A *margarita*," the bartender sneered. "The lady wants a *margarita*." This was back when margaritas were as rare east of the Mississippi as Coors beer.

Once again, Amy rescued me. "It's always safe," she whispered, "to order a gin and tonic in the summer and a vodka tonic the rest of the year." Until then, I didn't realize drinks were like shoes, with rules about before and after Memorial Day, but I ordered the vodka tonic.

I took a big sip and looked around at the group. Amy was dressed simply and elegantly, but her friends' outfits were like none I'd ever seen. The girls wore hairy pastel sweaters with Icelandic patterns circling the neck, and delicate gold jewelry. The guys wore wide-wale corduroys with layers of polo shirts under button-down shirts under sweaters. Shoes were leather boating shoes with gold eyelets, or loafers with no socks. Later, when I spent the night at Amy's, I was shocked to see that her roommate had neat stacks of Fair Isle sweaters in every color and in Gatsby-esque quantities.

Despite the intimidating, correct-yet-casual way my cousin's friends dressed—I would eventually come to recognize and disdain the preppy look—I decided to go to Wesleyan.

Back in Colorado, when I graduated from high school, my father took me to buy a new pair of cowboy boots. I had always loved cowboy boots, ever since my first pair of red ones at age five. I didn't have much in the way of a defined personal style in high school—I was always copying other people and trying to look thinner—but one thing I was sure about were cowboy boots. In my mind they were, and always would be, unassailably cool. My dad had always worn cowboy boots, lined up in his den near his collection of silver belt buckles, and while he hated anything having to do with fashion, he had his own effortless style that was different from that of other dads. We picked out a pair of Tony Lamas in soft brown antelope, and I couldn't wait to wear them.

Nevertheless, when I packed my trunk for Connecticut, I left the boots behind. With the advice of a back-to-school issue of *Mademoiselle,* I'd gone shopping for clothes I thought Amy's friends would wear. I bought a pink cashmere sweater, a blue Fair Isle one, some pleated wool pants, a beige corduroy skirt, and a blazer with leather buttons. I drew the line at Topsiders because they were just too ugly. I lost some weight and stopped curling my hair to rodeo queen proportions, which I'd always done to compensate for the fact that I was fat.

I didn't feel comfortable in those new clothes, but they were a uniform, and I was uncertain enough of myself that I just wanted to blend in. I sensed that everything I'd ever learned about how to dress right was wrong.

Most of us learn about style from our mothers, and I'm no exception. But in my mother's case, in the mid-'70s, the message was complicated: Fashion was oppressive, but also a guilty pleasure. Mom grew up in a white-gloved atmosphere, where ladies wore matching hats, coats, and shoes. Her single mother (whose tastes ran to rhinestones) insisted she be ladylike, too, but it's clear in photos of Mom as a child that she was most comfortable on the rare vacation occasions when she was allowed to wear jeans. There are plenty of photos of her in pillbox hats and tiny-waisted skirts, too, but after moving to Colorado, she used the casual Western atmosphere as an excuse to rebel against all that ladylikeness.

My mother was early to join the feminist movement and the clothes that went with it. She liked bell-bottom jeans and chambray work shirts. She was one of the first women to wear hiking boots: On a trip to Four Corners National Monument, when my mother stopped to use the restroom, another woman came tearing out of the next stall, screaming that a man was inside there. I clearly recall in 1974 when she announced, ripping holes in nylon, that she had worn her last pair of pantyhose. She has never put on another pair, not even for weddings.

Mom didn't want to dress her four little girls in pink, so she didn't. We had a few Easter dresses along the way, but for the most part, Mom encouraged us to dress like little Gloria Steinems. Jeans and overalls were fine, and she cheered the day we girls were allowed to wear pants to school (though not jeans: I had to stand in front of the class next to popular Cheryl Wahl as the Bad Example in my frayed Levi's, while Cheryl, in her light green matching polyester pantsuit, demonstrated suitable sixth-grade attire).

The problem was, we were girls, and so we *liked* froufy pink clothes once in a while, as some girls will. My oldest sister in high school had a hippie look, and the next one was athletic, but my next-older sister and I, the "little girls," liked tea parties, where we dressed fancy and entertained our stuffed rabbits in British accents. But Mom was active and outdoorsy, and our parents constantly reminded us that we had the freedom to dress as we pleased—as long as we didn't dress too girlie. Makeup and frilly clothes were frowned on in our household as a waste of time, intelligence, and, for my Depression-era, anticonsumerist parents, money. Looks simply weren't important to them; only our accomplishments and goals were (which included, confusingly, losing weight to look better). The natural look reigned.

That worked for my mother, who developed a Western, artsy style with ethnic flourishes. Leather jackets and Navajo jewelry didn't qualify as too oppressively ladylike, so she piled them on. My mother had Sundance-catalog style back when Robert Redford was playing the Sundance Kid. From her, I got a taste for unusual pieces of clothing and jewelry, which I grew into as I got older (she is still the only person in my family I can buy gifts for from Africa or Vietnam). But in junior high and high school, I would've rather died than wear most of that weird stuff—Mexican ponchos, Peruvian sweaters—to school.

Growing up, I did have one release for my pent-up sartorial yearnings and girlish expressiveness: the dress-up box. For all her serious feminist intent, Mom was also a big advocate of creativity, play, and imagination, so she went to Goodwill and brought home piles of ball gowns, cocktail dresses, Chinese kimonos, lacy slips, and fake-fur stoles. Grandma added to the mix with 1940s dresses sprinkled with rhinestones at the bodice. Femininity was okay as long as we weren't serious about it.

So my next-older sister and I made elaborate dramas to go along with our costumes. We were princesses and opera singers, dragon ladies and Southern belles. Once, on a hot day, we dressed in Clothing of the Future and ran around the back yard stark naked, looking for our spaceship. The baby sitter yelled at us, and we worried we'd get into trouble with our mother, but, liberal as she was, she merely told us to keep our outer space attire safely indoors.

Our grandma encouraged our dress-up parties. Once when I was visiting her, she threw a tea party where all her friends brought their favorite old frocks and veiled hats so I could do a fashion show for them. They had long since grown out of their flapper dresses and holiday gowns, and they applauded when I came down a makeshift runway modeling memories of their former selves. One neighbor, now gone, gave me the outfit I loved most, a light lavender silk dress with petticoats and real whalebone stays. I've grown out of it, too, but one day I'll have a twelve-year-old put it on for me.

I loved costumes and dressed up for any occasion, Halloween or school plays, with attention to the details of shoes, stockings, and jewelry. It's telling that in eighth grade, when we had to dress up as a character from a book for a book report, I chose *Fascinating Womanhood,* by Helen Andelin—an early backlash handbook on feminine submissiveness and how to attract a man—giving myself an opportunity to dress in full floral feminine style, with lots of makeup, while slamming the retro, antifeminist message of the text. When friends held a *Gilligan's Island* party, I had a perfect Mary Ann dress, red and white gingham. Did I go as Mary Ann? No, I took the rare opportunity to be Ginger.

But when I wasn't playing dress-up, it was Levi's and drab shirts. I wore mainly brown, which matched my eyes and made me look thinner, or at least less obviously fat. Part of me always wanted to rebel and wear something bright and tight and flirty, but not only did I recognize the validity of Mom's feminist critique of fashion, I was too fat to carry it off.

The older I became, the more I felt like a drag queen when I put on feminine clothes or makeup (my mother only wore lipstick—Lavender Frost—when she dressed up for a fancy event and had exactly one pot of green eye shadow in her drawer, which, as far as I remember, was used only for Halloween). I never felt feminine, pretty, or remotely glamorous in my day-to-day life and marveled at girls in school who could effortlessly wear eyeliner, short skirts, or heels every day. I never felt very attractive to men; no matter how desperately I wanted attention for my looks, I dismissed their compliments as shallow, unimportant, or untrue.

I suppose having a mother who was into the natural look was better than having one who insisted I curl my hair and wear confectionary dresses. It's a tough balance, feminism versus femininity, and it took me years to work it out. I see my sister dress her four-year-old head to toe in pink, and I wonder whether she is living out her own illicit princess dreams through her daughter, or if her daughter just likes to dress that way. Will my niece grow up feeling as uncomfortable expressing her independent and free-spirited side as I did feeling feminine? These days, little girls don't get their sense of style so much from their mothers as from marketing geniuses. They get to play, but the roles are limited to being pink fairy princesses. I wanted to dress like a princess sometimes, too, but I also wanted to be a witch, a movie star, a diva, a Victorian, a rodeo queen. I wanted to be more colorful and creative with clothes, but in real life I felt constrained. In feminine clothes, I felt like a fraud. Instead, I wore a jean jacket with a woman's fist embroidered on it and wondered why I never had a date in high school.

At college, armed with those preppy clothes—a very safely asexual version of femininity, to be sure—I still felt like a poseur. While I had the blond hair and WASP features to go with the outfit, preppy was a look for a certain group of people that didn't include me; I'd never been to boarding school or stepped aboard a sailboat. I didn't have the money to carry off the look authentically, either. I settled back into Levi's, but I felt completely uncool. Freshman year, my roommate looked in my closet and pronounced everything "shit brown." She made me buy a bright pink long-sleeved T-shirt, which I always felt called too much attention to myself.

I scouted my peers to try to find a way of dressing that would feel comfortable. There were plenty of factions to choose from—the feminists, the hippies, the punks, the artsy crowd. I tried out all the looks, within the limits of my resources and timidity, but always got them wrong. I bought a pretty pink Indian blouse, and then I happened to see my women's studies professor. She praised my paper on Victorian women as consumers and objects of consumption themselves, but I overheard her laughing on her way out the door with an older student about my cutesy blouse. When I tried to be sexy, going to a black-and-white ball in a black coat with a big fake-fur collar I found at a thrift store, I took off the coat, revealing a very suburban white T-shirt with black piping, and one guy told me what a disappointment I was.

My sophomore year, I had lunch at an eating club populated by Upper East Side New Yorkers trying to look like they'd just stumbled in from King's Road in Chelsea, in ratty plaid skirts, black tights, and leather jackets held together with safety pins. I ate dinner at a WASP fraternity where the other girls wore scarves patterned with horses and saddles. I changed clothes between lunch and dinner, but never fit in anywhere. The only time I seemed a success was when my friend Jim complimented me on my taste in clothing, telling me I was the only feminist he knew who wasn't afraid to wear pink socks. (Jim later became Jennifer, and so was also dealing with issues of expressing politically correct femininity.)

I finally gave up trying to fit in, brought my cowboy boots back from Colorado, and wore them with jeans and a black T-shirt, just so I didn't have to deal with the whole issue. Ironically, I suddenly became cool.

That became my uniform, which I wore when I moved to New York, and then to San Francisco. I tried to expand my style, because I still liked dressing up—mainly in 1940s vintage dresses that I found in thrift shops and that were feminine but campy and made for women like me, who had waists and hips. I found that I could dress in pretty clothes as long as I did it with an ironic wink. I didn't buy many interesting new clothes because, as a freelance writer, I was too broke and couldn't justify spending a lot of money on something I would love and wear forever because I never knew what I liked to begin with. As a result, I ended up with a hodgepodge look. One day I showed up at a newspaper I was working for wearing a taffeta plaid skirt I'd found at a secondhand store. An editor (who went on to work at *Vogue*) looked me up and down with an amused smile. "Yesterday you looked like a punk rocker, and today it's Mary Tyler Moore."

Heading into my thirties, I had to figure out a more reliable, grown-up look. Writing for women's magazines, I visited New York once or twice a year to have lunch with editors, which always made me anxious for weeks in advance. My cousin Amy wisely counseled that I should buy one good Diane von Furstenberg wrap dress, but that was both out of my budget and too clingy for my generous figure. I had no idea what to wear, so I always tried on everything in my closet before packing black pants and a black sweater.

That seemed to be acceptable, until I had lunch with an editor from *Vogue* who was a longtime friend. We were in the Royalton, a posh lunch spot for the Condé Nast crowd, where Anna Wintour and Si Newhouse and other fashion luminaries were picking at their salads. The waiter sat us in a dark corner next to the kitchen. Then he recognized my friend as a *Vogue* editor, apologized, and offered to move us elsewhere. I realized that we'd been seated in Siberia because of what I was wearing. My editor said we were fine where we were and, sensing my discomfort, made a suggestion. "Maybe you could find something with a little more *structure*," she said.

So, before my next New York trip, I visited Ann Taylor, where I bought a navy blue suit. It was double breasted with a short wrap skirt; apparently, one designer went to lunch and another took over. But I was panicked, it seemed to have structure, and it was on sale. When I arrived in New York, I realized I couldn't wear it; it was far too corporate and sartorially clueless for lunching with editors at fashion magazines. I looked like I was up for a PR job at Chevron. I put my head-to-toe black back on and hoped no one noticed how cheap it all was.

Finally, when I was in Italy one year, I decided to solve the problem once and for all. I was after serious structure, and willing to pay for something I could wear with fashion editors for years to come, something absolutely, unassailably correct.

I didn't mess around: I went straight to Armani. I pointed to a jacket hanging up and asked to try it on. The *commessa* shook her head no. Was I too fat? Was it obvious I couldn't afford it? Was I just wrong for Armani? *"Perche no?"* I asked. She shrugged her shoulders and explained the problem in that very matter-of-fact Italian way. "This jacket is too short for you. You have a small waist and a large bottom, so you must always wear a long jacket fitted to your waist, which is your figure's best asset." Italian saleswomen take their profession very seriously, and unlike American salespeople, who will be happy to ring up anything hideously unflattering as long as they get a commission, they don't want to be responsible for any aesthetic mistakes walking around on the street. Finally, at least, someone had given me a rule I could follow about getting dressed.

The *commessa* didn't give up on me. She helped me pick out a gorgeous suit, in a light green and gold fabric that looked pretty with my hair. The jacket fit perfectly and was slimming. I spent more on that suit than anything I'd ever bought, including my VW Bug. It would be worth it to never again worry obsessively before I went to New York.

It was the '90s, and the suit had big shoulder pads. The next season, it looked ridiculous, and no amount of tailoring would make it look right. Sometimes I still pull that suit out of my closet, slip it on, and marvel at how I looked so correct for a few days in the spring of 1994.

I did have a chance to wear the suit on national TV, though, on *The Today Show*. The woman who ironed the jacket in the Green Room examined the black label and then told me she loved it (they iron your clothes before you go on *The Today Show* if you arrive looking as rumpled as I did; Judith Martin, Miss Manners, happened to be there at the same time and reassured me, politely, that she always has her ironing done at *The Today Show*). I also wore the suit on *The Maury Show*—where they revisited my old rodeo queen hairstyle—and I shudder every time I see the clip: Along with my impeccable Armani suit, I was wearing black sandals—with beige socks.

The Armani suit incident made me a little less fearful about spending money on clothes, even though, in the end, it hadn't been a very good cost-per-use value (I hold out hope and space in my Clothes Museum closet that it may yet come back in style). But I did realize that if something looks great and will last, it's worth spending money on. Even my parents, who pay top dollar for sturdy outdoor clothing, more or less agree with this philosophy (although to them, if an article of clothing wouldn't help you survive a sudden hailstorm in the Rockies, it isn't worth paying full price). I had also spent some time in Europe, with Italian friends who had few clothes but lots of style; they wore the same wildly expensive sweater day after day. That became my new goal.

Around that time I met Marijka, who owned a tiny boutique in San Francisco, now closed (her psychic told her to move to the South of France). Marijka is warm and engaging, with a wacky clothing style that always looks fabulous. I was afraid of the three-digit labels on her clothes, not to mention the very unusual European styles. But from the day I walked in, she took my measure. "You dress too boring," she told me. "You're an outgoing, exuberant person. You should dress that way! Why not?"

At the time, I was married to a man with very conservative taste in clothes, who liked me best in a gray polo dress or a fleece pullover and disliked my turquoise high-top tennis shoes and anything with leopard print or rhinestones. In a moment of honesty before we split up, he told me that he'd been attracted to me for my exuberance, then did everything he could to dampen it.

When I split up with him, I felt a new freedom—and also a need, now that I was single again, to dress a little sexier, to have a little more fun with what I wore, and to be as exuberant as I damn well pleased. I was depressed to be getting a divorce, too, so I wanted to wear clothes that made me feel cheerful. Off I went to visit Marijka. I began cautiously, with clothes that were safe but had just slightly softer fabric or a witty little detail in the cut. I started to pay more attention to which clothes made me feel good about myself.

One day Marijka held out a garment that seemed outrageous—a thick, orange hand-knit sweater, held together at an angle with a large safety pin—with an equally outrageous price tag. I tried it on, but thought I looked foolish. She pointed out that the color was great on me and the sweater had a one-of-a-kind personality. I bought it, full of buyer's remorse, until everyone I saw complimented me and asked where I'd found that fabulous sweater. I wore it, with a Spanish black wool skirt, for an entire week in Paris and another in New York, where I was dressed perfectly every day for lunch with a different person.

Every six months—well, three—I would get another piece from Marijka. She did me a favor by being honest, always letting me know if I came out of the dressing room in something unflattering that I should take it off as quickly as possible. She also introduced me to the concept of flaunting my curves, not hiding them, but without letting things be too clingy or tight. If I came out of the dressing room complaining that something was "too sexy," Marijka would roll her eyes. "There is no such thing as too sexy." Marijka was feminine but completely confident and unconventional, with a touch of outrageousness. The great thing about fashion, if you don't follow it but use it, is that you can express whatever you want.

Soon, I started falling in love with the oddest pieces in the store. One day Marijka handed me a Krista Larson skirt with layers of pink satin and tulle—a princess skirt. I tried it on and it brought a smile to my face. Marijka urged me to buy it, and offered a discount, but I replied that I had nowhere to wear such a skirt. "Wear it *everywhere*," she said, adding that I had to dress it down, not take its girlishness seriously. I wore it with cowboy boots and a jean jacket, and people marveled at my confident taste. Then it was on to asymmetrical skirts and hand-painted tops by obscure Spanish, Danish, and German designers.

I have gone a little overboard buying clothes in the past few years, but almost everything in my closet looks good on me, fits me the size I am, and has personality. I no longer ask salespeople their opinion when I try something on, because I know what I like and what looks good on me. My style is eclectic and cheerful, a mix of simple basics with strong dashes of color and originality. I buy pieces that rarely go out of fashion because they were never in fashion to begin with. If I see a fabulous embroidered coat in colors that look good on me, I'll pay a price that would make my mother faint, because I know I'll wear it forever. I love it when women on the street, strangers, compliment me on something I'm wearing; fashion is a form of communication and connection.

Last year, I visited Hoi An, Vietnam, which is filled with tailors' shops. The city was like a giant dress-up box. I'd walk into a store, admire the colorful silks stacked floor to ceiling, and imagine a jacket, a dress, a pair of pants. I drew designs on paper, they measured me, and I ended up with several pieces I love—a brilliant blue silk tunic, a long gold and brown Chinese brocade jacket, a multipaneled coral linen skirt, a black wrap dress—all custom fitted. The experience made me realize how assured I've become about fashion, knowing what looks good on my body and what suits my lifestyle. When I got home and stuffed all the new clothes into my closet, it also made me realize that as much as I love clothes, I have enough.

These days, people in San Francisco compliment me on my style. Even in New York, I've been making an impression. When I was meeting with several editors at a women's magazine recently, one said, "Look at her—she's positively blooming in all that color, and we're all in black."

I had lunch with the *Vogue* editor I'd known, too. I was wearing a skirt of heavy Irish linen shot with silver thread, unraveled at the waist and hem, with a simple brown fine-gauge sweater and a chunky turquoise necklace. "You always dress so well," she said. I smiled, and under the table I tapped the toes of my cowboy boots.

Lighten Up, It's Just Fashion: How to Be a Gorgeous Revolutionary

FRANCES VARIAN

"We should not have to apologize for reveling in beauty."

—Camille Paglia

I AM NINETEEN years old and standing in front of Jackson Pollock's *Autumn Rhythm (Number 30)* at the Metropolitan Museum of Art. My best friend, Meryl, and I have escaped to the city during winter break. Meryl is a lot like me, a misfit, working-class teenager ensconced in the bewildering world of near–Ivy League academia. But she is also different. She is worldlier, more sophisticated, and ethereal. She teaches me about abstract art and foreign films in a way that feels simultaneously safe and exhilarating. I teach Meryl how to smoke spliffs and get what she wants out of her cafeteria dining experience. We are attached at the hip.

"This is my favorite," she says, standing reverently next to me in front of the painting. I wonder how another poor girl from the Hudson Valley could become so acquainted with the Met that she has a favorite anything. At the time, I know nothing about abstract expressionism, but as I stand there I come to realize that Pollock's masterpiece had been painted for me. I am meant to understand something about the way the world moves through an artist's hand and imagination because he chose to convey the message. Dead old Jackson and I are suddenly involved in a conversation. *It is so beautiful,* I say to myself, and then I say it out loud to my friend.

Eleven years later I find myself working at a dead-end job, trying desperately to reconcile the fact that life-sucking employment drudgery does not afford me as much writing time as I had hoped. I sit in a room with very straight, diet-obsessed women who generate "must have" lists full of Gucci purses and Coach shoes, despite the fact that our salaries place us below the poverty level in the city of San Francisco. I'm a leftist, fat, queer femme, chained to a phone, sitting in a room with people who hate themselves for every cookie they munch, who are none too fond of the gays, who think their lives would be much better if they could only afford the newest Coach loafers. It would be funny if it didn't tempt me to puncture my own eardrums with office scissors.

Still, I am fond of some of them, especially the woman who said to me the other day, "I like the pink fur on your collar. I could never wear anything like that; I'm always trying to blend in and not be noticed. But I like the way you dress. It's almost artistic." All of the feminist theory in the world cannot prepare you for the heartwrenching, maddening, and completely unexpected experience of coming to know other adult women. Of all that is stolen from us and all that is withheld, the loss of a true and spiritual relationship with beauty strikes me as uniquely tragic and problematic on countless levels.

Because I studied feminist theory in the mid-'90s, I did not read Camille Paglia until the summer of 2005. I would have rejected her, as my peers did, if I had read her in the '90s. I spent the better portion of my time between college graduation and reading Camille Paglia working in abortion clinics. Abortion: the bastion of good, middle-class, white feminist ideology—or, I should say, "choice." "Pro-choice," because endorsing actual bloody abortions is still considered gauche in most feminist circles. I was a passionate pre-abortion counselor, the best hand-holder in five states. I went bankrupt working in abortion clinics. The feminists did not pay me a living wage. I went a little bit crazy, too, coming to terms with the fact that I, like many of my clients, am not a good middle-class feminist. Coming to terms with the fact that if I wanted to claim feminism as my own, I would have to carve out a place for myself and other outsiders, and the work would not be easy.

Fashion and feminism are both infused with the theoretical and practical limitations and opportunities presented by the female body. They can be symbiotic or deadly, depending on the way the light shifts. They are parasites and I am the host. Without me they both die. And yet in varying similar and dissimilar ways, fashion and feminism would have me believe it the other way around. I stand metaphorically naked before you—how problematic!

How else to make my point? I have a white body that is considered a plus for both feminism and fashion. I have a fat body—a huge minus for fashion and a slightly smaller subtraction for feminism. My body holds the scars and modifications of thirty years' worth of femaleness: cuttings, stretch marks—minus, minus. My queer body earns me bonus points as exotic from both camps, unless I qualify my queer identity with the truth of my femmeness, at which point my rating takes a major dive in the feminist arena. Being born working class means I've been repeatedly indoctrinated against presenting myself as easy, available, and wanton. The belief that my body can be easily taken has been drilled into me since a tender young age. The world is all about power, and money is a bodyguard. This fear of the body I live in, the notion that without my consent my body can and will betray me, has been beneficial to both fashion and feminism in countless, insidious ways. Why, then, do I find myself turning to feminism and fashion time and time again for comfort, for inspiration, and, perhaps most important, for community?

I have a fondness for the outrageous, the theatrical, but the unquestionable foundation of my aesthetic is beauty. Simply because I am drawn to it, and because it is the single most revolutionary choice I can make. If it is shiny, pretty, delicate, fantastic, sparkling, hot, and dangerous, I want it. If it is deviant, audacious, ironic, humorous, difficult to launder, and slightly inappropriate, then I most likely already own it. White lesbian feminists often tell me that this predilection of mine is traitorous. Frances of the big hair, false eyelashes, and fuck-me red lipstick is a sellout. The skirts and the stockings and the arch-killing shoes all point toward my poorly hidden heteronormative nature. I am told by all kinds of women that this predilection of mine is wrong for another reason: Frances of the wide hips and big, soft stomach ought not to wear tight clothing. My lack of shame is shameful. Shocking. More than once a straight acquaintance has come to watch me perform, only to approach me after, eyes huge and unblinking, and stutter, "You . . . you . . . were sexy," almost a question, not quite an accusation.

I try to keep track of all the ways women die in the world, but I cannot. I try to conjure the dead women when I'm walking by myself late at night and pray to them for protection. I make friends with their ghosts, especially those who left in broken, twisted bodies: raped, burned, stabbed, poisoned, strangled, shot, the ones who left by their own hand when it all became too much, the women who died tortured and grieving for their unfulfilled dreams. Their numbers are legion. I watch little girls on the bus, search their eyes to see if they've been extinguished yet. I search my own eyes in the mirror to see if I've been extinguished yet. The global war waged on women amounts to nothing short of genocide. And, even more horrifying, the global war waged on women remains unexamined, unchecked, and largely unspoken. We are dying as I write this. We will be dying when you read this. And what the hell does any of this have to do with fashion?

Fear is a powerful weapon, much more powerful than violence. It's cheap, easy to market, and effective. The current administration had little more to do than organize primary colors on a posterboard and print the words TERROR-ALERT CHART on top to convince a country of people who knew better to acquiesce to a gruesome, senseless war in Iraq. For women, the fear training starts at birth and never ceases. We are served a constant visual meal of all the dangers that can befall our fairer sex. The fear of being alone, the fear of being different, the fear of being raped, the fear of being beaten, the fear of being ugly, the fear of poverty . . . and yet structuring our lives to avoid these fears seems to have little to no effect on preventing them from occurring in the first place.

Furthermore, structuring our lives in such a way seems to occur without much conscious thought. The point of marketing fear is to make it seem natural, normal, to be afraid. With every Lifetime movie about bulimia (starring Valerie Bertinelli) and every *CSI* episode featuring a raped and strangled coed, the message becomes more clear: The world is an unsafe place for women. Then, rushing in on the white horse of our fairytales, is a perfect, thirty-second nugget of relief with a seductive message: "Diamonds Are Forever." Rinse and repeat until you've got us all so brain-wiped, we're policing ourselves and each other: *I can't believe she's wearing that dress at her age. Did you hear she slept with four different people last month? She's too skinny; I don't think she eats enough. She's such a bitch. I can't believe she's so ambitious. How can she be a queer feminist and*

wear all of that girlie crap? It's like she's giving head to the entire patriarchy.
She has such a pretty face, it's a shame she's covering it up with all that fat.
She's so pretty I hate her.

My own life has been plagued by fear. It seems to be the most po-
tent legacy the women in my family possess. At the same time, I am no
stranger to beauty. No matter how dim my prospects, regardless of how
hopeless I have felt, beauty has always found its way to me and reminded
me of the bigger picture. Perhaps I should have wondered what right I
had to fall in love with *Autumn Rhythm,* but I didn't. Meryl made it clear
to me that art exists for my pleasure as much as it exists for the pleasure
of the more privileged. This has been my saving grace.

So I found myself at the age of twenty-nine crying on a downtown
Seattle bus while reading Camille Paglia. For all that I find wrong with
Paglia, and there is a lot, what I cherish beyond measure is her insistence
that beauty is not the enemy of feminism. I can make an argument here
about how brave I am to dress extravagantly. How fat women and poor
women and women who live on the margins of society in every way are
especially encouraged to not draw attention to themselves. And I would
not be wrong.

I am often unsure if the stares I receive are stares of admiration,
disbelief, or disgust; my best guess is that I've received my fair share of
all three. But when I dress, I dress to arouse and please my own sense
of beauty, my own aesthetic. It is as internal a process as I can honestly
make it. There is no way for me to dissociate myself fully from the culture I live in, and therefore I have to admit to an active external process
as well, but my core motivation is my own pleasure. Because I claim
ownership of the aesthetic and the pleasure it brings me, I am actively
dismissing the culture of fear that infiltrates my life. This is not a flaw-
less strategy; I flounder all the time. I, too, find myself full of doubt
and preoccupation. I have experienced some major fashion panic before

important events. But more often than not I found myself authenticated in a surprisingly delicious way.

I have no prescription for beauty and fashion, just as I have no prescription for how to be a "good" feminist. I'm not particularly interested in writing one, either. There are millions of ways to delight the senses, and I fully trust my fellow humans to explore each and every one. I am mostly interested in exploring and detailing survival strategies. I am interested in voicing the emergent, critical situation that women find themselves in. I am interested in preventing, if possible, the sacrifice of our children to this mindless, brutal drone of normalcy that is the enemy of free thought and exploration. I want to prevent the senseless abdication of personal liberty for the myth of safety. Safety does not exist. We will be raped. We will be beaten. We will be poor. We will be silenced. We will continue to live as second-class citizens until we decide, for ourselves, that we are not.

But we do not have to die by our own hands. We do not have to grieve for the death of our dreams. If you cannot walk yourself to the movies at night for fear of what will happen to you, you are not free. If you cannot wear whatever makes you feel alive for fear of repercussion, you are not free. If you cannot allow your spirit to soar because you have never been told it is your inalienable right to be moved by something beautiful, however you define beauty, you are not free. It takes courage to reach for freedom and it requires strength to fight for an authentic life, but both require far less energy than a fear-based existence.

Feminism is an important weapon in the war against women. I am indescribably thankful to feminists who have come before, but I want to sharpen its blade. I want feminism to be useful for all kinds of people, including women who are not feminists. We need to think three-dimensionally about the problems women face. We need to think globally, and that means that we, a global community of women who face violence every day based upon our gender, desperately need to train ourselves to think outside of the box. We have to understand that the "Diamonds Are Forever" commercials are mind-washing exploitation, while simultaneously accepting our enjoyment of the lovely couple with good lighting and romantic music and remembering that illegal diamond trafficking has caused enormous destabilization in Sierra Leone, which contributed in part to the murder of one of Africa's great queer and human rights activists, Fannyann Eddy.

The intrinsic artistic merit of fashion is not diminished because the world of fashion can be unsafe for women. The intrinsic political value of feminism is not diminished because many feminists fail to check their privilege long enough to understand the countless women they are leaving behind. It's up to each of us to decide when and if we will use these tools and, if we use them, how we will modify them to better fit our hands. What is not up for interpretation is the desperate condition that women face globally. If we do not find a way to bridge our differences and reach for each other, we are likely to face even more disastrous realities. The first step to thinking outside of the box is to step outside it, and for most women that means claiming beauty, claiming ownership, and claiming personal freedom. The battle lines were drawn before any of us were born, and up until now we have not been able to sustain any kind of unified resistance. I can't guarantee you a safe and easy outcome if you fight, but I can promise I'll be standing next to you. If we have to go down, we might as well go down together and looking fucking fabulous.

A Torrid Affair

COOKIE WOOLNER

WELCOME TO A DAY at the mall in twenty-first-century America, home of the escalating "war on obesity." Where fat girls shop at stores displaying ads with models wearing a size the store doesn't sell because "studies show" that not even fat girls want to see pictures of actual fat girls wearing clothes. Yes, folks, if we see an image of a happy, healthy, sexy big chick who's not making a self-deprecating joke or planning her next starvation diet, the world as we know it just might implode.

Us beefy babes who want to keep up with the trendy teens shop at Fat Topic. Okay, so there's no store called Fat Topic, but there *is* an alterna-chain called Hot Topic, and it has a little sister chain named Torrid. Fat Topic is the nickname my friends and I have bestowed upon this chain. It sells big clothes for big girls with prices much bigger than they deserve. But fat girls don't get to complain about our few clothing choices—that would be looking a gift horse in the mouth. There used to be only Lane Bryant and Avenue and Elizabeth by Liz Claiborne, and every one of those stores is a bore unless you're a yuppie who craves bland beige work separates or hideous floral knee-length sweatshirts. Skinny girls get tiny midriff tops and belly button rings, and fat girls get looong shirts, because god forbid our asses or tummies show. That's called "making a spectacle of yourself," which is cool for dudes, but not a lady's prerogative.

"Making a spectacle of yourself" is an art form I perfected at a young age: one day when I was in third grade, rocking my new sporty ski jacket, a turquoise CB Sports jacket that the preppy WASPs at my suburban New York elementary school had decided was de rigueur. A popular girl named Liza saw me, despite my total lack of interest in skiing and all things sporty, trying to strike a pose, and declared, "I didn't know they made those jackets *in your size.*" Damn, she put me in my place. How dare some chubby girl in glasses with knots in her hair try to be stylish, try to look good, try to be something she was obviously not?

On field trip days we didn't have to wear uniforms. Everyone else would be wearing their Ralph Lauren and L.L.Bean, and I'd show up in outfits like the ones Chevy Chase and his family tried on in *National Lampoon's European Vacation* when they got stranded in Italy. I'm talking weird baggy sweatshirts covered in rubber studs, wrinkled satin pants with wacky pockets. It was the '80s, and my parents were art fags who took me to SoHo and Greenwich Village on the weekend. I was marchin' to my own beat—experimenting, if you will.

At that age (eleven, twelve), I wanted to be a fashion designer. In my later teen riot grrrl years, I became so ashamed of this previous "un-punk" dream that I eventually disclosed it in my zine in the hushed tones usually reserved for baring deep soul secrets: "I know this is so unfeminist, and totally uncool, and probably classist, but I used to want to be . . . a fashion designer!" Oh, the horror! Looking back, I think that designing clothes seemed to the young me like a creative outlet that was acceptable and plausible for girls, as well as a way to form identity.

I wanted desperately to connect with people and culture and ideas, and fashion seemed like the way to go.

A few years ago I thought I had come full circle when, on the cusp of turning thirty and freaking out over how to make a living doing something I wanted to do, I decided I should open a cool fat-girl clothing store. Although I never had an interest in business, or selling products, or sewing, someone had to do it, and it might as well be me. I had spent the past decade as a fat crusader, talking and singing and dancing about fat positivity in my zine, in workshops, at school, in my bands, in my burlesque troupes, and mostly in one-on-one conversations. Sometimes I challenged people's negative assumptions about fat, and sometimes I scared people enough into never talking about their diets in front of me, but either way, everyone knew that I was a local expert on the topic of fat oppression. So why not start a fat-girl clothing store?

It soon dawned on me that I didn't want to run a business, learn to sew, or learn marketing or any other aspect of opening a clothing store. What I wanted were magic powers. Magic powers to snap my fingers and give myself and every other fat girl in the world a closet full of clothes that fit them, that were stylish, that were well proportioned for their bodies, that weren't made from polyester and elastic, that weren't more expensive than skinny-girl clothes, and all that other good stuff that skinny girls can take for granted. It's rare for me to talk to skinny girls about my troubles finding stylish, well-made fat-girl clothes without their jumping in, saying they know *exactly* what I mean, because they're so small, or one arm is longer than the other, or whatever. And I know that everyone has his or her own struggles with their bodies, and most folks do not conform to commercial sizing, but still, it's just not the same.

Being a fat girl shopping at a thrift store is like being a vegan at a Las Vegas buffet: You have to search so damn hard to find the one thing that fits, half the time it's not even a question if you like it; it's just all there is. I spent my twenties sifting through everything, looking for the special treasures, but as I get older and bigger I just can't be bothered to spend all that time looking and hoping for the one vintage dress in my size. So I end up buying crap on sale at Macy's Woman, looking through brands I would *never* glance at if I were skinny. Tommy Hilfiger? Carol Little? Supersquare soccer-mom brands. These days I'm performing less and teaching more, and that translates into needing less "going out clothes" and more "work clothes."

Am *I* Macy's "Woman," and in denial of my new place in the world?

Of course, this brings us back to Torrid, the store that kicks major ass compared to the other fat-girl chains. Lip Service stretch jeans? Not only for skinny tweaker metal chicks! Skirts, bracelets, panties, and bondage pants? Buckle up for safety! T-shirts with Bettie Page, Pirates of the Caribbean, and Emily the Strange in size 4X? Check! Torrid even has a perfume. I think the ad should have Liv Tyler's hot sister, the plus-size model Mia Tyler, crooning sultrily: "Torrid Perfume: This is what a fat alternative girl smells like." I think it would be a big hit, don't you?

If there had been a Fat Topic when I was a young, chunky punk, sitting at home, ripping my jeans in half and safety-pinning them back together to fashion a crude, slutty miniskirt, I'm not sure what I would have thought. I wasn't as fat as I am now, so I didn't have to shop at fat-girl stores, but I would have appreciated the message of Torrid. Fat Topic cries, "Ahoy, fair fatties, adorn your bod with stretchy faux-corset tops and bedazzled miniskirts, and rock a thong and a push-up bra underneath!" Which pretty much translates to: Fat can be sexy and desirable. Granted, there are as many ways to be sexy as there are things to wear, but as far as cultural conventions go, Torrid sells the merch that Americans call "spicy." When I was a teen afraid of cute boys, cute girls, my reflection in the mirror, and voices in my head implanted long ago by all my peers telling me I was a big fat loser, Torrid's message might have rocked my little world.

The Hot Topic execs are smart. They know Americans are getting fatter and fatter and aren't going to stop wearing clothes anytime soon. Torrid's existence has even been dubbed controversial by fat-haters who think giving "corpulent consumers" one measly stylish option is going to send the message that—gasp—it's okay to be fat. And we can't have that! How will all those gastric-bypass doctors and pharmaceutical execs pay their pets' acupuncture bills if we stop trying to lose weight? What I don't get is why more clothing brands don't make plus-size lines. You'd think the dollar would always be the bottom line. But this is fashion, dahlings, so something else counts even more. Prestige. Envy. That's right, can you imagine how ghastly it would be to see fancy designer clothes on a body bigger than a size 8? How unsightly! Something must always be out of reach, someone must always be turned away at the velvet ropes, or else it wouldn't be any fun for those allowed in.

Body norms have been an increasingly hot topic (if you will) in our current cultural moment, with growing vocal distaste for bone-juttingly thin models. The rallying cry against the human-clothes-hanger look became frenzied when a model *died* after being told to cut back on food. Spain announced a ban on fashion models whose body mass index is below the average. Message boards have been filled with people spouting off pros and cons: "Models should represent realistic beauty standards for young women," versus: "Hello, this is fashion! Couture designed by gay men who idolize Audrey Hepburn! Don't ruin our fantasy!"

Complicating matters, Jean-Paul Gaultier, designer of Madonna's pointy cone bra, sent a three-hundred-pound smokin' hottie named Velvet D'Amour down his runway recently. While the regular minus-size models around her wore sporty workout clothes, D'Amour wore lingerie suited for the boudoir. Critics were quick to say one extreme was just as bad as the other: "Underweight" is unhealthy and "overweight" is, too, not to mention that they don't want young girls to start taking fat chicks for role models! Others cried "freakshow spectacle" and "token." I just cried, "Hell yeah! There's a really hot fat girl in a fancy French fashion show!" However, as the badass Marilyn Wann of *FAT!SO?* fame pointed out to me, cool as it is, Gaultier actually doesn't *make* clothing that fits fat girls. Sure, he's got the guts—or nerve, depending on how you see it—to send a large lady down his runway, but he doesn't care about fat girls enough as a potential market to make clothes that fit us. Perhaps he just sent her out there for nothing more than to get some press and to take advantage of the model size controversy of the moment.

Another problem with the image he created on the runway for D'Amour was the contrast of her indoor look with the thin models' outdoor one. Most folks believe the following fallacy that one message board critic wrote: "You can't put a fat person in workout clothes because fat people don't exercise!" When it comes to fat, fashion, and sexuality, things get very complicated. Sure, some fat people work out, and sure, some don't, because they're scared to death to walk into a gym and get laughed out the door. It's that whole "making a spectacle of yourself" issue again. And let's not forget that many thin people don't exercise, either. And yeah, it's cool to put a fat girl in sexy clothes on a fashion runway and celebrate her beauty and sensuality. But the contrast of one fat girl in lingerie and a bunch of skinny models in sports gear cries out, *I lie in bed all day eating bonbons!*

That's really the clincher: Everyone wants to lie in bed all day eating bonbons. But most folks think that if they do, they will get punished by becoming fat. And they can't hang with that, so they work really hard to not get fat. Then a hot fat girl comes along, rockin' some French couture lingerie, and thin people are like, "How dare you enjoy food and your body! I spend all my time avoiding both, and here you are, celebrating while I suffer." Americans' fear of fat is the same as their fear of losing control, or letting go of their willpower. Fat girls in lingerie symbolize sumptuous excess and untamable appetites for food and sex.

It's okay to be a consumer, society tells us, as long as you don't show it with an expanding waistline. We're all bombarded daily by words and images telling us to supersize it, just do it, be sexy even if we don't have sex, snap into a Slim Jim, and FedEx it overnight. Order your videos and books and pet food and groceries online. Consume consume consume. Sit in front of a computer screen all day and a TV screen all night. But as long as you can miraculously stay skinny, you'll never be told you're lacking in moral fiber. Us fat folks get the full share of the blame. So, to offer a f(l)abulous "fuck you" to our ever-expanding yet fat-hating country, I will end with my list of revolutionary fashion tips for big girls.

Ready? Get one of those *What Not to Wear* books and rock every "fashion don't" in it. Yes, it's that easy! Horizontal stripes? Clingy tops? Exposed upper arms? The muffin-top special? Love handles blaring out of low-cut pants? Chubby ankles popping out of high heels? Bring it. Just think about it: Every fashion tip you've ever learned is to help "flatter" your body, which translates to "make you look thinner." Thinner equals smaller. Smaller equals taking up less space in the world. The 1920s saw women finally get the vote—and called in the waifish flapper era of bound breasts. The 1960s brought more women into the workplace and the university—and Twiggy ruled the fashion world. A big woman symbolizes power and presence, so why be a shrinking violet?

After you've violated all those fashion rules, use that copy of *What Not to Wear* to kindle your fire on a cold winter night. The mainstream fashion and beauty industries exist to keep us alienated from our bodies and desires, in a constant cycle of consumption and false expectations. Fashion should be about joy and expression, not fear and loathing— loving and truly inhabiting our bodies, not hiding from them.

Style Outlaw: How a Genderqueer Fashion Label Was Born

PARISA PARNIAN

1980: PLANTING THE SEEDS OF FASHION DISSENT

At the tender age of ten, I discovered the power that fashion holds. It had been six years since my family had immigrated from Iran to the United States and settled down in the desert resort town of Scottsdale, Arizona. The year before, 1979, I had gone from being the curiously wild-eyed, dark-haired gypsy child that little blond girls liked to chase at recess and kiss behind the orange trees to being the root of all evil when the Iran hostage crisis took place. I no longer held a place of intrigue and fancy in the eyes of those girls; now I was feared, distrusted, an object of repulsion. I walked into the classroom to the jarring voices of little boys yelling, "Terrorist! I-ray-neyan! We're gonna bomb you!"

My only salvation during the long hours of fourth grade was the fact that I was smart and had figured out how to quickly finish the math, reading, writing, and science projects given to us by Mrs. Harris, our pretty, redheaded teacher. This meant I could sit in the back of the class and draw and doodle and sketch while the rest of the kids had their heads down, concentrating on finishing up the pop quizzes and math exercises doled out to us.

I had developed an intense curiosity for what the female anatomy looked like underneath clothing. I began to blindly draw what I imagined women's breasts, hips, arms, and bellies would look like if I had a chance to pull up the layers of clothing that covered them. On a particularly stifling Wednesday afternoon, after I sped through another spelling quiz and found myself bored and restless, I started to sketch what Mrs. Harris might look like underneath her flowery blouse and A-line tweed skirt.

Totally oblivious to my surroundings and completely wrapped up in perfecting the round, bouncy breasts I had drawn on my sketchpad, I was startled to hear one of the cute and popular girls in my class squeal, "Are you drawing a naked lady? Like, oh! My! God!"

Mortified, I looked up to see two of the cool girls turned around at their desks, craning their necks to take a look at my sketchpad. My entire body burned up with shame and fear of being discovered. I had to think quickly, so I said, "I'm not drawing a naked lady. I'm going to be a fashion designer one day, and that's just my model that I'm about to design clothes for—duh!"

With that, I quickly started sketching a blouse, skirt, jewelry, hat, shoes, and handbag on top of the naked drawing of Mrs. Harris. By the time I was done she looked very much like a fashion plate à la Oscar de la Renta, coming down a Paris runway. I just prayed that I was convincing and that these girls wouldn't discover what a weirdo I really was.

"Wow, you're really good! Can you design some clothes for me? Like, I'll totally model for you at recess if you'll draw me, too." And then another girl: "Me too, me too! Can you design my wedding dress for me at recess? Pleeaaaase?"

The clouds parted at that moment over my dark and gloomy social existence at Desert Coyote grade school—the cool girls wanted me to spend recess with them, look at them, and draw them. At that moment, I solidified my destiny: Fashion helps you get the girls.

1990: COLOR ME QUEER

My early fashion influences were Coco Chanel, flamenco dancers, and the dark-haired, pale-skinned vixens in the Robert Palmer video "Addicted to Love." So in the '80s, when acid-washed Guess jeans and pink over-size sweatshirts were the rage in my high school, I walked around in sophisticated, floor-length tweed trench coats and pencil skirts that I made for myself. I fancied myself a worldly young lady in the middle of a dusty desert landscape full of rich bigots and rednecks. Needless to say, I was viewed as odd and often mistaken for a teacher rather than a student when I walked down the hall.

When I started college in 1990, my whole world changed. I was still in Arizona, but I had exposure to people from all over the world. I was introduced to my first out gay person—the sweet little pixie boy who gave manicures in the student union's beauty salon. I found myself sketching and designing clothes for both men and women when I wasn't studying. From those early sketches, it became clear that the way I was using clothing on bodies did not correlate with traditional ideas of femininity and masculinity. My fashion illustrations were often viewed as "queer" because my men had a feminine aesthetic and my women had a masculine edge to them, often sporting a mysterious bulge in their pants.

It's interesting to point out that my own queer identity had yet to emerge. However, I found myself drawn passionately to people and stories that showed a gray place in a world that I had known to be black and white up until then. Gender ambiguity—not fulfilling one's social roles or obligations in a predictable manner; challenging the eye with beauty that did not conform to society's ideals of what is attractive on a male body or what is beautiful on a female body—consumed me.

By the time I graduated with a degree in marketing and business, I was well aware of my sexuality and that, indeed, I was truly queer in more ways than I could have imagined as a child. My queerness moved beyond my label as "gay" or "lesbian." I found myself constantly pushing the envelope and at odds with many aspects of my upbringing—as a devout Muslim, a first-generation Iranian American living in a culturally unsophisticated, suburban sprawl of strip malls and bottle blonds.

Arizona in the '90s was starting to develop a queer culture of its own. It revolved around a small handful of dyke and gay bars located in the seedy part of town. But everything was very mainstream gay and predictable. As a lesbian, you were admired for looking as feminine and straight as possible. The only kind of drag anyone had heard of was a drag queen. The bars were somewhat racially segregated. Latinas hung out in one bar, whites in another, blacks in a third. And the very few Asian dykes—or, in my case, a single Arab/Iranian—just floated to wherever the girls were the cutest and the music was the best.

As a well-bred Persian girl, I was groomed from a young age to be an über-feminine woman. When I started hitting the lesbian bars in the early '90s, the sort of femininity and grace I carried myself with made me a big hit with all sorts of women. Yet, although I was having fun in my role as the exotic, femme temptress, I found myself hungry to explore an aspect of my identity that had lain dormant since my childhood.

Soon I got the chance when I was asked to go-go dance at a big gay men's party. I was rather confused about why they would want *me*—a femmey lesbian—to entertain them. So, the night of the party, I decided to use the event as a platform to debut my genderqueered male self. That night I worked the go-go box in an exaggerated gangster suit and fedora, a pencil-thin mustache and sideburns adorning my face, and a butch sneer. The crowds went wild. It was the first they had seen of what I would later find out was called a "drag king."

Around the same time, I debuted my first clothing collection, called Gigolo. It was highly colorful, patterned, dandy clothing for men. Today we would say the clothing was for "metrosexuals." Back then we didn't have quite as many labels.

I knew that what I wanted to do more than anything was be a professional fashion designer. I knew I needed to get out of Arizona and go where the industry was alive and I could thrive. So, with the help of a few talented pals, I put together a full-color faux fashion magazine called *Parisa Journales,* filled with photos of my designs, editorials, a gossip column, and even shots from a fashion show I held at a drag queen bar, called "Paris Is Burning." I sent my magazine to Parsons School of Design and was given a scholarship to go to New York and study fashion design.

1996: NYC, FASHION CAPITAL OF TRADITIONAL FEMININITY

During my years at design school in New York City, I continued to play with and develop my own relationship with masculinity. By my junior year, I had cut all my hair off and was sporting an Elvis-like pompadour. I was going to all the drag king shows in New York and was highly inspired by Mo B. Dick, Murray Hill, Dred, and all the major drag performers of the mid/late '90s.

Design school turned out to be quite challenging, in a way I had not expected. My assumption had been that the premier fashion design school in the most cosmopolitan city in the United States would be encouraging of subversive fashion expression. What I realized was that even at the most liberal of liberal schools, there was a limit to what was considered acceptable in terms of gender expression in fashion.

For my senior project, I tried to bend the rules and create masculine clothing for people born with female bodies. My concept board included pics of butch dykes, FTMs, drag kings, and other genderqueer imagery I had been collecting since coming to New York City. My professors—who themselves were predominately flamboyantly gay men and really hip, artsy women—quietly dismissed and disapproved of my direction. Dressing Cindy Crawford in a men's suit and fedora was about as subversive and genderqueer as the fashion industry was ready to get in the late '90s. You could play with bringing masculinity into the realm of female fashion, as long as the object wearing the clothing represented a very feminine, mainstream ideal of beauty.

My professors strongly encouraged me to just focus on traditional menswear for my senior project, and I reluctantly accepted. I graduated from Parsons with menswear as my specialty and began my fashion design career as a men's designer.

2000: TWENTY-FIRST-CENTURY FASHION OUTLAW

As destiny would have it, I landed my first design job as the result of winning a national design competition. It was sponsored by Target and the CFDA (Council of Fashion Designers of America). My winning entry, ironically, was a collection of womenswear that had lots of the style and functional elements found in menswear. I called the collection UTILITY. As the grand-prize winner, I was hired to design a young men's brand for Target called, interestingly enough, UTILITY. I accelerated quickly to senior designer. Mostly I was designing clothes for young surfer and skater dudes. It was during these years at Target that I noticed how many dykes and genderqueers were shopping urban and skater men's brands for their own wardrobes—and, dare I say, shopping Target's boys' and men's sections for a lot of their wardrobe as well.

The next stop in my corporate fashion career was designing menswear for Old Navy. I had the similar experience of witnessing lots of folks from my queer community shopping the boys' and men's sections of these fashion labels for their clothing needs. It got to a point where, as I was designing clothing for this mass retailer, in my head I was imagining I was designing clothes for my own genderqueer community.

The seed was planted. In 2003, I decided to leave the world of corporate fashion and see what I could do on my own. Being a self-employed fashion designer in New York City was about as crazy a career choice as any girl could make, but with all my heart and soul I felt it was the right thing to do. I had started to feel somewhat alienated within the traditional confines of the fashion industry. Though this was probably one of the most liberal, and the gayest of gay, industries I could be in, I felt palpable discrimination against and dismissal of the dyke and genderqueer point of view within the fashion community.

During the summer of 2004, during my first experience at the Michigan Womyn's Music Festival, the big lightbulb went off inside my head that would lead to the birth of RIGGED OUT/FITTERS. Wandering around the craft area, where all sorts of women were selling their designs and handiwork, I noticed a significant lack of clothing targeting the queer aesthetic. What I did see were mostly the gay pride–themed T-shirts you could pick up at most gay pride stores and festivals.

I suddenly realized that with my background in young men's design and my love of graphics, silk-screening, and thrift store shopping, I could pull together a line of subversive, genderqueer clothing that would appeal to female-bodied folk who didn't want to wear feminine clothing.

And so RIGGED OUT/FITTERS was born. I had no idea what I was getting myself into, other than wanting to see how this little experiment in fashion would fly in the real world. Where do you gather information about how to market, sell, and communicate to a demographic that has been totally overlooked and disregarded by the fashion industry? Every aspect of launching my first collection was done with no technical history or consumer information about my genderqueer market; everything I did came from instinct. The first collection was featured in a stunning photo shoot in *Velvetpark* magazine during the winter of 2005. It was kind of a historical moment in many ways: As far as I know, there had never been a major fashion editorial done in which all the models were real-life, bona fide butch, queer, genderqueer, or FTM-spectrum transfolks *and* in which the clothing collection was designed specifically for that market. We didn't try to pretty up the models or dilute the message of the fashion story. It was bold, unapologetic, and made some waves.

Soon, every major queer publication and website wanted to do an article or photo shoot with RIGGED. I made a point of selecting all the models myself and never allowing the editors to try to create a more mainstream lesbian or gay image of what RIGGED stood for. After all, the tagline for this brand was "Style for Outlaws," and it was really important for me that this highly overlooked portion of the fashion market got its time in the spotlight.

Since RIGGED OUT/FITTERS was launched, I've had to really think long and hard about what I am trying to do with this fashion label and what it stands for. I think the brand is still evolving. The main interest I have is in challenging the fashion industry's perception of how gender and fashion and sexuality should relate. Defying the fashion status quo is definitely a big personal motivator in my designs and marketing philosophy.

With the advent of *The L Word* and a whole slew of LGBT reality TV characters out in the media today, products geared toward these markets are popping up at an exponential rate. Now there is queer jewelry, an entire *L Word* fashion line, gay colognes, and designer denim by gay and lesbian celebrities. Gay Expos are popping up in every major urban city in the United States, and major corporate brands are aggressively wooing the LGBT market with targeted ad campaigns and event sponsorship.

I look back nostalgically on my design school days, when I tried so hard to convince my professors that marketing fashion products to the queer community was where it was at. I have a funny feeling that if I were a student at Parsons today and I proposed a graphic-driven, vintage-inspired line of clothing for the subversive queer market, I might actually be supported in my vision . . . and would maybe even win the Design Student of the Year award. It could happen.

Antifashion: A Punk Style Memoir

ADELE BERTEI

FASHION AND IMAGINATION have been linked in my psyche since childhood, and by 1973 music had become an integral part of my fashion equation. I had morphed into one of Bowie's androgynous "Moonage Daydream" kids, but the style was petering out by 1975; you can only sport an orange mullet and green glitter platforms for just so long, and thankfully the Thin White Duke felt the same. Although I loved the look and music of the Warhol/Velvet Underground set, its women were too femmey for me to imitate—with the exception of the seemingly sexless Mo Tucker. But, though she was the first female musician I ever admired, I could not be moved to imitate the style of someone who foreshadowed *Saturday Night Live*'s Pat character.

Clueless about where to find my true tribe in the industrial hellhole of Cleveland, I finally found inspiration in the form of an album called *Horses*. Patti Smith broke the whole shebang open for me when she appeared on her album cover with that "How cool am I, and fuck you" look dripping from her eyes, dressed in a men's white shirt, a skinny black tie, and a suit jacket thrown casually over her shoulder. Add to this the fact that she rattled off prose that would singe your scalp and dropped names like Jimi Hendrix, Edie Sedgwick, and Jean Genet in the same breath—well, now, *this* was a style to be admired. Patti taught me that fashion was equal parts art, romanticism, and rebellion. All the girls I knew in the gay scene of Cleveland dressed and thought like disco bunnies in glittery spandex, or like man-hating granola dykes in Birks and flannel shirts, or like smart-ass pimps in garishly colored bell-bottom polyester suits (which would be me). But even I knew my look was getting tired.

That same year I met Nan Goldin in a Cleveland gay bar while she was running around the country, snapping her glorious photos of drag queens. Nan came upon me in the midst of a severe style crisis—dressed in a goofy Sgt. Pepper military jacket with glitter on my eyelids—but thankfully she wasn't offended. Her curly red hair was pulled up in a chignon. She had on a skintight pencil skirt, black high heels, stockings with seams, a sleeveless top exposing plenty of cleavage, and an elegant string of small white pearls, her only other accessory a sexy Nikon strung over her shoulder. As if she had stepped out of a classic film noir—the Nikon might as well have been a gun—I fell in love immediately. Propelled by my parallel visions of Nan and Patti Smith and the bullshit diatribes of guys like Crocus Behemoth of Pere Ubu, who blathered on about how "girls don't have the balls to play rock 'n' roll" and demanded, "Name me one great female artist," I couldn't get out of Cleveland fast enough.

New York's East Village in the mid-'70s provided all the new sound and vision I'd hoped for. Everyone who was there knows well who started the "punk" look that Malcolm McLaren would later appropriate—it was Richard Hell, who got busy one night when his tatty wardrobe left much to be desired, painting drunken triangles on a ripped T-shirt, sticking safety pins in it to cinch the holes together, and voilà, a style was born.

Back then Richard was a poet and bass player high on French symbolism, and his broke ass was living in a tenement flat on a heroin block with a bathtub in the kitchen. Inspired by the detritus around him, he was merely taking advantage of the resources at hand and would begin the East Village trend of wearing the inimitable distorted geometry of your head on your sleeve. But it's important to note that Richard was also known to wear a floppy black tie with a blousy, ragged white shirt, like the poorer French artists wore in fin de siècle Paris, so it wasn't all about nihilism. This style had everything to do with mood, imagination, poverty, of course, and whatever befit your fancy at the moment.

When Brit purveyor of punk McLaren returned to New York City, toting his and Vivienne Westwood's Seditionaries line and trying to sell it back to its Yankee provocateurs, it was like the Boston Tea Party—none of us were having it except for the bridge-and-tunnel wannabes, and poor old Malcolm found himself homeward bound again, where he kept busy dressing up his very own meat puppets, the Sex Pistols. McLaren also approached incendiary Brit girl band the Slits, raggedy, white-dreaded rastas who created an utterly unique skank/punk/reggae hybrid. Rumor has it he tried to woo them into management via ridiculous faux-punk posturing, telling them he hated music and hated women. (Surprisingly, they turned him down.)

Where McLaren and his Pistol gang were the essence of punk fashion, post-punk New York was the quintessence of antifashion, and, for the first time in the history of rock 'n' roll, internationally inspired girls were included equally as architects and innovators. While the commercialism of the Sex Pistols nailed the coffin on punk, the magnificent *ping* of girl-marionette strings being severed rang out new music on both sides of the pond.

Downtown NYC in 1977 was all squalor and haunted emptiness, caverns full of abandoned buildings, ruinous streets all groaning for some kind of new warfare. The fucked-up, nihilistic fairytale look of the No New York band of renegade post-punk misfits had more to do with words, music, film, art, and unspoken visionary gender politics than it ever had to do with fashion or feminism as anyone knew it. Post-punk was a slap in the face to commercialism, and when the ugly "isms" happened to rear their little pinheads, the more idealistic among us ignored them as idiotic. Sure, some of us chose to shoot spitballs at Granddaddy Burroughs or the Warhol Queens in the back room at Max's. But for others, hanging with them was a privilege, and no matter what your age or sexual inclinations were, sleeping with them was even better.

One of the things I initially admired most about the way the new breed dressed was their penchant for black, which was, is, and ever will be, supremely sexy. Although the black leather jacket remained a staple of rebel uniformage, everyone in the post-punk scene had his or her own individual take on style. The Brit punks had our initial inspiration regurgitated into a very specific uniform of mohawks, safety pins, and Seditionaries. We No New Yorkers took our style cues from Marlene Dietrich, Jean Seberg, Barberella, and actors in the films of Pasolini, Fellini, and Godard; from Antonin Artaud and Anaïs Nin, Monique Wittig's *Les Guérrillères, Valley of the Dolls,* Bertolt Brecht, kabuki, the Zulus, Kerouac, Jackson Pollock's paint splashes; and from terrorist groups like the Brigate Rossi and the Baader-Meinhof Gang.

Girls felt free to express their animus in their thrift store choices. It was exhilarating to dress like a fucked-up Catherine Deneuve in *Repulsion* one day and a black-and-blue Artful Dodger the next, fashion as perfect complement to sex and theater. One could be a no-wave filmmaker on Friday and a neosurrealist poet on Saturday night. The boys all looked gay, even when they were trying to ape Belmondo's machismo, rubbing their black-panted ass cheeks against a brick wall while dangling a Gitane from their bottom lip, a Borsalino cap cocked over one eye. Girls worked this French gangster look with equal heat. The only boy I ever really loved in the scene was a part-time transvestite—a stunning English boy who made for one ugly woman in drag, and I loved him anyway.

Sexuality had no boundaries. If you wanted to get with someone, you did it without needing or having a label slapped on your ass. You appreciated the girl in the boy, and vice versa; it was fascinating and seductive. Where clothing was antifashion, fluid sexuality was fashion, even if you didn't act on it. And yes, there was definitely a French thing going on then in New York, and it was damn sexy. Even Stiv Bators of the Dead Boys wore a boatnecked striped T-shirt and a fey little French sailor scarf around his neck on occasion. Stiv is a great example: Although he was butt ugly, one had to admit he was sexy, because sexy was about style, not conventional prettiness or good looks. After succumbing to heroin, he was fatally hit by a taxicab on the streets of Paris. Style to the end.

Lydia Lunch was another perfect example. A teenage Anna Magnani in black slips, cleavage barely covered by a leather jacket, with a perpetual sneer, she had the anarchistic growl to support the look, as if Rochester, New York, had given birth to its very own Kali. Lydia penned the anti-anthem that just about sums up the whole scene visually, its only line being a repetitious screech of: "Little orphans running through the bloody snow!" My bandmate in the Contortions at the time, the guitarist Pat Place, resembled a hermaphrodite raccoon from *Andromeda*. I remember her once pinning little wiggly rubber dinosaurs to her torn shirt and chopping hunks of her white-blond hair out—you could see the hot spots on her scalp from her recent dye job. Sounds nasty, but she looked sublime. My friend Lizzy Mercier wore flea-bitten suits or a crazy mix of prints à la Zimbabwean women, her wild hair tied up in weird geometrics with multicolored rags she'd pick from the garbage. Post-punks backed up their looks; infatuated with Africa and hyped up on her own hormonal ecstasy, Lizzy played rhythms on her guitar that no master musician could follow, and Pat perfected her sound on the guitar by using a beer bottle as a slide.

This art war against commercialism inspired and was equally spawned by some of the greatest feminist artists, women like Barbara Kruger, Kiki Smith, Jenny Holzer. Art as life as personal style = antifashion. My friends and I were infamous for taking advantage of art openings by gobbling up the free food and causing scenes. I wore black ballet slippers with my vintage boys' suits and French sailor gear, or full, gathered black skirts stuffed with fake bustles, and I'd singe the edges of my clothes. Still working the pimp look on occasion, I'd refined it and gotten rid of the "I'm gonna git you sucka" nuances. I kept my hair buzzed to half an inch short until some art-yuppie guy at an opening had to ruin it for me, with his "You remind me of a French prostitute." Just as I was tensing up to spit a glob in his eyeball, he fell all over himself exclaiming, "No, no, the Nazis shaved their heads because they worked for the Resistance! It's sexy, no kidding!" I soon commenced growing my hair out when I discovered it was the just the opposite—French patriots shaved their women's heads to shame and mark them for collaborating and whoring with the Nazis.

We girls were skinny for the most part, but our eating disorders stemmed from poverty more than from compulsion. Blissfully, we didn't yet have huge billboards of Auschwitz-shaped models in haute couture underwear imploring us to join their ranks from every visual angle imaginable. Not that advertising ever would have swayed us. Even though we were hungry, the comfort of food just wasn't a priority—we preferred to live by our arrogant, independent wits over working normal jobs in the piss factory or wearing its assembly-line styles.

Buster Keaton became a style obsession of mine, initially because his suits were as cool as his blank expression, but the fact that he did his own stunts made him a great role model for all those drunk and disorderly nights I was unceremoniously tossed down a few flights of stairs by a bouncer at an after-hours joint. Which brings me to the well-positioned bruise or cut being as antifashion as you can get, more or less stemming from some type of "romantic" violence. It could be a fistfight provoked by the lead singer in your band, ending in a free-for-all between band and audience members in front of the stage, or, in some instances, strenuous forms of loveplay, or out-and-out abuse by a lover during a drunken, druggy squabble. And if you sliced up your fingers while playing your guitar onstage, or got smashed in the lip by a swinging microphone, the blood was all the better and stayed ad infinitum on whatever garment or cheek was fortunate enough to be spattered by it until it caked and flaked away into dust.

Already deep into dipsomania, we didn't see Madame Heroin coming until she'd banged us all over the head and dragged us away caveman-style. The call to junk was compounded by AIDS in the mid-'80s, and the powers that be must certainly have rejoiced as they watched all that rebellious imagination practically bleached right out of existence.

Add to this the rise of the girlie stars in the mid-'80, strings pulled courtesy of the new corporate media moguls as they served up a supposedly countercultural message to hypnotize the future women of our nation with the idea of young woman as sexual aggressor. Everybody! Girls just wanna have fun! Translation: Dressing, thinking, and acting like a hetero-promiscuous-dolly-bird-sexpot-who-just-wants-to-dance-flirt-and-fuck was in. It's not Madonna's fault; she was merely reveling in the ambitious, slutty infancy of her becoming the consummate chameleon, performer, and queen of England that she is today. And Cyndi Lauper has always been a damn good singer, not a politician. Both were merely the perfect specimens to promote, put in the right place, to pave the way at the right time.

Being an imaginative, anarchistic lover of outsider lit, art, and ideas, and reflecting that in your wardrobe choices, was now out. Truthfully, it was never allowed in when it came to commercial exposure. Girls knelt at the altar of MTV for its fashion and cultural cues, and what they were getting for the most part were conventionally pretty, straight-looking femmes devoid of ideas in dress and message, aside from the predictable sexual provocations. Not surprising that you never saw the Au Pairs or Lydia Lunch on MTV.

In the ensuing '90s, this backlash against feminism continued, as fashionistas and advertisers searching for their new sartorial designs went into frenzies over Nan Goldin's photos, seizing on the concept of "heroin chic" like piranhas to a bloodbath. Boy, they sure know what to exploit and what to ignore when it comes to women and fashion.

I went back to dressing in all black, this time in mourning as friends died, "feminism" became a dirty word, and the corporate rulership we know today began its ascent. Some of us survived to create careers for ourselves, learning to combine art with commerce and maintaining some semblance of integrity in the process. In the '90s, the only fashionable thing that I found both provocative and exciting was the new tide of gays and lesbians rushing out of their closets, with its stellar moment of Cindy Crawford giving k. d. lang a sexy shave on the cover of *Vanity Fair.* But overall, new geezers in old Cointel suits had successfully brought another countercultural revolution to its knees.

My wardrobe still reflects those times, less by choice than because of the designer aspirations and peculiar tastes of my cat, a gargantuan screaming bulimic queen. (Try to imagine the personification of a civil union between André Leon Talley and the ghost of Stephen Sprouse in black pussy.) The cat has a penchant for chewing holes in my clothes, especially cashmere sweaters—then the fussy little bugger will throw up a steaming wool chunk to add insult to injury. In Los Angeles, Swiss-cheesy cat spittle is not a coveted look. Where it would have been haute couture in NYC circa 1978, it now demotes me to the ranks of a style catastrophe on a brief sojourn from the soup kitchen at the Rescue Mission.

I rarely perform these days, but when I do, I still wear the vintage boys' black leather motorcycle jacket I bought from Nan for a whopping twenty bucks back in 1979—whether or not I may appear as "mutton dressed as lamb," like my friend Anita is always so quick to point out. And each time I put it on, I make a wish to the gods and faeries of science fiction that these young fireflies I catch glimpses of will spark the somnambulant night with a new fashion, one that reaches beyond the confines of a costume—a fashion that will make me catch my breath with the promise that the dust will rise again.

New Coat Reverie

BETH LISICK

I GOT A GREAT coat a couple weeks ago from my neighborhood dry cleaner. You know how they have those racks of clothes for sale in the front of the store? I love those. The items that have been abandoned by the forgetful or tragic or deceased, some so hideous or bland, it's difficult to believe that anyone ever brought them in for specialized cleaning in the first place. Strange gabardine slacks and man blazers with enamel crest buttons.

When I saw this coat, however, I knew immediately it was for me. It's an ivory-colored, hip-length winter coat, wool and lined in acetate, with a cut so plain and humble it could have been manufactured any-where between 1940 and the present. No discernable era. The fit is nearly perfect, sleeves a little short, and the lady sold it for $12, surely the price it would have cost the owner if she had ever returned after dropping it off three years ago. It's been cold lately, and I have worn the coat every day since acquiring it. It's really good.

The coat got me thinking. What was so "me" about it? It's a fucking boring coat. No extravagant details or fancy buttons, no cool lapels or interesting sleeves. It is as nondescript as a woman's winter coat can get while still being visible. The most exciting thing about it is the label on the inside, the jaunty font of the words WEST COAST and then, wrought in a sophisticated cursive script underneath, FOR L. C. MAE. There's a rad red jet airplane swooping across, with a little arrow beaming out its nose, implying the adventure one will hopefully experience when wearing this otherwise very ordinary thing.

My first thought is that I like the coat so much because it doesn't "say" anything particular. And now I'll cop to being a hypocrite.

Of course, in some way, everything we choose to put on our bodies is going to say something. Even my oldest brother, who at age forty still wears whatever my mom buys him for Christmas, is guilty as charged. From tighty-whities to brown braided belts to synthetic sweaters with a thick, snug waistband, he will forever carve his path on the earth wearing the garb bestowed upon him by a third party. And that says a lot.

When I think about my own style (and I will contradict this later), what comes to mind is that I don't like to attract attention to myself. I like to blend in. On most days I wear my Levi's and a sweatshirt, usually paired with the same pair of black boots I have been trudging around in for the past four years. Getting dressed in the morning takes a couple minutes. My hair is its natural color. My ears aren't pierced. I don't have tattoos. I own two lipsticks. I never paint my fingernails. While others live by the motto "Make Yourself a Work of Art!" I usually like to feel more like a frame or a nail. Or even, to use words that bring to mind a '70s-era Laurel Canyon folk song, an empty canvas. Part of me likes to be blank.

Now to get into some Psych 101 with a semiotics chaser. It's also true that I don't want to *be seen* as a person who tries to attract attention to herself, and I like being *thought of* as a person who is low maintenance.

Just as someone who feels rebellious or sexy or creative or capable will likely dress in the manner they perceive as expressing those attributes, I put on the clothes I do because I want the world to see me in a certain way. They feel right for who I am. I want to wear clothes that allow me to sit down on the sidewalk if I have to. I like wearing shoes I can walk all over town in. I don't like being cold. I want to throw all my clothes in the washer together on the same cycle. Black and navy blue forever.

The hypocritical part is that I do love interesting clothes. I love seeing them on other people and I love them on myself. For every T-shirt I put on, there is a rayon mock turtleneck covered in tiny Liberty Bells sitting in my basement. I own a lot of clothes. I once bought a pair of '70s elastic-waisted polyester pants that had a green and blue flame-stitch pattern. Then I cut them into shorts, took one of the legs, cut it in half, and wore it as a tube top to create an instant matching outfit. Twenty years ago I went to the prom in a fuchsia sari with a shaved head. I recently auctioneered a citywide art event in San Francisco wearing a horribly unflattering belted pantsuit. Just last month I hosted my birthday party wearing a floor-length coffee-and-cream negligee with a slit up to the hip that came with a matching pair of hot pants for underneath. Part of the thrill for me is not planning to do these things, not laboring over creating a look, but just letting the fashion bug bite when it's going to.

Like for the birthday party thing. My son and I had come into San Francisco that morning from our house in the East Bay. We were going to fart around together at some parks or museums, and then my parents were going to whisk him away before the party started at my friend's apartment. I was wearing my jeans, my boots, and a sweatshirt. Around 6:00 PM, as my friend was figuring out what to wear, I got a little anxious. There were going to be fantastic appetizers, two delicious cakes, special punch, and a shitload of our favorite people. Why hadn't I thought about bringing something special to wear? It was too late to make a round trip back to Berkeley to dig through my basement (for something that would likely smell pretty moldy anyway), so I got in my car and drove to a consignment shop. I walked in, went up to the guy behind the counter, and said, "I'm having a birthday party tonight and want to wear something that a lady in the early '70s would wear if she were hosting a key party and knew she wouldn't be leaving her house all night." He pulled out this bizarre garment, truly like nothing I had ever seen before. (Did I mention the gold brocade lining on the cuffs, collar, and hem of the hot pants?) I tried it on, laughed my ass off, and handed over my thirty bucks. The party was fun, and if there were a way to measure such things, I'm pretty sure that the party was made that much more fun precisely because of my ridiculous outfit.

Now I think I'm bragging. Fashion has always seemed like it's a little bit about bragging, which is why I hate it sometimes. My obscure vintage pumps, my unearthed thrift store jacket, my boutique designer sweater. I have a notion that they make me a tad more clever and precious than I'd care to be. I like to think that I would wear absolutely anything, but it's not true. Even when I find something I like because it's ugly or confusing, it has to be ugly or confusing *in the right way.*

About a year ago, I dropped my cell phone in the bathtub and needed a new one. My husband, Eli, was out shopping for it with one of my oldest friends, Miles. Here's what they say happened.

ELI: Let's get Beth a pink cell phone!

MILES: Yeah! You know she won't return it, because she doesn't want to be the kind of person who cares what her cell phone looks like.

ELI: Totally. She'd be all, "Fuck you. It's just a cell phone. Who cares what it looks like? I'll use it." But the truth is, she'd either be embarrassed or would have to explain the story behind it every time she pulled it out. She'd act like she didn't care, but secretly she would.

In the end, they got me what I really wanted, the most nondescript one they could find. That's what I prefer in a cellular device and the clothes I wear every day, but I've never given much thought to why. Why keep everything so plain when there are endless variations and mutations to choose from?

Part of it has to do with a serious utilitarian streak that runs through my blood. If something serves its purpose, that should be good enough. There's a tiny, irate man inside me who occasionally reveals himself and shouts to passersby, *Stop trying to "say something" with your purse or your socks or your leopard-print tennis shoes! Quit "expressing yourself" with your hairdo and car seat covers and iPod cases!*

I realize this sounds dismal and harsh and hypocritical, as well as immature and unrealistic, and that if everyone did this the world would be boring and sterile, but such is the intermittent torture that fashion brings.

It's countered by the other voice in my head, the elementary school art teacher, who says things like, *Well, if you're going to have to use an umbrella, why not find a wacky one to make your day brighter! That man's outstanding fedora just brought a smile to my face!* and, *How creative to wear the cutoff leg from a pair of polyester pants as a tube top!*

Here's another clue to why I might choose to be so unadventurous in my day-to-day style of dress. When I meet someone for the first time and they are impeccably dressed, working an outfit, flying a freak flag, or otherwise demonstrating the prowess of their personal fashion, I get a little distracted. We may be carrying on a conversation, but I'm also furiously trying to piece together a story by looking at their shoes and buttons and tattoos and haircut. We all do this anyway, no matter what someone is wearing, but with these people my mind goes into overdrive. I wonder how long they took to get ready, how much money they spent on their ensemble, if they're vain or fun or catty or damaged. What do they do for a living? Do they go to work like that? Is their house a mess? Or is it immaculate? Are they working through something from their past? Or maybe throwing up a screen because they're insecure? Or perhaps they're superconfident? Perhaps they're really into clothes and are simply having fun? The questions they inspire! There's almost something "noisy" about it that turns me off, which says a lot more about my brain than their outfits. They don't turn me off from looking. I will always love to look, but sometimes I think I'd rather let those people, the seriously fashion savvy, remain a mystery.

However, when I meet someone whom I might not have noticed at first, someone standing there in a boring outfit, and that person turns out to be interesting, I am doubly intrigued. The part of me that values the humble and ascetic thinks they're that much cooler because they're not making a big deal about how they dress. It's misguided, I realize, but I find something virtuous in it. So I think, when I put on my regular pants and regular shirts in the morning, that part of me wants to be that person to someone else. The understated one they may have overlooked, but who is secretly amazing.

I think this is the reason I like my new coat so much. Because I want to *be* my new coat. Kind of plain on the outside, with something cool and surprising inside. Dependable. Warm. Accessible. Found by accident.

Slippers, Bring Me My Slippers

ALI LIEBEGOTT

I LOVE PROJECTING humble innocence onto inanimate objects, especially animals in little outfits. My favorite fodder for this kind of projection is 1950s children's illustrations. Let's make a simple half-inch line for the deer's mouth. Now it can eat its perfect, bite-size green leaves humbly and unobtrusively. God, I love a clean line. The first time I saw the drawings in the original *Winnie the Pooh,* I envied Piglet's striped unitard. There he was, debonair and elegant. No piggy camel-toe or varicose veins creeping toward his crotch and screaming, *I'm washed up! Divorce me!* No, Piglet in his unitard was a regular Cary Grant.

Fashion is fantasy, right? Look who we can be in our sexy little ensembles. Why not push the fantasy envelope and crawl right into the children's book to live alongside bears in furnished apartments? It's the fake civility that I find so appealing. Or maybe I want parents, still. Bear parents with their slippers and newspapers. Bear parents smoking a pipe in a distinguished fashion, instead of working ten thousand jobs. I want to be with the bears, drinking tea in their modest yet clean living rooms. We can all put on our regular matching cotton pajama sets with plain slippers. Excuse me for a moment while I call out to my subservient bear wife. "Subservient bear wife in plain slippers, can you bring me my tea?" Puff, puff on my pipe. Now I'll return to Joyce's *Ulysses*. Excuse me while I become a learned bear.

One day it occurred to me that I thought of the illustrations in *Goodnight Moon* as a kind of J.Crew catalog. The problem was, I'd never find these outfits in stores. Someone had drawn the perfect pair of pants for the bear in the book to wear, but they'd never gone and sewed them. I wanted to live in a world where my simple slippers with their simple curved toes waited for me at the end of a long day. There they are now, half pushed under the bed and sitting neatly on an oval rug. When I get home from work, let me change out of my monkey suit and into my color-coordinated, powder-blue pajama top and bottom set. As I step into my simple old-man pajamas, let me appreciate the austere crest embroidered on the pocket. Now I can ease my sore feet into the slippers.

In my fantasies, small-town streets are loaded with shops that sell my matching pajama sets and slippers. The problem is, the real world doesn't. The other problem is, sometimes the real world gets close. When I lived in Brooklyn, I kept myself nourished fashion-wise on clothes bought from hole-in-the-wall businesses that were a second from going under. The neighborhood was changing and the working-class men's clothing store was vanishing. I hit a few going-out-of-business sales at these places. Some old man would send his grandson up a creaky ladder and into the attic to look for any other matching powder-blue cotton robe and pajama sets. And, of course, you could get the whole set for under $10. The beautiful original packaging, just a little dusty. Soon enough, these last holdout stores went out of business, and my remaining pajama sets became more and more worn.

Now I live in a cultural wasteland, San Diego, with my double-Taurus wife. Anna has great style, but for years we fought over what kind of slippers she wanted me to wear. She often wanted to give up the quest for humble coloring-book slippers and buy me ankle-high suede moccasins that had sheepskin on the inside.

"I don't like them," I'd say as she showed them to me. "I'm not looking for fancy slippers."

"You call everything that doesn't cost two dollars 'fancy.' They're not fancy."

"I just want to find some regular slippers."

But we couldn't. I looked in 99-cent stores, in the old-man section in Sears, in all the places I thought I'd find a traditional slipper. Alas, they'd disappeared. The times had changed, and I hadn't changed with them. We all know what happens to those creatures in an evolutionary picture. At the same time, am I the only one who's noticed the gross perversion of the slipper in the last twenty years? How the slipper has become high tech and sneakerish? I saw the pinnacle of this perversion one day in the mall. At first glance, I mistook the slipper for a rock-climbing shoe with its giant, gummy rubber toe.

"How does the guy who designed that sleep at night?" I asked, somberly touching the rubber toe.

Anna, zodiacally predisposed to practicality, defended, "It's so you can wear them outside, too. So you can drink your coffee in the morning and then go outside and pick up dog shit."

I thought the whole point of wearing slippers was that they signaled the end of the workday. By the time the slippers come on, picking up dog shit is out of the question. It's time to read the paper and cross your legs, regally, in front of a roaring fire. Let me tinkle the ice in my highball glass as I bore my wife with the details of my day at the firm.

Hunting for my traditional slipper became a wedge between Anna and me over the years. I'd hear myself explaining to clerks, "It's plain.

Like a drawing of a slipper in a coloring book." Or, "Have you ever read Nabokov? It would be like the slippers one of his toothless old man characters would wear."

"Can't you just get these temporarily, until we find the kind you like?" Anna would say, gesturing toward a canvas-backed moccasin. "These are plain," she'd say.

"Those wouldn't be in a coloring book," I'd remind her.

"Yeah, well, there weren't dykes in 1950s coloring books, either. They don't make the kind of slippers you want anymore. I hate to break it to you, but the slipper has changed in the last sixty years!"

We didn't talk about the slippers again after that day. I walked the house in my old-man socks, which thankfully you could still find, and managed to forget, for the most part, ever finding my coloring-book slippers. Anyway, I probably wanted the ritual more than I actually wanted the slippers. I wanted to come home at the end of my day and say, "Hello, slippers" before slipping each foot in.

Or, "Let's retire to the drawing room, slippers."

I'd buy a purebred hunting dog and name it Slippers.

"Slippers, bring me my slippers," I'd joke in front of financially virile friends.

Oh, how they'd chuckle at that one! Then we'd retire in front of the fireplace, the hearth, with its flames colored perfectly orange and yellow. I'd stretch my legs out, unfold my newspaper, and contentedly notice the perfect geometry of the small mouse in the corner of the room, eating his perfect triangle of cheese.

After years of living inside the coloring book, I came home from work to find Anna sitting on the edge of the bed in a red vintage slip.

"Close your eyes," she said. "I have a surprise."

When I opened my eyes she was holding a pair of muted olive green coloring-book slippers.

"Where'd you find them?" I cried.

"IKEA."

Apparently, there was an enormous bin near the exit filled with $3.99 coloring-book slippers.

I put the slippers on immediately. They were so comfortable. The lines were so clean. I kept my word, and when I came home from work, I said, "Hello, slippers." And later, when I took them off to get into bed, "Goodnight, slippers."

Within a year they were worn out. I kept pulling them out of the trash.

"This is no longer a slipper," Anna'd say.

And then I'd retrieve them.

"Your scarcity issues freak me out," she'd say. "It's okay to throw things out when they're used. Anyway, these were meant to be disposable slippers."

"Why would IKEA sell disposable slippers? Why would someone want to buy disposable slippers?"

"For guests," she said.

But I'd seen disposable slippers when I was in the mental hospital. They were nothing like *my slippers*. The slippers at the mental hospital were made of blue foam and had embossed happy faces on the toes. No one believes me when I tell them about the embossed happy faces, but it's true.

Soon I began to admit that the slippers were done. The foam sole had deteriorated and the fabric was shredded. Anna and I began a new dance around throwing them out. Sometimes I'd go to the trash can first with them and say, "It's time," and drop them in dramatically, but by the next night I'd fish them out again. Then Anna began to approach me like the mediator they send onto the roof for the jumper.

"We're just going to walk those slippers over to the trash can. It's okay," she'd coax, stretching her hand out toward me. "Okay, now give me the slippers. They've been great slippers and they've done their job. . . ."

This particular dance ended with my clutching the slippers and her calling me a money anorexic. If I knew I could buy a new pair, I could let the old pair go more easily, but we never saw them at IKEA again. Then Anna went away on a trip. I decided to surprise her when she came back by throwing out the slippers. So I went to the outside trash can and dropped the slippers in. Then I piled dog shit on top of them so I wouldn't be tempted to take them out.

"I have a surprise for you," I said when I picked her up at the airport.

"What?" she said, and then, a split second later, "You threw the slippers out!"

She's good.

The Undressing of America

MARY WORONOV

THE FIRST TIME I went to Las Vegas was during Frank Sinatra's reign. Women glided noiselessly across the carpets of Caesars Palace in cocktail dresses and evening gowns, children weren't allowed in the casino, men wore tuxedos, and only Frank loosened his tie for the last smoky song. Standing behind the velvet rope I could watch my mother at the baccarat table, looking like Grace Kelly in her icy pale green cocktail dress with the halter strap and a double strand of pearls as big as blueberries. The man she was with never spoke to me, and when he spoke to my mother, he referred to me as "the kid." His name was Mickey, and he resembled a well-fed, sleek, manicured rat. I figured he must be related to the famous Disney Mouses because he dressed in the latest Italian suits with gold cuff links, handmade shirts, and patent leather shoes to match his elegant black tux. During the day he wore tan wing tips to go with a beautiful cream-colored suit and a panama hat tilted over black sunglasses . . . all that just to go down to the pool for five minutes to say hello to Mom.

Years later, while revisiting Las Vegas for its film festival, I wander down to the casino to watch the baccarat table and get the shock of my life. The place looks like a tacky TV game show, with flashing colored lights and ringing bells. Families with their kids in tow migrate across the endless casino floor, looking for lines to queue up in and different ways to lose their money. I am uncomfortably aware of lots of skin and leg hair. Most men are wearing T-shirts and shorts cut like baggy underwear. A few women have on halter tops but seem to have forgotten the dress that goes with such tops, and the majority of footwear is flip-flops or sneakers. Everyone looks ugly, sloppy, and sort of dazed, like they don't know what hit them—should they shop? Or gamble? Or eat? Rest is out of the question, since there is no place to sit that doesn't cost money. Looking tense and exhausted, they move like cattle being prodded through their chutes.

Comfort, I decide. They are dressed in their underwear because they want to be comfortable, because vacation is stressful. It used to be a time to be seen, to socialize, to dress up and express yourself while impressing others, but not anymore. These people have forgotten how to dress up, something that sounds like a lot of work, and now that they're on vacation they can enjoy looking ugly. But if comfort is the object, why don't they just stay in their rooms? Bed is the most comfortable place I know of, in the prone position, with lots of dreams to replenish the soul. I retreat to my room and turn on the TV. Perhaps they're happy and I'm the one who's exhausted. Feeling very out of it, I get into bed.

I can't sleep. I keep thinking of all those sheep downstairs in their T-shirts. After centuries of incredible inventive dress—the toga, the suit of armor, the corset, the high heel, the wig, the tie, magazines full of the latest makeup, the fortunes made on the Paris runways, the '40s, the '50s—after all that, my generation will be known for *underwear*, the T-shirt, the baseball hat, the sneaker. How humiliating. Being seen in underwear used to mean only one thing—sex—but nowadays, when everything else from wedding dresses to raincoats is sexy, I suspect the T-shirt's popularity is not about sex. Just because Marlon Brando looked sexy in a T-shirt doesn't mean the T-shirt is capable of making someone look like Brando. Besides, the fat stomachs I saw downstairs in the casino didn't look like they wanted to have sex, and if they did, wouldn't they go back to their rooms and fuck each other in private? Certainly if you're not getting fucked, the worse thing you can do is advertise it by walking around in your underwear. Nobody fucks someone who can't get fucked, no matter how good looking they are. In our culture death is better than not getting fucked, so why let everyone know you're not getting any?

Having gone to bed early, I'm up at six in the morning, attempting to re-enter the casino, when I see *them*, the same mob walking around in their underwear, like zombies in a cheap movie, so cheap they couldn't afford costumes. Only the hotel employees and a few foreigners seem to have made an effort to dress. Perhaps it isn't comfort; perhaps it's laziness, or everyone just forgot to dress. Their alarms didn't go off? They slept in their cars? They weren't allowed to sleep, due to the hotel policy of lacing all alcohol with methamphetamine? Everybody's clothing was stolen? There was an infestation of clothing-eating insects? Tired of thinking up excuses for them, I order breakfast and stare at the table until my eggs arrive.

I am not going to let this underwear fad ruin my mood. After all, fashion is a perverse game. One day it's about beauty and the next day it's about being ugly, but there are those rare times when it's about making a statement, the way French courtiers did when they wore a single red ribbon around their necks while they danced the minuet in the shadow of the guillotine. I stare at *them*. Obviously the T-shirt is an affected look. No one is wearing a T-shirt because they are here to fix the plumbing, nor are they so poor that they can't afford other clothing. On the contrary, when people arrive at your party in T-shirts, it means they don't think much of you because they don't have to. They want to look as if they are so busy, they didn't have time to dress for your party; they are so rich, they don't have to impress anyone. Everyone is so busy proving that they are better off than their neighbor that we are all sitting in our underwear, looking like shit.

It's not the T-shirt's fault. Historically speaking, the T-shirt was invented by the army in World War I to replace itchy wool underwear. It escaped from under the shirt in World War II when a picture of sailors working in their T-shirts hit the cover of *Time* magazine. Its sex appeal soared when Brando wore it in the T-shirt named desire, but when did this piece of underwear get invited to the dinner table? I suppose some people refer to it as casual, relaxed indifference, which is accomplished by dressing down with the utmost care and then seeming oblivious about it, like a movie star going on the late show with his shirttails out. You might think it looks like the audience means so little to him, he forgot to tuck his shirt in, but in fact he is so nervous that he has hired a makeup artist, a dresser, a coach; he has memorized a million one-liners; and he just threw up in the wings. It's gotten to the point where, unless you are a drag queen, dressing up makes you look conservative, uptight, like you're trying too hard, like an asshole and a fool. So while the all-American dad is in the bathroom with his porno mag, Mom is in the closet with that expensive dress she can't be seen in.

Wearily I go upstairs to see the director of the movie they are showing, and I find him digging into his third lobster at ten in the morning. He tells me to sit down and have some. The food and drinks are on the house. When I tell him eating too much is not good for his health, he looks sad, and I can tell he wants me to leave. He is in his T-shirt and a pair of corduroy pants that are worn out at the knees, but he is a director, and he can dress any way he likes. I'm a has-been actress, and I still have to look sexy. I think I'll go change into my black jeans that I never wash, my black torn T-shirt that's skintight, and those fucking boots that make me look nine feet tall and absolutely unfuckable. At least I still know how to dress when I do have something to say.

That night I get drunk and things don't look so bad. After all, it's just fashion, and our fashion at the moment is to look like everyone else, not to stick out, just a million clones advertising corporate logos on our chests. At two in the morning I slap the bar with my fist. That's it! The T-shirt has become a form of camouflage, the uniform of the group. We are all afraid and we need to be in hiding, hiding in the pack, a paranoid nation of fearful lemmings. "What happened to the individuality Americans are so proud of," I ask the bartender in a loud voice, "the underdog we like to see win, and the rebel we all fell for in high school?" The bartender is trying to ignore me but I press on. This is information he should know about. "Remember tie-dying? T-shirts used to be the great democratic leveler, the Phrygian cap, the opposite of the crown, a political statement. I had one with a pot leaf on it. T-shirts used to be cheap, but now they're expensive, they have labels that turn your chest into a billboard, or, worse yet, there is someone else's idea on it and you're just a fucking mule.

"No one thinks of a T-shirt as a sign of democratic equality anymore, unless democracy means 'lack of style,' the same way communism means 'drab gray uniform,' which is preposterous because the men who forged our constitution had great style. So why does our president wear a baseball cap instead of a homburg, or a bowler, or a panama? Kennedy was the first president to show up without a hat, probably because he had a great head of hair, but a baseball cap? Is Bush trying to invoke the memory of his last job? Last night I saw him on TV in his shirtsleeves without a tie. Next he will have fake sweat rings under his arms, trying to convince you that he is one of us, that he is working hard. Bullshit—he doesn't have to impress us because we're not the boss anymore. He is the boss. The people used to be the boss, but now we're just something he pats on the head like a dog."

I'm on a roll. I can feel everyone at the bar listening to me. The bartender comes over and says people here are republican and I should go to another bar, but I don't let him intimidate me. "You don't dress up to pat your dog," I tell him, but there is no real conviction in my voice so I shut up and leave. Let's face it, the rebellion is over and I just want to get through the rest of my life without any problems. Some would call this an intelligent decision. I call it hiding in the pack, T-shirt anonymity; sure, my country is fucked-up, but I just live here. I'm a liberal, the kind of liberal who talks a lot at the dinner table but doesn't do anything else about his fucked-up government. Did I buy an electric car when they came out? No.

Back to the room to watch more TV. What's puzzling is that it's not just America; everyone wants to wear this piece of underwear. We are not the only people who feel middle aged, declining, and humiliated. Go anywhere in the world, visit any shrine, and you will be faced with thousands of little vendors trying to sell you a stupid T-shirt. I'm embarrassed to say that I still wear T-shirts most of the time. T-shirts and blue jeans and sneakers are my magic cloak of invisibility—my grandmother would be horrified and my great-grandmother would have shot me on sight, but my mom just smiled sadly as she slipped off her high heels, rolled down her silk stockings, shimmied out of her beautiful icy-green cocktail dress, unhooked her bra, and squirmed out of her girdle. By the time she laid the double strand of pearls as big as blueberries gently on the bureau, I swore I would never get that dressed up for any man. Well, maybe for James Bond, but certainly not for someone who looked like a sleek rat, whose eyes flickered around the casino like a pair of whiskers sensing things Mom and I could never be aware of. I pass out on the bed.

Next morning everything is crystal clear. The real reason that my generation and I wear T-shirts is that we don't want to grow up. It's completely retarded. I am wearing the same outfit I started wearing in high school: blue jeans, sneakers, and a T-shirt, and I'm over fifty. I own a string of pearls and a rather large collection of high heels. I never said I didn't like buying things, but I rarely wear them once the novelty wears off. They are the dreaded costume of responsibility that I still think I can get out of. My routine outfit is the Peter Pan T-shirt: *No, I'll never grow up*. My generation has replaced the gray flannel suit, the sign of adulthood, with the T-shirt, our sign of infancy. *Mary Woronov was buried this morning in her underwear, the first person ever to be interred in a T-shirt.* I always knew I would make history. On the plane home to L.A., I tell the stewardess that I like her outfit. I mean it, but somehow she looks insulted. I close my eyes and Mom's pearls slide off her neck. The rat slips me a twenty. "Okay, kid, get lost." No amount of cologne can make up for the rat's five o'clock shadow.

In the LAX car park I finally find my car and get in. I breathe a sigh of relief. I love L.A. and it loves me. Unlike Las Vegas, L.A. immediately gives me my revenge on the underwear craze. The new gang fashion on the L.A. streets is to wear one's pants below your ass so all your underwear shows. It is so far over the top, it's laughable. It's also maniacally ingenious; the reversal of cleavage for ass crack, from female to male, deserves an essay all its own. I see this overt display of underwear as a hip rebellion against the generic T-shirt uniform of my generation. This wonderfully ridiculous getup is usually worn only by teenage boys or copycat lesbians. I'm not sure if they mean it to be sexy or insulting, and, even better, I don't think they know or care. I certainly didn't think about it when I walked out the door twenty years ago in nothing but a black slip and black army boots to a punk club called the Lingere. I just wanted to get loaded and dance.

Stuck in traffic on Sunset, I sit in my car and stare dreamily at the billboards. Suddenly I'm depressed again. The billboard in front of me is an ad for Abercrombie & Fitch that shows only the hips of a young boy in nothing but his jockey shorts. It is so overcalculated that you can't tell what the fuck they are selling anymore—it's certainly not hats and coats. If I were a gay man this might mean something to me, but now I just stare at it, uncomfortably confused and pissed off. The first time my mom took me to Abercrombie & Fitch in New York, I was so impressed. On the ground floor they had a real stuffed elephant's head just for decoration. It was exotic and wonderful, and I've never forgotten it. The blast of a horn wakes me up and, flipping off the guy behind me, I plunge recklessly into the traffic ahead of me. Life sucks. I can't even remember why I was so happy to be back home.

Scrunchies & Bite Marks

NICOLE J. GEORGES

Doctor Drew continually ruins the tasteless good times of his callers. If you call and mention wanting to be bitten until you bleed or vice versa, he would delve into your psyche & let you know this comes from watching your parents fight, or that you were hit with an object by your mom.

He is usually correct, but who wants that rattling around while getting innocently straight/not me!

One day while dishing out conservative advice to a lesbian friend, my eyes focused on her feet.

I keep my psychological talk show findings in a pocket marked Advice, and go over it as i ride the bus or take a bath later.
I think to myself, Are there really that many abuse survivors, or is it the demographic of Loveline callers in particular?
and
What does it say about me when i repeat Dr Laura advice to friends disguised as my own?

Beaming at her sensible saddle shoes, i had a horrifying memory and realization,

1st day of school in Bethesda Maryland, my mother sat stuffing me into brown and white shoes., as i kicked in protest. Handling my legs a little more roughly, she offered the merciless:

Because I'm the mother, that's why.

nobody else will be wearing these! why me?

Nothing seemed more awful than to wear this hideous pair into first grade, even after my geriatric teacher commented on their beauty & old fashioned sensibilities.

With this I realized THE FASHIONS THAT WERE FRIGHTENING TO ME AS A CHILD ARE WHAT I AM DRAWN TO IN ADULTHOOD.

Not only am i wearing secret scars from rough sex in an effort to liberate my 26 year old self from childhood visions of terror, I'm wearing peter pan collars as well.

In Catholic school i was sickened to have a powder blue polo

hate it

obscure my much sought after grunge apparel.

With the sound of the afternoon bell, i was found racing into the bathroom, oversized flannel & Nirvana teeshirt thrown on in a futile attempt at portraying my angst & authenticity as i waited with my carpool for a ride home.

My adult dream outfit has been this: Peter Pan collared shirts of different shades and sizes, perhaps a jumper or velvety dress with a bow, orthopedics or saddle shoes, sweater vests and ribbons, eyebrows eliminated. If i could choose my own uniform this would be it.

hey

don't worry about leaving a mark

The girls I'm attracted to? Those i seek out for forever purposes? They look like the boys i ratted out for sniffing glue in math class.

Made appointments with the school counselor to tearily confess i saw a jar of Elmers rubber cement passed between them. The pale boys in the PusHead illustrated metal shirts, one complete with stomach turning phrase "I'M INSIDE YOU. SAD BUT TRUE"

It's disappointing to admit Yes, I am the living embodiment of Pop Psychology. Go ahead, ask. I had no father figure and now i'm a lesbian. I was forced to attend Catholic School and now harbor a uniform fetish. All of my likes and dislikes, interests and favorite foods are probably the result of what I saw in babyhood. I have no control over these preferences.

I can't do it. missionary and i can't wear a scrunchie.

the end. NG06

14

A Condensed Autobiography of My Life in Clothes

CHELSEA STARR

MY PERSONAL STYLE was a long time coming. When I was a kid I didn't have very many clothes, and the clothes I did have were usually dirty and ill fitting. My mom was young and had what you might call a "hands off" approach to parenting—but, given her propensity for blind rages, you might not be very accurate. In any case, the kids in my family were mostly left to our own devices when it came to matters of eating, clothing, and grooming, and as a result we were a pack of greasy-haired ragamuffins.

At any given time, we'd have one set of functional clothes each, which could get kind of sticky. Once, in second grade, my class had a substitute teacher who didn't know that when playtime came I was supposed to chip away at my long list of unfinished assignments instead of playing with the other kids. I had been wanting to get my hands on the Little People's barbershop since the school year began, and here was my chance. I had to pee pretty badly, but not as badly as I wanted to play with the barbershop toy, so I held on to it. As the situation became do or die, I scrambled to the front of the room for the bathroom pass, but it was out! I stood waiting at the door for the person to come back and return the pass.

The sub saw me dancing all crazy and suggested that I go to the bathroom without the pass. "Thanks, man!" I yelled as I tore down the hall. Once I got into a stall and slammed the door, I started unzipping my pants, but the zipper got stuck. I eventually unstuck the zipper, but not before I had peed all over myself. "Gosh dang it!" I cried. I sat down on the toilet, completely unable to come up with any other plan. I stayed there for the whole rest of the afternoon until the end of the day, when a classmate named Tish (whom I hated because of her beautiful Velcro shoes) was sent to look for me. She was so sweet to me, it made me hate her even more. I went to catch my school bus and everyone avoided me and called me "Tanya," after the girl at school who always smelled like pee. To avoid my pee, the kids all crowded three to a seat at the front of the bus, while my ever-loyal sister and I had the back ten rows to ourselves.

We didn't have a washer or dryer at our house, and there was hardly ever money for the Laundromat, which was hard to get to anyway since it was more than a mile away and we didn't have a car. In a rare motherly moment, my mom washed the pants out in the sink and hung them up to dry. It was winter, and the next morning they were still soaking wet. Having no pants to wear, I was forced to stay home from school. The next morning they were still damp and my mom tried to make me put them on anyway, but I refused. She threatened to send me to school in my too-small pajama bottoms, but I crawled into my closet and would not be moved. The pants were dry the next day and I went to school. By then everyone had almost forgotten that I'd ever peed my pants. Lucky!

I'm sure this doesn't come as any shock to you, reader, but when you are a filthy little urchin, people treat you much differently than they treat your well-kempt counterparts. I'm talking teachers, librarians, store clerks, you name it. To these people, you're either totally invisible, or you're all too visible and are treated like a repugnant little rat.

I was always the last one to be called on in class, the first one to be singled out for any small infraction, and the very least popular person at any school. We moved a lot, and every time I kept hoping to make a decent impression, but it's hard to make something out of nothing. I remember once starting a new school wearing a too-small purple sweater that my mom had yanked out of a bag of dirty, mildewing laundry that morning. After a few hours I got used to the smell, but other kids could smell it, and I felt like my teacher was looking at me disdainfully whenever it rode up, so I kept trying to pull it back down over my belly. Another time we moved during Christmas break. I had gotten a pair of moon boots, about three sizes too big, from my grandpa for Christmas. It was snowing, so I delightedly put them on. Because I'd been wearing the moon boots, my one pair of actual shoes got lost in the move. It stopped snowing. I prayed it would start up again before Christmas break ended, because I knew that snow or no snow, I would be starting my new school in moon boots.

Having the wrong clothes can make for a lot of shame. There was a church bus called the joybus that would come to our apartment complex and take all us poor kids to church. The joybus was a good Sunday option, since there was never anything on TV but televangelists and *Star Trek,* and I hated creeping around the house like a church mouse all day while my mom slept off her hangover. Plus, they served a snack. On the joybus we'd sing songs and play games, and usually on the way home they'd show a filmstrip. Once the filmstrip was called "Rude Ruth." It was about a little girl named Ruth who was in all ways uncouth. She talked too loud in Sunday school, squirmed in her seat, and snacked on communion, though she had not yet been baptized. She bore such an uncanny resemblance to me that the filmstrip could very well have been called "Rude Chelsea."

The part that really got me, though, was when they picked apart what she was wearing, saying that you really have to go to God's house in your best. Instead of wearing proper kneesocks and Mary Janes with her raggedy dress, Ruth was wearing striped tube socks and tennis shoes—my exact outfit. I was filled with shame. My cheeks turned red and hot as I discreetly rolled my socks down so that instead of looking like Rude Ruth, I looked like I was wearing two cloth doughnuts around my ankles. I liked the way it looked, and I kept wearing my socks that way for several months, until someone said, "You look like you're wearing dirty doughnuts around your ankles."

I had a cool outfit in fifth grade. My brother's dad took me to Fred Meyer and let me pick out an outfit each for my sister and myself. I picked blousy black tops and plaid jeans that were poufy on top but tight at the ankles. That winter I also had a pair of stirrup pants, which were very cool at the time but were the cause of great sadness for me. My grandpa gave my sister and me each a pair for Christmas, but when I opened mine I said thank you and then excused myself to the bathroom to cry. They were white and flimsy and see-through, and I hardly had any underwear to wear under them. Plus, I knew they were going to get dirty and ruined so fast. My sister's were black. Unfair.

Around junior high I started getting a few bucks here and there from baby-sitting neighbor kids, and a couple of times I was able to get my Aunt Marlene to take me with her to the Red White and Blue Thriftstore. I found a pair of light blue Guess jeans there, their only problem being that they were straight leg instead of pegged. I'd roll them up tightly at the ankles as a quick fix. I also found a Coca-Cola T-shirt and a cute antique bowling shirt with Chinese characters on the back and cool metal buttons. This I would wear with my Guess jeans. For shoes, I had a pair of real Keds that my grandma had gotten me for my birthday. I wore them for a year straight, until my toes were poking out, the whole tops of the shoes were ripped, and the soles were worn clean through. Then it was back to $2 hard-bottomed fake Keds.

When I was in ninth grade, my mom had a boyfriend who had a job and a car and took us school shopping. A hundred bucks each on his JCPenney card. I got a pair of Nike Airs, a Paula Abdul T-shirt, and some socks and underwear. I still fit into the Guess jeans, which were now shorts, but just barely. A few months later they got married, and we were taken to the mall to pick out a wedding outfit. My sister and I conspired to wear all black in sullen protest of our mom's marrying a fuckwad we hated. I got the cutest little brown and black baby-doll dress and black bike shorts from Rave, and a pair of witchy shoes at The Wild Pair's going-out-of-business sale. My sister got the same outfit, but a little different. The "family" photo from the event shows my mom, sister, brother, and me standing together awkwardly with my mom's new husband. The only clue that could tip you off to the fact that we're at a Vegas wedding and not a funeral is that my mom, who is for some reason also wearing black, is holding a bridal bouquet. Also, the new husband is smiling wildly.

My mom's husband got a job working on the Hoover Dam, so we moved to Boulder City, Nevada. With my Nikes, Guess jeans, Wild Pair shoes, and baby-doll dress I felt pretty optimistic about starting a new school. It was amazing to have two outfits that looked so clean and normal. I didn't make any friends, but walking through school without constant harassment was a dream come true. It was definitely the first time I'd ever blended in with my peers.

We moved back to Oregon, and by that time I was almost old enough to get a job. I turned sixteen, and the next day I went and got a job at McDonald's. I bought a pair of Birkenstocks with my first paycheck. When I came home with my next check, however, my mom's husband had left, and she bullied me into handing the money over to her as a "loan" so the lights wouldn't get shut off. In fact, whenever I got paid

I was bullied into forking over most of the money, so, though I had had visions of tons of cute shoes and clothes, I eventually stopped working. I was just as broke working as I had been when I was not working, and I was greasy and exhausted.

I finally turned eighteen and went off to an expensive college I couldn't afford. My guidance counselor and everyone at the college tricked me into taking out huge loans to pay for this stupid fucking school, saying once you get out you can get a great job and pay them off in no time. Sounded plausible to me—I hadn't ever known anyone who'd gone to college. The college was in a town with the best thrift stores I've ever been to this day: Spokane, Washington. I started what would become a lifelong love affair with vintage clothing. I didn't know it was called vintage back then, though; I called it "old" or "antique."

Just when I was starting to get a little panache, I realized I was a big lesbo. I mean, I had known for as long as I could remember, but I finally decided it was time to come out. The effect on my style and wardrobe would prove to be disastrous. I started hanging out with some gays (we didn't use the words "queer" or "dyke") and, due to their internalized misogyny, I had to start dressing the part in order to be taken seriously or listened to *at all* when I spoke. I shaved my head, got a pair of overalls, some Doc Martens boots, and a couple thermals, and I was good to go. Looking back, I can see that my more feminine side was making itself known in tiny ways: My overalls were tighter than was cool, my thermals were flowered. I dressed this way for several years, and it felt okay but not amazing.

When I finally started dressing up and feeling amazing, I had moved to Austin, Texas, and made friends with Flip, the most beautiful girl I'd ever seen in my life. She had the most incredible fashion. She'd wear whatever crazy, pretty thing she wanted, and her risks paid off. She always looked perfect, even when she was slouching through the house in the morning, half asleep in her underwear. She rubbed off on me. I rode my bike to the thrift stores and bought frilly, little-girl church dresses, maid uniforms, fancy silk cowgirl shirts. We decided once to have a contest: Who could keep up leaving the house either totally dressed up, or looking like we might be in costume, the longest? We both won, because neither of us ever quit.

I moved to San Francisco with a backpack. In it: my journal, a pair of red cowboy boots, a red T-shirt with a metallic tiger on it, electric-blue tights, a furry aqua-and-navy-blue miniskirt, two T-shirts, a pair of New Balance sneakers, a pair of jeans, a red slip, and a checkered cowgirl dress. I got a job right away and started buying things on the street. A wedding dress, a glittery scarf, a leather vest. I also started taking a big empty purse to Thrift Town and filling it with whatever struck my fancy. Turquoise Nikes, knee-highs, '80s spandex dresses. I'd wear anything. I'd be a fancy lady one day, in suit pants and a tie the next. I was often asked whether I was butch or femme. I had never heard those terms before, so I said, "Neither."

I've gone through a lot of fashion in San Francisco. From 2000 until about 2003 was pretty '80s, but then people started being able to buy leg warmers and other things I'd spent years digging around for at thrift stores, so I moved on to the '90s: bejeweled bra tops, lots of gold chains, shiny spandex. People began to wear a lot more spandex, a lot more gold; I moved on to a more Victorian look. This, too, was co-opted by the mall. And then I wore a giant bouffant, bell-bottoms, and hippie tops, followed by a disco phase, which I'm still quite fond of. Somewhere in there I wore prairie dresses and made Holly Hobbie bonnets to match them. Also, I like just about any vintage dress that fits well: mod, hippie, '40s sexpot, whatever. And I've almost always worn hot pants in some form or another to my dance party, "Hot Pants," which is now in its fifth year.

My current look is sort of hard to characterize. I like bright colors, I like billowing frocks. I am into things with designs, things that are out of scale, huge or tiny. When I go out, I almost always sew a new outfit for the night. I like anything that's one piece. I make a lot of things with hoods or matching hats. I overdo the matchy-matchy. I look at fashion magazines when I can't think of anything good to make. I also really like perusing Style.com; nothing like watching a runway show to dig you out of a fashion rut and get your little motor running (my favorite designers right now are Jeremy Scott and Alexander Herchcovitch, in case you were wondering). I also like to go to thrift stores and pick out the ugliest, most garish thing and transform it into an outfit of beauty.

I'm happy with where I'm at fashion-wise, and I'm even happier about where things are heading now that I'm getting better at sewing. Given my humble beginnings, I'm a little surprised by how things turned out for me, but I also always knew it would be this way. My sister and I used to say, "Just wait till we're eighteen. We're gonna have more clothes than we even know what to do with." When I look around my apartment at the million zillion clothes and the two different sewing machines and the giant heap of fabric exploding with possibility, I am ridiculously glad we were right.

15

Fifty-Cent Fever at the As-Is

TRINA ROBBINS

It's 3:00 PM on a blustery December afternoon, and I'm freezing my ass off in a long line in front of the Goodwill As-Is Store. Even on an ordinary day the As-Is is something to write home about. Bins fill a huge room, piled high with every conceivable kind of clothing, and everything sells for $2.25 each. On Sunday there are bins overflowing with books, and booksellers crowd in by the droves. Sometimes bins might hold shoes, belts, or handbags, even stuffed toys still bearing their original tags. The name As-Is might make a body think that what you find here is trashed beyond all recognition, but such is not the case. I have found torn T-shirts and I have found leather jackets with the original store tags still attached. Apparently Goodwill just gets so many donations that the surplus is detoured to its As-Is Stores all over the country. There's one in Santa Cruz and one in Honolulu. And on the first Saturday of every month they have a special sale: Everything in the store, from leather jackets to torn T-shirts, goes for fifty cents, so help me god.

Clustered next to the entrance are the resellers. They're regulars at this place, been coming here daily for years to score fabulous vintage clothes and hot new styles. Some of them sell their finds at vintage and hip new/used clothing stores; others sell their stuff at local flea markets. They know each other and save places for each other at the front of the line. Some of them are nice, most are obnoxious. They grab the choicest items by hogging the bins, elbowing out of the way any plebeian who might want a chance at that red leather coat or silk leopard-print wraparound.

Us ordinary though intrepid and addicted folks have to stand behind them in the line. We are a motley crew, composed of Russians and Filipinos, African American church ladies, Japanese art students here to buy clothes that would cost hundreds of dollars in Tokyo, multipierced young men and their maroon-and-blue-haired girlfriends, and a drag queen or three. I have brought friends in the past, but not everybody can handle the experience. Most of those I've brought here never come back. It is, after all, intense.

At three-thirty, the manager opens the door and the crowd surges forward, a tsunami of bargain hunters. A veteran of these sales, I am dressed for the hunt. A long full skirt, beneath which I can slip on pants to see if they fit; a tank top beneath my sweater for pulling shirts over my head; slip-on loafers in case there are shoes to try on. A small crocheted shoulder bag hangs diagonally across my chest, freeing my arms for yanking, dragging, and hauling; inside is the bare minimum: lipstick, keys, a hanky, money. No ID. If there's a raid I'm out of luck. (Somehow, I feel a place like this *must* be illegal!) No scarf, even though the weather's arctic. If I find a nice scarf, I'll wear it home. Pulling the look together is a canvas tote bag to hold my booty.

Even though I'm close to the front of the line, by the time I get inside the room is already filled with frenzied maniacs tossing the contents of the bins over their shoulders onto the floor while the manager ineffectually yells—in Spanish and English—for everyone to pick up their mess. The resellers, who got there first, have already claimed the bins closest to the entrance, and their discards form small cloth mountains over which I have to climb. I spot a promising plaid peeking out from a pile of clothing, reach under a reseller's arm, and drag it out. She gives me a dirty look and moves in front of me so I can't take anything else from "her" bin. "Bitch," I mutter, but I see that I've found a great little vintage plaid shirtwaist! I stuff it into my canvas bag and move on.

Already the place is a madhouse. Everybody here has learned about this place by word of mouth—the As-Is definitely does not advertise. Now here I am, spilling the beans to the whole world, and some of my fellow thrifters will hate me for it.

Most of the clothing is mounded on the floor, with people rummaging through piles of velvet, wool, cotton. A woman passes by, arms full of clothes, laughing out loud—she just can't believe it, it's so outrageous!

"Hey, you want this coat?" It's Ramon, one of the nicer resellers. Actually, he's a fussy bitch who complains about everything, but I cheerfully listen to his rants against the government, the transportation system, and the homeless, so he likes me. He knows I adore vintage. The coat is red wool, with a fur collar, from the Jackie Kennedy era, but I have a closet full of coats, all bought here, and anyway, it's too heavy for San Francisco winters. "I know you can sell this," I tell him. "Keep it. But thank you." Maybe he'll even wear it.

A maroon-haired woman lifts up a blue-and-green garment from one of the piles, and *ohmygod ohmygod!* Palm trees and tikis unfold before my eyes. It's a long Hawaiian barkcloth dress from the '60s, this Hawaiianophile's Holy Grail. I breathe a prayer to the Thrift Goddess: *Please let her not want it.* And she doesn't want it! I follow up with a prayer of thanks, snatch the dress as it falls from her hand, and add it to my bag. Can't have enough Hawaiian barkcloth dresses. When I finally amass an entire closet full of Hawaiian barkcloth dresses, I can move to Hawaii and wear them, right?

I paw through some hideous stuff. Much of what you find at the As-Is is a drag queen's nightmare: party dresses from the '80s, all humongous shoulder pads and cheap glitter; last year's flimsy, ruffled rayon crop-tops; teeny-weeny miniskirts made in India. But here's an embroidered linen tablecloth. If I have too many coats, I have more than too many embroidered vintage tablecloths; yes sir, three drawers full and not enough occasions to use them. So, tablecloth in hand, I search the room for Joan, who collects old linens. There she is, across the room, next to two large Russian ladies who discuss the merits of a lavender terrycloth bathrobe. Joan has already found a seriously cute tea towel with an aproned teddy bear and the word THURSDAY embroidered on it, and now she has the tablecloth.

Lana sits leaning against the wall, sorting through a huge pile of rayon and silk. She has a consignment store in San Mateo, but she dresses like a ho, in gold hot pants and high-heeled boots. Judging from what she keeps, a lot of Victoria's Secret lingerie in size 0, her anorexic customers dress that way, too. But she discards things I can use, tank tops and T-shirts that aren't trashy enough for her shop, and I'm not too proud to go through her rejects. Sure enough, on top of her reject pile is a sea-green baby tee in a medium, my size.

Jeez, is it four-thirty already? Time flies when you have fifty-cent fever. I have already circled the room and am back where I started. Now to try on my finds, decide what to keep. There's one full-length mirror in the place, and I join a small group of women, sharing the mirror and trying on clothes. None of us are resellers, because resellers don't need to try anything on—they're just gonna sell everything—so we're all nice to one another. A woman compliments my pink suede jacket: "Just your size, and it goes so well with your hair." Another woman asks me to pass on to her anything I don't want, which I do. We are all sisters in the rag trade, and suddenly sisterhood really *is* powerful. Somebody else offers me a black leather jacket, but I already have two black leather jackets at home, and this one has a small rip in the collar, so one of the Russian guys takes it.

The Hawaiian dress is too small! My heart breaks but I keep it anyway. I'll put it up on eBay. Sweaty and rumpled, I count my score: the pink suede jacket (Can you believe a pink suede jacket for fifty cents?); the baby tee; the vintage cotton dress (A perfect fit! It will become my favorite day dress!); a silver leather belt by Nine West; transparent plastic kitten-heeled slides by Chinese Laundry (When will I wear these? But they're absolutely gorgeous—and they're fifty cents!); a three-tiered cotton skirt with cowboys printed all over it (I have already named it my *"Brokeback Mountain* skirt," and once you name something you have to keep it.); and a dark green nylon slip from about 1960 (maybe I'll wear it as a dress).

I join the long line at the checkout counter. In front of me, a Filipino woman drags two overstuffed garbage bags full of clothing for her family back on the islands. The line moves with the swiftness of a snail, and along the way I continue to pick up and discard dresses, blouses, jackets, and sweaters, mostly ripped and unwearable. Just about anything in decent condition has been taken. I decide to keep a pair of embroidered brown linen capris, then check the size and see that they are an extra large. As I toss them back onto the heap, a woman rescues them and makes off with them.

By now there is nothing left unclaimed that anyone could possibly want. The room resembles the scene of some massacre, with rejected clothing littering the floor like so many broken bodies. I finally reach the checkout counter. My total is $4 for the most fabulous wardrobe on the face of the planet. I am completely disheveled and so exhausted that I want to cry. I can't wait until next month.

Ideas of Fashion from the Great Depression to Today: 33 Ruminations

DIANE DI PRIMA

1. In Red Hook, Brooklyn, where I was born, the templates of fashion I found around me included Sicilian women in long black dresses, all the women on the block in housedresses and sensible shoes, and my mom's youngest sister, who lived with us and had to be peeled in or out of her tight-fitting rayon dresses with ruffles and flounces and a zipper on one side—at least two women doing the peeling—whenever she had a "date." I was not amused.

2. I learned early on that anything I thought looked good would be laughed to scorn by my mother in the department stores of downtown Brooklyn.

3. Also, anything I wore to school (chosen by Mom from those same department stores) would be laughed to scorn by my schoolmates at St. Mary's Star of the Sea on Court and Luqueer Streets in Red Hook.

4. I quickly discovered that starched organdy pinafores wore holes in my skin, and the "picture hats" so loved by my mother and her sisters were definitely not cool.

5. Once, in high school, I endeavored to dye my entire wardrobe black in the family washing machine. I loved the resulting subtleties: brownish-blacks, blueish-blacks, et cetera, but I learned unequivocally that from my parents' point of view this was not a good idea. They also didn't like what it did to the machine.

6. Generally, I took to jeans, berets, and peacoats. After only a few years, my beloved peacoat with anchors on the navy-blue buttons was tossed into the garbage by my mother.

7. As a sophomore, I discovered Keats and Shelley, as well as the pirate novels of Rafael Sabatini. Added long red sashes to my jeans. Searched everywhere for what were later called "poet shirts" with wide sleeves and tight cuffs (available much later from mail-order catalogs).

8. Up to this time, I had been unable to cop a single fashion clue from the movies, since the only flicks I had been allowed to see were *The Little Princess,* starring Shirley Temple (whom I hated on sight), and all the Walt Disney offerings, which I was lucky enough to abhor from the get-go. Not a clue there.

9. At fifteen I discovered modern dance and took to wearing black leotards and pink ballet slippers to school. My father chased me frenetically about our four-story brownstone, declaring that leotards were "underwear" and not fit for the streets. On the upside, all this being chased about made me fit and trim and prepared me for life to come on the Lower East Side.

10. And so I went off to college with a trunk full of plaid pleated skirts, Gibson Girl blouses, and oxford shoes—all newly purchased for the grand occasion by my mother. I stashed it all in a footlocker under the bed in my dorm room and continued with the blue-jeans-and-red-sashes look. Having by then actually *seen* some pirate flicks, I began to cut off my jeans at the knee (leaving plenty of ragged fringe). I had also managed to acquire red ballet slippers (instead of the regular wimpy pink ones).

11. In college, I turned a look into a lifestyle by rushing about the two acres of campus woods with my ass-length hair streaming behind me, or by lying on the lawn under a flowering fruit tree to chant Shelley at the moon. I added a bit of *La Bohème* to my dorm room by casting out all furniture except the bed and lining the walls with orange crates. I hung a whole, very ripe provolone from the eaves, stuck a knife in it, and put busts of Beethoven and Nietzsche and a white bisque figure of a veiled woman on top of the crates.

12. Since my classes were dull, I stayed in my dorm room for days at a time. Whenever I *did* emerge I found many proper young women in pale cashmere sweaters and single strands of pearls keeping vigil outside my door, speculating in low tones about whether I had died—the consensus leaning toward suicide. Decidedly, the pastel-sweater look was not one I yearned to acquire. I began to play Tchaikovsky very loudly on my phonograph while I arranged to drop out of college, return to New York, and get a crew cut.

13. Back in Manhattan I found some like-minded folk. We took possession of the night streets, dancing and cavorting in gay bars, on loading platforms, in empty lots, at the Plaza Fountain—wherever we pleased. As for fashion, there were two basic requirements: Could you dance in

it, and did it leave you free to defend yourself, climb a building, or run really fast if you had to?

14. I became friends with an anarchist sandal-maker on McDougall Street who radically extended my notion of footwear. I designed my very own sandals, complete with rawhide laces that crisscrossed at the ankle and on up the leg. *Very Greek,* I thought, *and decidedly very sexy.*

15. Within a year I stopped doing office work and dumped all my remaining skirts, blouses, and straight shoes (mostly left over from college) into a large sheet, tied it up at the corners, and left it behind in an apartment I was abandoning. My friends and I then took the time to courteously cover the walls of this place I was leaving with paintings, artistic admonitions, and anarchist slogans, all in enduring enamel paint from a hobby shop. The effect was stunning.

16. As they tell us unendingly in new age magazines, fashion is an ever-changing, ever-evolving life study. I next discovered army surplus stores, which at that time were flourishing like mushrooms. My wardrobe took on variety; I added oversize sweatshirts and green corduroy workshirts. The most important fashion advancement of this period was the advent of black peg-leg jeans. "Blue" jeans would never again be quite as interesting.

17. Black peg-legs met black leather "motorcycle" jackets—architectural feats of gratuitous zippers, silver rivets and studs, and pockets inside and out. Diagonal zippered pockets on the sleeves. Need I say more? With my red crew cut and black "engineer" boots from the army surplus store, The Look was complete.

18. But one can never settle into complacency. I started having babies, and was forced to develop a whole new wardrobe. However, I am sorry to say that during my first pregnancy, "style" was not a major consideration. Survival was. But by the second time around I was sporting handmade red-and-purple dresses with slash-cut huge sleeves sewn for me by my friends in California. Floor-length, handwoven robes were also coming into downtown Manhattan from Jordan. Like the first robins, they were the harbingers of hippie styles to come. With their beautiful embroidered yokes and one-size-fits-all design, they were good for all occasions—you could sleep in them, wear them to dinner on the Upper East Side, fuck, meditate, and even give birth in them. Though for the actual "lying-in," I found that antique stores abounded in quilted bed jackets and other diverting oddities from the Victorian era, many of which I proceeded to destroy as part of the happening called "giving birth."

19. Of course, when one has children, one desires to extend one's unifying vision of high fashion to include the entire family. The Free Boxes of the 1960s and early 1970s made this stunningly possible. I suppose you could say that Free Boxes and communal living were a great fashion influence on everyone in that period. You were perforce displaying other people's visions, living them out, to some extent . . . like using someone else's dreams in your poems. Kind of a surrealist exercise, actually. I began wearing things I'd never tried before.

20. An inadvertent assist with my "look" at this time was that every time I had a baby, I lost a lot of weight. Pregnancy for me was better than any diet. A couple of weeks after giving birth, I predictably weighed twenty or thirty pounds less than I did before I had conceived. In 1968, after I had my fourth child at home in bed at the Hotel Albert, I took advantage of my postpartum ninety-three-pound but shapely self. I bought myself a purple minidress with wide, gorgeous sleeves and a tiny waist. I loved

that wisp of a dress; it was hardly there. I floated about New York in it, garnering come-ons and compliments (much needed when your husband is not at all interested). Alas, like so many well-loved things tend to do, the Dress left me one day without warning. John Wieners, the great gay poet, was living next door at the Hotel Albert. He slipped into my apartment one day when I was out and absconded with the Dress. By the time I found him, mournfully writing a love letter to Robert Creeley, my Dress was torn and stretched badly out of shape, its beautiful purple smudged with pancake makeup. I bade it a fond goodbye.

21. One of the most stylish places I've ever lived was Tim Leary's commune in Millbrook, New York. And definitely, beyond argument, the most fashionable occasions ever seen on this planet were some of our acid trips there. Indescribable, the robes and costumes, the jewels real and imagined, the things stuck in our hair. In the firelight, in rooms full of mattresses and banked with flowers, in the light of a thousand "mikes" of acid and then the light of dawn.

22. Soon after my six months at Millbrook, I moved to California. I must say, it took a while to get used to West Coast fashion. The main difference, I think, is a kind of rough-and-ready edge the folks here sported. They used a lot of fur trim in the West and lots of magickal symbols, painted or embroidered. Capes abounded. When I was still a new arrival, I made the faux pas of washing my lover's jeans. He was devastated—told me it had taken a couple of years to build up the patina, the sheen of oil and dirt that made that greasy black-over-blue denim shine.

23. From those days, I remember fondly one of my finer moments of haute couture—a fashion statement unto itself and for the ages. I arrived one late afternoon at the Tassajara Zen Mountain Center in

San Francisco, having just driven down from an outlaw "commune" on the Oregon border, where for various reasons I was living incognito. I was just in time for evening meditation and, leaving my boots outside the temple as decorum required, I strode into the *zendo* in my black jeans and tie-dyed shirt, with my buck knife in its leather sheath tied to my waist with a sash. I bowed decorously to my cushion and sat down for a round of armed *zazen*.

24. When the Free Boxes left us in the early '80s, it was necessary to improvise. To make choices. In fact, to actually *buy* clothes. Except for the purple minidress, it was something I had rarely done—not since those army surplus stores had gone out of my life.

25. This was the time that I started to get rounder. I don't know if it had to do with menopause, or the start of working as a psychic and healer, as my healing teacher assured me. (I personally have never seen or heard of a skinny psychic—have you?) Since the Free Box stuff had come in all sizes, I hadn't noticed my change of shape till I actually had to go shopping.

26. First I had to get over my phobia about going shopping at all. I am terrified of department stores to this day. I only venture into them for underwear and sheets. I had to find places I was sure I could find my way out of, that wouldn't blind me with lighting and overwhelm me with Muzak. Then, when I actually did get inside, I found that nothing fit.

27. I had picked just the wrong time for getting round. The '80s were crazed about many things—not the least of which were health and body image. Everywhere around me, people were jogging, running as if that invasion from Mars had finally happened. Running from demons, from the future, or from their upcoming deaths. It was live-forever time in

San Francisco and Marin. No one ate oil or meat. The Deva realm spread like some proud, new British Empire.

28. I did make a few worthwhile discoveries. During my twenty-year shopping hiatus, there had come into existence the comfortable dress! A dress that did not dig into one anywhere. It hung loose from one's shoulders or came in two pieces, sporting an elastic waist. I immediately acquired a few of these but—alas! For the most part it hasn't been warm enough to wear a skirt in the Bay Area since I moved here in 1967. The dresses mostly languish. And since many years elapse between one wearing and the next, and they are undatable in any case—looking more like robes from the Golden Dawn or costumes from a DeMille epic than like clothing, per se—I'm sure I'll have them for the rest of my life.

29. Wonder of wonders! While dresses were getting comfortable, so were the pants. Elastic waists, loose cut, lots of "give." Definitely the way to go. I currently have two kinds: light and a little warmer. At first I acquired these gems in many colors, but over time I have more or less settled on black. Mainly because my T-shirts are of such variety and striking madness that I am hard put to find pant colors that will "go" with them. But at least there has been no denim at all in my closet since the advent of Roundness.

30. The "tops" I eventually scored are also of two kinds: short sleeved and long. For the two kinds of weather we get in the Bay Area: chilly and freezing. And to go with the two kinds of pants. The short-sleeved shirts can be "real" tees, with pictures (see Rumination no. 31), or solid-color raw silk tees I buy from a catalog, or all-blue V-neck cotton-with-something-synthetic. (All my life I have mostly been a purist with leanings toward puritanism: Against my skin I want only cotton, silk, or wool. I still remember the days when "synthetic" was a dirty word. As

dirty as it gets.) But to get back to my shirts: The long-sleeved ones don't seem to run to pictures. There are tee-type cottons and there are humongous sweaters (good in the coldest weather with a silk tee under them).

31. A note about T-shirts: The pictures on your T-shirts are very important. I myself tend to favor baseball players, anarchists, and jazz clubs, with the occasional wolf or otter. One shirt I love goes back to the '60s and is still going strong. It is bright red and features a black line drawing of several dinosaurs with dinosaur grins chowing down, one with a necktie protruding from his jaws, another drooling a shoe and part of a leg. The caption reads EAT THE RICH. I rescued this prize in the early '70s from one of my kids who was giving it away—where he got it I don't know. Another nice option is the "art tee," though these have become harder to find in recent years. And after fifteen years or so, my Magritte shirt with bowler hat floating among the clouds is fraying at the seams. And the Matisse tee has definitely given out.

32. Shoes are simple. They are either sneakers or Birkenstocks, depending on the weather. (Boots if you're traveling east in the winter to give a reading or to pursue some other madcap adventure.) I do have a special pair of "dress" Birkenstocks with laces that I reserve for the opera. That particular style hasn't been made for almost twenty years.

33. As you can see, this style is modular and can be assembled to fit any occasion from the most casual to the ridiculously formal. (Ragged and beloved clothes are never simply discarded; they moved to a bag in my closet, which I reserve for "gardening," "house-cleaning" (incredibly rare), and "painting" days. But the "dressy" version of all this is a nice solid tee with a sexy neckline and aforesaid black pants. Add earrings—noticeable ones if possible. If the occasion is *super*formal, the tee as well as the pants should be black, and I add a scarf. Through the years, I've

collected all sorts of scarves: hand-painted, cut velvet, beaded, tie-dyed—scarves of every color, mood, period, and implication. Long and extra long. (Hint: Eschew square scarves, as they tend to bunch up at the neck. One wants the flowing look, to offset basic clunkiness and override any hint of underdressing implicit in tees and pants.) I make sure the earrings and scarf are compatible, *at least in my own mind,* and voilà! Poetry reading, museum opening, dinner party—whatever. As Ezra Pound said in another context, "The splendor! It all coheres!"

The Slimming Effect

SHERILYN CONNELLY

IN EARLY 1999, a few months after I came out as a male-to-female transsexual, I was asked to write a fashion column for a goth webzine. Nobody thought to ask if I actually knew anything about the topic. It was accepted as a given that the most approachable transsexual (transvestite, drag queen, female impersonator, whatever it was I called myself, they weren't going to split hairs about a boy in a dress) in the San Francisco goth scene would have plenty to say. Weren't people like me always talking trash about other people's clothes and style?

Being reduced to a catty-queen stereotype was more than a little offensive, and in terms of practical knowledge, being asked to write on fashion made as much sense as asking me to write about quantum physics. Hell, after a few hours at the library I could probably fake the physics thing, but I had not a damn thing to say on the subject of fashion.

I agreed to do the column because it got me an email address I'd been coveting, any reason to write was a good thing, and—who knew?—maybe I'd actually learn something about fashion in the process. I had a pretty cool name for it, "The Slimming Effect." (It's the answer to the unasked question "Why does Sherilyn always dress in black?") I managed to pound out a column and a half before the zine imploded in a cloud of conflicting egos. But fashion, also known to my estrogenating brain as "how to dress on the outside like the girl I was on the inside," remained a great mystery.

Being born in 1973 didn't help. By the time I realized that the male thing wasn't quite right for me and started paying attention to how women looked, the Reagan era was in full swing. The order of the day was excess. What was the point of consuming if you weren't going to be conspicuous about it? The fashion influence of *Dynasty* alone caused more damage to the culture than *Beavis and Butt-Head* or *South Park* could have hoped to in later years: big makeup, heavy on the scary rouge. Big permy hair. Big fugly jewelry. Big floppy bow ties made from scarves. *Shoulder. Pads.* Shoulder pads were confusing and frightening, making me want to run deeper into the closet like a spooked tabby cat. I couldn't figure out why a girl would wear something that made her look like a football player. I *still* don't get it.

I knew what I liked when I came out, but as much as I appreciated how Shirley Manson looked on the cover of the June 1997 issue of *Spin* (beautifully pale and scrawny, her eyes dark and her hair tousled, a strung-out Kewpie doll), that was a million miles from the monochrome jigsaw that was my face and body. I had no idea what to do beyond attempting to find clothes that fit and weren't overtly male. Those rare moments when something actually clicked (usually the occasional top) were revelatory; pieces suddenly, if briefly, coming together. Whatever it was, I would buy as many as I could.

Aside from those fleeting moments of victory, shopping was a miserable experience. It felt like a snipe hunt. Lots of trannies claimed it was their most favoritest thing to do, since, well, girls like to shop, right? Many an online profile of a new girl contained lines to that effect— "HOBBIES: shopping, of course *giggle*." Not me. It was a necessary evil, but I could achieve the same emotional effect by staying home and jabbing a fork into my eye.

It's not that I didn't want to be fashionable, to wear stylish clothes, to look good. I did, very much. While some trannies were focused on surgery as the answer to all their problems, I knew that my immediate appearance was going to determine whether I was parsed as female. I'd even managed to acquire a few simple black velvet dresses from places like Ross, affectionately known in some circles as "Cross-Dress for Less." I was fine for clubbing, but daily wear remained an issue. (Years would pass before I felt comfortable wearing clubwear on a daily basis.)

I had recently dropped down to one hundred and sixty pounds from a peak of three hundred, but I was six feet tall and had only been on hormones for a few months, with no breast growth to speak of. Even though I was relatively skinny, mine was not a body shape that existed to manufacturers of women's clothing. The few companies that made larger sizes logically assumed that their customers were genetic females, and would thus be contoured like genetic females. It's possible to fake such things, but in my obstinacy I would no sooner wear breast or hip padding than I would wear a wig. My long, thick hair was one of my few natural assets, and I was proud of it. Of course, since irony is the motivating factor of my universe, people often complimented me on what they assumed to be a wig.

It would have been different if I had been four inches shorter, or even six—though, as long as I'm fantasizing, why not go nuts and drop my height down to 5'4"? If I could have walked into Forever 21 and said, "I'll take it," there's no doubt in my mind that I would have been a shopping fiend, the clotheshorse to end all clotheshorses. I would have been a goddamn clothes stampede. As it was, I towered over the average customer at the stores with the clothes I liked. I couldn't shop off the same rack as them, but I could tell when their roots were starting to show. Shopping was too frustrating and painful to pretend that I got all giggly about it just because of the stereotype.

When something fit, it was by accident, not design. And "fit" was a relative verb. Even if something wasn't overly snug in the shoulders, if I could raise my arms without fear of the seams ripping—and I've destroyed a number of nice jackets prematurely due to shoulder erosion—the sleeves would never be quite long enough. Cold wrists were something I'd have to learn to live with if I wanted to wear women's jackets.

Shoulder and arm issues are also why I developed an affinity for tank tops and sleeveless blouses (*blouses, not shirts anymore, blouses*): They didn't draw attention to the fact that my arms were so long, I could scratch my ankles without bending over. Okay, not really, but that was the impression I felt was created by sleeves that barely made it past my elbows. I was the inverse of the Rockwellian image of the small girl playing dress-up in front of a full-length mirror, barely visible under her mother's clothing and requisite large floppy hat.

What were designed as knee-length hems on genetic girls went considerably higher on me, and a complex about my height kept me from enjoying the miniskirt effect. I didn't want to be leggy, to have what I felt were my disproportionately long gams emphasized. I wasn't auditioning for *Dreamgirls* anytime soon. Tall boots eventually helped me achieve the illusion of proportion. Flats, of course. I never wore heels. What's more, women's shoes in my size (lucky number 13) that weren't fugly lunch-lady shoes were almost *always* extra-high heels, as it was assumed that only genetic males would need fashionable women's shoes in that size, and strictly for fetish/drag stuff.

❁

The webzine editor and I went thrifting a few times, and she got frustrated because I didn't try on as many things as she did. I tried to explain that thrift stores tended to have far less decent clothing in my size than regular retail stores, since they were governed by the law of the secondhand jungle. As usual, the law was slanted heavily toward the bias of the enforcers, in this case the (inevitably) tiny girls working the purchasing counter.

She accused me of being "negative," as though the reason a petite size 2 skirt, which looked barely larger than my hand, didn't fit was that I didn't have enough faith. After all, she could wear plenty of stuff, right? So what the hell was my excuse for not trying? Out of necessity, this admonishment was often delivered with her head craning upward so she could see my face.

My being a head taller on average than the girls around me was a good thing, she insisted, because I was "like a supermodel." Ugh. The fucking S-word, the bane, the cop-out, the extreme condescension. This is not to say I had a problem with supermodels in general; I had a crush on Christy Turlington, and I thought the controversy around them was a bit absurd. Critics made it sound like teenage girls didn't have eating disorders before that Calvin Klein ad campaign. Then again, I never thought Kate Moss looked *too* skinny. She looked the way I wanted to look, but I had neither the willpower to not eat nor the intestinal fortitude to stick a finger down my throat and yak said intestines out. And even if I did make it down to skin and bones, my bones were not small.

The popular if anecdotal belief that supermodels are tall didn't do me any favors. For starters, aren't their clothes custom-made for them? Sure, what they wear while grocery shopping is probably a bit more modest in origin, but they are still genetic females and I am not. Even if Kate were taller than the average girl (which I doubted), it's unlikely that she was ever called "barrel-chested," as I had been ego-shatteringly described a few years earlier.

I quickly learned there was no point in bringing up the genetic issue, since the preordained response was a smirk, an eyebrow raised in victory, and: "How do you *know* none of them were born male?"

The short answer: "Because I'm a goddamn psychic. Bite me."

The long answer: "Ever heard of Caroline Cossey, also known as Tula? Beautiful, highly successful model whose career was destroyed when the tabloids discovered that she was transsexual. She was very passable, had had surgery, was undetectable clothed or naked, but it didn't matter—suddenly, nobody could see past the fact that she, quote, used to be a guy, unquote. Besides, even in the unlikely event that a tranny becomes successful in today's climate, without her past being discovered and made public knowledge, I seriously doubt she would be built like me, so the speculative possibility of a tranny supermodel doesn't do me much good. Besides, I'm a goddamn psychic. Bite me."

As an overall style, going goth felt natural. It appealed to my existing sense of aesthetics—I was aware of the slimming effect long before I'd ever heard the word "goth"—and the scene itself was open to gender fluidity, the confusion over the difference between me and the boys in skirts and eyeliner notwithstanding.

For as unkind as genetics had been in terms of skeletal structure and metabolism, I got fairly lucky with my face, which was never especially masculine to begin with. I had my hair cut and colored in the standard-issue Bettie Page style several months before I came out as transsexual —causing no small amount of strife with my mother, who was deeply troubled to see her youngest son wearing such a blatantly feminine haircut—and electrolysis was slowly eliminating my facial hair.

My conscious role model was my friend Rudha, a tiny goth girl. Though she'd long since moved away, the few pictures I had of her were my aesthetic inspiration. I wanted to be her when I grew up. That she was about ten inches shorter than me and actually knew what the hell she was doing was irrelevant. I mean, I was conscious of the disparity between us, but if Rudha could do it, so could I, damnit. I was like a dog who thinks it's a person.

Though the occasional girl (such as the editor) would develop a momentary fascination with me and promise to take me shopping for clothes and makeup, their interest would burn out as quickly as it had flared up, leaving me in the same vacuum as always. Growing up, I didn't have any sisters or local female cousins or even casual female friends beyond the second grade. My first girlfriend, though supportive of my transitioning even after we broke up, was not necessarily the most fashion-literate creature on the planet and couldn't offer much help.

So I was more or less on my own, trying to figure out how I could somehow manage something kinda sorta close to how I wanted to look, even if you had to squint and use your imagination some. Like any other special effect, it was smoke and mirrors, the success of which depended on the spectator's willful suspension of disbelief. Nothing ever quite worked, though. It was always false, as special effects are by definition.

I was false, an approximation, an attempt to be something I wasn't. Yet the something that genetics and most forms of logic suggested I was—a boy—wasn't me at all. In spite of how much simpler it was to dress as a boy (easy to find clothes that fit, no pressure whatsoever, I could look as schlumpy as I pleased and nobody gave a shit), I was absolutely not going back in that direction.

For all the frustration, I tried to be conscious of it as a period of experimentation and discovery, to enjoy the adventure as best as I could. Since Rudha was elsewhere, the closest thing I had to a makeup guru— and the only person to fulfill a promise of assistance—was an enigmatic little goth boy who called himself c0g. He lived out of town, and I didn't see him often, but one trip to Rite Aid to stock up on supplies (I still have the receipt dated January 24, 1999) and an hour of patient instruction were enough to get started, and I'll be forever grateful.

c0g said he envied me for starting out, that he missed the sense of excitement from his early goth days. He was not a tranny girl and he understood better than most that I did not identify as male in any way, but the sentiment still rang true. For as much as attempting to find my style sucked at times, that I had the opportunity to do so at all was pretty wonderful. It felt like I was exploring uncharted territory and could fall off the edge of the world at any moment, but that was part of the thrill. If I wasn't going to take risks, I may as well have remained a boy.

As 1999 progressed and I continued to stick out like the sore thumb I was, I began to care less and less about how I looked in terms of fitting in. I didn't fit in—I couldn't—so why bother?

One of my favorite pictures of myself is from Shrine of Lilith, my preferred goth club. It was August, by which point I was bored with the few black velvet dresses I owned. Instead, I was jarringly resplendent in red-and-black stripey tights, sheer black knee-high stockings (which were calf-high on me), gray bicycle shorts, a Mystery Science Theater 3000 T-shirt, a leather jacket, my long black hair under a black beret I'd unintentionally inherited from Rudha, dark glasses, white makeup, and thick black eyeliner as lipstick. Sitting next to me is my friend Serena, a goth girl who looks the part.

In contrast to Serena's luminescence, I appear neither fish nor fowl, not necessarily goth or girl, not following any known standards, yet improbably beautiful. Most people are embarrassed by old pictures of themselves attempting to look contemporary, though in this case, the sheer *wrongness* of my look transcends time. After all, there's never been an epoch in which wearing stripeys and bicycle shorts qualifies as fashionable. Far from embarrassed, I'm rather proud of it. I remember being in a good mood that night, and even though I'm wearing sunglasses—

nonprescription sunglasses, inside a goth club, after midnight—it shows. Rather than being tortured by my alienness and evident inability to wear clothes that match, I'm rolling with it.

The only cringe-worthy aspect is that I couldn't blend makeup for shit: The stark white ends abruptly halfway down my neck. I got better at it with practice, as I did that look a lot.

Along with the clothes, I'd happily embraced the gothling makeup aesthetic, though my faux-chiaroscuro interpretation was a few years out of style: the most unnaturally pale skin I could manage, with the darkest lips and eyes. I used Manic Panic Dreamtone foundation (in Violet) for the former and the late, lamented Street Wear Tar eyeliner for the latter two. The foundation was intended for use on skin of the opposite tone, which for Violet was sallow and yellowish. My skin was already pale and light, not especially sallow at all, and the foundation gave my face a slight purplish hue. We're not talking Violet Beauregarde levels, but it was there. I. Looked. *Weird.* I know it now, I certainly knew it then, and I did it anyway, because I wanted to. I liked what I saw when I looked in the mirror, and that was the only barometer I could trust. Some friends fretted politely, and let out not-so-secret sighs of relief when I evolved to a more natural look, but their approval (or lack thereof) didn't matter.

Paradoxically, there was something comforting about the extremeness of my appearance. It was a mask I hid behind, even though the anonymity of a mask is arguably compromised when nobody else is wearing one.

Seven years later, the mask has gone away, though I occasionally trot it out for nostalgia's sake. c0g was right; I do miss the heady sense of experimentation and exploration of those days, and tend to remember that more than the frustration. Even the frustration served a higher purpose, as it was a necessary step in figuring out not just who I was, but how I would look.

I'm not a fashion expert and never will be, but I continue to know what I like, and I can actually write about it when asked.

Shopping still sucks, though.

Reflect Me

LAURIE STONE

I HAD A FACE-LIFT after a man I loved dumped me. Not that I thought I could get another boyfriend. I didn't view the age in my face—the downward pull, the loss of muscle tone—as a souvenir of experience. I saw no safety in submitting to gravity. The marks could be erased, which wasn't the same as reversing time. Erasure was a kind of mark, too. And it wasn't like I meant to pass for younger than I was.

The operation caused almost no pain. The scars in front of my ears faded in a few weeks. There are thicker scars behind my ears that you can see if you look carefully, though they are set in the creases and hair obscures them. I'm not trying to keep them concealed.

When I first had the face-lift, I made a point of being out about it, and it pissed some people off. I wanted friends to be interested in the transformation, view it as a science experiment. I told myself they would want to see me upgraded. This was true of men and women who were younger than me, but the decision rattled some women my age.

My friend Madeleine said she was disappointed. Madeleine was gorgeous, with long auburn tresses, and she was eating-disorder thin. (She alluded to it once at a dinner party, as I watched her move braised rabbit and wild mushroom risotto around her plate without eating any of it.) About my face-lift she said, "We were supposed to change everything. We were supposed to make it okay and sexy for women to age instead of cutting our bodies. That's what feminism was supposed to give us, and what we were supposed to give feminism."

I wanted to squash her like a bug. Her argument reminded me of the early days in the women's movement, when everyone knew women were supposed to present a new, radical image of what we were, but no one agreed on what that look should be. Some people believed they knew what a woman was and thought it was different from what a man was. In the early days of the women's movement, tongues would wag if you dressed in femmey clothes and looked like you wanted to fuck a boy. If you looked like you wanted to fuck a girl, that could make people crazy, too. Some people went nuts if anyone got dressed up to get fucked by anybody. Some people thought there was no way to be a new kind of woman if you looked like a slut and enjoyed behaving like one, or actually were one, and some women thought all this packaging business ought to be up for grabs.

Me, I liked a smooth surface back then, too. After an accident or sex, when I checked myself for damage, I didn't like finding a mark. I had a habit with people I met: I wouldn't put their number in my phone book; I would keep it on a piece of paper I could throw away. I liked a smooth surface, but I could admit there was murk underneath it. I could absorb grainy truths, while lots of people with gravelly faces simplified internal complexities.

I objected to talk that equated something's virtue with its being *natural.* I was a friend of the unnatural—which wasn't a real thing any more than something classified as natural, but at least it didn't build altars to granola and wrinkles. I like technology—including surgery. To me technology encompasses the opposing thumb, so it isn't outside of or opposite to the body. Machines are inventions of the mind and therefore on a continuum with DNA-based forms. I imagine technology as a strap-on, a power prosthetic that levels the playing field for people lacking penises, or those apportioned a smaller amount of muscle mass and height, and others who want more things or different things from what custom and metaphysics had ordained for them.

The face of age on both males and females, what does it tell us? That we will die. To see goodness in being reminded of this all the time privileges a process that's inevitable. I see body modification—extreme weight loss or gain, piercings, brands, and tattoos, radical haircuts or the lack of hair, fashion statements that incite policing—as defiance of systems that place arbitrary ideas about *the natural* on top of the value heap. I could have argued that cosmetic surgery was intrinsically feminist, in that it thumbed its nose at all essentialism—the false idea that the biological is unchanging, and that there is some kind of intrinsic and teleological meaning in things that simply exist. Essentialism invariably backfires against women, becoming an argument for why they are other, less.

And that is what I did basically say to beautiful, thin Madeleine. I told her my goal as a feminist had not been to carve out a new aesthetic in which sags and puckers were fine for both sexes and erotically appealing. I said I understood that for some women and men, getting off the desirability train was a relief. I said I was sorry if my face-lift made it harder for her to accept the age in her face, but I didn't mean it, and that's when I smelled a rat in myself. Madeleine was saying that the way to oppose the double standard—whereby men could age and still be sexy while women couldn't—wasn't for women to look younger, but was rather to stand our ground and insist on a different way of being perceived. That's what we'd done with the other views of us we wanted changed. She was pointing out that I resisted living out conventional ideas about women in every other quarter of life—except in the way I looked.

Appearance was linked to excitement, possibility in my mind. Why surrender pleasure and opportunity if I didn't have to? I didn't have children, so there was nothing in my daily life—like the seminude form of a nineteen-year-old—to remind me of my season in life. It was fun to be aggressive, ambitious, independent. It was fun to look good, and gratifying to have control over something concerning my body when so much change was beyond my agency. I started losing my hair in my forties, and although it hasn't proved calamitous, it's a situation, due to genes, I've had no say about.

More than anything, though, Madeleine made me want to squash her because she kicked up fear that I'd abandoned the girls' team. There was no getting around this: A woman who had a face-lift made it harder for women who wanted to stand their ground, and although they were making a point I didn't in this particular case endorse, I admired their stance in general.

Does looking pulled together smooth my path in life? I have assumed so. Does it give me power with men? Only a tiny bit, now that I'm not young. Am I willing to forfeit sex because of ideas that make me unsexy? Yes. Am I willing to be thrown off the girls' team for wanting to preserve my looks? I suppose I run that risk. I don't think anyone should have dominion over how we treat our bodies. I have no fixed feelings about the marks of time, the marks of sex, the marks of loss, the marks of memory, the marks I leave on other people.

I lost a friend over the face-lift. Not Madeleine, Susie. Susie and I had been in each other's lives since college. She emailed me a few months after the operation, saying she was finding me increasingly alien. The surgery bugged her—also my ideas. In a conversation, I'd said I found Shakespeare irritating because his vision was often conservative.

She thought my positions amounted to "intellectual divorce." When I received her email, I was feeling lighthearted and wrote back saying she should take all the time she needed to sort out her feelings. I thought she must be very angry if she couldn't make fun of me, since I said outrageous things all the time and then changed my mind. I knew I could sound authoritative, but I thought there was an understanding between us that the things I said were provisional. Incisive, but not forever.

Years later, after our friendship resumed and I was back on speaking terms with the Bard, she told me the Shakespeare thing had been a ruse. It was the face-lift after all. "I didn't want us to walk down the street and for people to think we weren't in the same generation."

I like a smooth surface, and I don't like it. I don't like being reminded of what has been lost, but I like knowing that something has been there.

Layaway

JEWELLE GOMEZ

THERE WERE TWO types of clothes-shopping for me as a kid, two ways as unrelated to each other as a stroll in Golden Gate Park is to walking on proverbial hot coals. My favorite shopping was the intriguing forays to the rummage sales that my great-grandmother, with some magical power, rooted out in Boston church basements and abandoned storefronts.

The Olympics of rummage sales were held annually at the Horticultural Hall in the Back Bay; you could find clothes, antique furniture, dishes, toys, and an array of books that reached from first-edition Faulkner to paperback anybody. The line started forming at 8 AM for the 11 AM opening and was a startling cross section of the population—the poor (both black and white), who simply needed to clothe the family, and Beacon Hill matrons trying to match an old family silver pattern. It was heaven for me to dive into the piled-high tables of secondhand clothes delivered from places I could barely imagine—big houses with central heating and hot water, where people could afford to keep their clothes clean enough to pass on to rummage sales. Men's clothes were somewhat the same—dark suits, glaring white shirts with tiny but hard to conceal repairs, oddly patterned ties that had never really been loved.

But women's clothes all told stories. The colors, prints, hemlines, fabrics, and shapes stretched through time, from Victorian frill to Rudy G. mod. Shoes, purses, hats came from every stratum and neighborhood, each looking equally eager to go home with a new person. I could breathe in their pasts along with the scent of mothballs and musty trunks. It was a treasure hunt that was always a success.

Then there was the other kind of shopping: humiliating visits downtown for the obligatory brand-new outfit for Easter or the beginning of the school year. My great-grandmother was as generous as she could be on our meager income from Aid to Dependent Children ("welfare," as the comfortable middle class calls it dismissively). She loved being able to buy me absolutely new clothes twice a year, and I never let her know how horrible it felt to not be Shirley Temple—that is, petite and curly.

We'd troop through the children's departments of Jordan Marsh and Filene's, fruitlessly searching for something to fit my not-thin, eight-year-old body, and we'd always end up at the Husky Shop. It might as well have been called the "Fat Ugly Girls' Shop" because that's what the clothes said, and the salesclerks were cheerleaders for self-loathing. The waistlines were inevitably too high, the fabrics were all wrong, and there were never any shorts at all. The salespeople always tsk-tsked, as if it were my fault there were no clothes there for me. In the minds of designers, a child with full thighs or any ass at all was an anathema to the off-the-rack culture. I had to be hurriedly hidden in rough denim or huge flowers that were rarely cut to fit in proportion. The end result was that any pants we bought had to be altered to within an inch of life so the waist would fit—and then followed the acute sense that I wasn't "right" with the world. All the girls being dragged through the mindless torture of the Chubettes section looked as miserable as I, and we all probably thought it was our fault.

Soon, though, I began to understand that this was really about being a girl. My father wasn't thin, and he was a fashion plate. Like the '60s television star Jackie Gleason, he wore large, crisp suits and glamorous camel hair overcoats with the aplomb of a man who knows it's okay to be big. Husky on a man is a compliment; on an adolescent colored girl it was an epithet, a condemnation that distorted my self-image and diminished my self-confidence for the next thirty years.

My great-grandmother never scolded me for eating, or pushed eating as a salve for being poor. Her only food issue was not allowing me to read at the dinner table. Sharing meals was a joyous occasion, not the frightful manifestation of dysfunction that it can be. But even with her strong example, the external influences—movies, television, magazines—were way too strong, tipping the balance in ways that we still inflict on girls today.

I dragged myself through high school under a cloud of fashion panic that I suppressed by wearing three basic outfits that I knew weren't too tight or too ugly. When the miniskirt came into fashion, I figured out how high I could roll my skirt up and what dark-colored tights would keep me from looking like a cigar with a band around it. There were glimmers of possibility that I bent toward, like a housebound plant yearning for some sun, and when I look back I can pick out the seedlings of my current sense of style. At the time, when the little sprouts of prêt-à-porter confidence sprouted, some of my friends thought I was having a nervous breakdown.

Like the time I bought my very first item of clothing on my own. Well, not exactly on my own. I was about fourteen. I had a crush on Shirley (not Temple), who lived in my father's neighborhood. I usually saw her only when I visited him on the weekends, when we'd hang out on the stoop feeling sophisticated as we drank quarts of Schweppes ginger ale as if it were champagne. One Saturday afternoon I accompanied her downtown, deliberately avoiding the site of my earlier humiliations. We salivated in front of the windows of all the cheap shops that lined Washington Street—fishnet stockings and skirts with deep slits up the side were within our reach because of *layaway!* A dollar down and a dollar a week was the way to go before there were credit cards with 500 percent interest.

Impulsively, Shirley and I bought matching winter coats. Or, more precisely, we "laid away" matching winter coats. Then, studiously, we went downtown each Saturday to deliver our payment, for several weeks, until winter finally arrived and the coats were ours. The thing about layaway, though, is that you can kind of forget what the item looked like in the weeks that intervene between love at first sight and the day you bring it home from the pet shop . . . I mean boutique. And these coats were kind of like taking home something from the pet shop—three-quarter length, with huge hoods trimmed in white fake fur, the bodies were made to look like the hide of a brown-and-white cow. Hanging in the window, they seemed just the thing at first glance. The soft brown matched the sweet caramel color of Shirley's skin, the white was pure like our snowy New England winters, and the fake fur almost looked like a coat Sonja Henie wore in one of her ice-skating movies. Back at my father's house we modeled them like we were on the runway in Paris. My stepmother smiled indulgently, understanding what it meant for me to buy my very first piece of clothing on my own, even if it did look like a barn animal.

The frightful impact of the purchase only hit when I had to wear it to school, alone, because Shirley didn't live in my school district. Suddenly I was the cow stitched back into her hide who'd wandered away from the herd. But I wore it because it reminded me of Shirley and the smoky, mature sound of her laugh. And because I was stubborn and wouldn't admit that I felt like I had a target painted on my back and was waiting for hunters (the senior class) to pick me off. I can't remember who tired of the coats first, Shirley or I, but I know that when I donated mine to the rummage sale it was still in fairly good condition.

A couple of years later I bought a matching coat with my best friend from high school, Gwen, but it was much more conservative—a dark herringbone wool with a black leather collar. Herein lie the roots of my identity and my fashion confusion: I kept buying clothes to match those of girls I had crushes on. Wrong strategy! It took a while for me to get the concept of femme style, in part because all fashion that I would identify as femme never came in larger than a size 10.

The only satisfying fashion moments for the rest of my high school life were on gym day. I hated gym, of course. There was no way I was going to be able to do those air force exercises someone had decided were just what young people needed to survive in case the Russians invaded. My upper-body strength, like that of most girls, was barely noticeable unless we were carrying grocery bags. But gym days were great because I knew that my legs looked particularly good when I wore white sneakers and thick, white ankle socks. And I thought the other girls looked great, too; something about the firm calves and athletic shoes said, *These are girls with power.* Thursdays became my favorite fashion day. I stayed dizzy with the joyous sight of sparkling white cotton hugging shiny brown legs.

Then came college, where the specter of thinness was even more intense, in part because the most famous African American alum of my undergraduate school was the first nationally known black model, Beverly Johnson. How could I explain to the white students, "No, I'm not related to Beverly Johnson" and not cringe when they responded, "Oh, yeah, I can tell"?

The Black Power movement of the late '60s was almost my savior. No way I was going to be able to afford a black leather jacket like the members of the Black Panther Party, but all over town women were recreating African garb. You could almost see the smoke rising from racing sewing machines in Roxbury tenements, trying to keep up with the demand for brightly colored Ghanaian robes and loose-cut dashikis that draped easily around full-bodied black women. Grateful that I'd been taught to sew at a young age, I made my share of *geles, bubas,* and *lapas* and was liberated by the news that Africans liked large women.

But even when I was comfortable in clothes for the first time in my life, I felt like an impostor. There was more Wampanoag in me than Swahili, a language I could never quite master beyond pronouncing the name of Lieutenant Uhura from *Star Trek.* I did create a nice selection of brightly colored African outfits, and even wore an authentic Nigerian-made *lapa* under my gown to my graduate school commencement. Secretly, however, I really loved the gold-and-bronze-striped corduroy pants that took two people to zip me into. I'd wear them with a soft, low-cut blouse that cupped my breasts perfectly, but only when it was dark so no one could see how fat I looked. It was an outfit I wore from 1968 until about 1972, and anytime I put it on, I felt like the center of my own fashion world as long as I stayed in the shadows. But the time came, because I did depend on breathing, when it didn't really fit anymore. I gave that outfit to Goodwill, convinced my sex appeal was folded into the brown paper bag along with it.

As I read more and grew into my feminist impulses, I realized that I had to stop blaming myself that there were no clothes on the rack to fit me. I, and millions of other women, were the victims of mostly white, mostly gay men in the fashion industry projecting their own fantasies about themselves onto the bodies of ordinary U.S. women. I came to despise the fashion industry with a passion as I watched young girls succumb to anorexia and bulimia because the culture and fashion industries refused to see them. Twiggy had been a kind of a joke; to think that she was so thin that she was named after a tree branch was amusing. But it was no longer funny when young girls I knew couldn't face themselves in the mirror and tried to starve themselves to death.

I felt lucky that my humiliation in the Husky department had made me more angry than self-destructive, but the self-hating was still in there. Fat is a feminist issue and I, like other women of color, was my own worst oppressor. I read the magazines, even the black ones like *Ebony* and *Essence,* which rarely showed a woman who weighed more than 105 pounds and certainly didn't use models darker than a brown paper bag. The surge of Black Power had many successes, increased numbers of black publications among them, but it betrayed the masses of black women; that is, the black women who were ambitious and independent and wore anything larger than a size 14. I compared myself to those glossy images and found my body lacking. Or, I should say, not lacking enough.

Then I went women's-liberation wild. Part hippie, part kibbutznik, the look of freedom from dieting and ill-fitting clothes beckoned like a mother calling me home. I finally figured out that I had to take my style into my own hands, and there was a period when I felt I had the fashion tiger by the tail. New York City sprouted shops that experimented with every kind of mix-and-match. Anything was possible: drawstring "combat" pants dyed bright orange or purple and worn with matching leg warmers; skintight leotards topped with thirteen-button, wool Navy dress pants; full skirts that swirled around me midcalf; and huge knit sweaters or full-cut, deep-dyed baker's shirts. I was a happy camper! The memories of department store Husky Shops almost evaporated.

I knew for the first time that I was not a cast member on *Mary Tyler Moore,* and I didn't have to dress like one. My style might still have been shaped by what clothes were manufactured to fit me, but I didn't have to try to re-create only the images I saw. I could bend the mirror to fit what I *wanted* to see. As I had in high school, I figured out the several pieces of clothing that made me feel good and replicated them, either searching out duplicates or sewing my own. It was sometime in the early '90s that an acquaintance commented that she liked my style. I was so stunned, I had to ask her to repeat it and then ask what she meant by it. I picked through the memory of my closet, imagined what she saw, and noted what an eclectic collection of items I'd assembled there. No hooded cow coat, but enough interesting things that felt good on me.

Things crystallized when I started doing readings from my books and lecturing on college campuses. I had to pull together clothes that looked good onstage, but most important, they were clothes that made me feel good so I could talk with confidence. I had outfits that reflected who I thought I was, and each time I stood before an audience I knew I looked good. At some point I decided that I didn't have to be onstage to feel that way—or maybe that all the world's a stage. The clothes I wore every day started to say something about me, not about what was on sale. How I decided to put clothes together by feeling, rather than just taking what stores wanted to hand me, finally made me feel like I owned my own life. It was as if I'd finally reached that period of rebellion that teenagers get to much earlier. But I was rebelling not against my family, but against the straitjacket of Madison Avenue.

Sometime around 1997, I was putting some papers away in boxes when I came across a picture of myself in those gold-and-bronze-striped corduroy pants. My heart did a double thump as I peered at the very crisp image. There I was, the outfit clearly as sexy as I used to think, and I looked great in it. In the picture I wasn't "husky" at all. I looked regular. I looked like all the women I knew. The outfit didn't look wrong or vulgar. I didn't look outlandish. The pants and blouse looked perfect for the size 16 I was. I looked healthy and average. I cried looking at the picture.

I cried for the tormented teenager I'd been, with not a strong enough sense of myself to know I could trust my own image. I cried for the years that I'd tried to diet down to the "right" size. I was bereft for those years that had passed when I'd choked on the distorted image of myself that had been shoved down my throat by the media, the fashion industry, and the department stores.

And even if I had been huge in the outfit, even if my stomach had been spilling out over the top of the pants and my breasts had been bursting from the confines of the sexy blouse . . . so what! It was the outfit that made me feel great. I wasn't wearing it to meet the queen of England or to go to work in a law office; I was wearing it with my friends. Why did no one want me to be happy in it?

Department stores today do have plus-size departments, as if they couldn't dare to have the fat people's clothes next to the skinny people's; they're usually tucked away discreetly. They are, however, happy to give you the secret map and code word if you'll just ask. But try going into one of those cute boutiques that line the malls, selling clothes cluttered with glitter, chains, painted hearts, or fake rose petals. You won't catch a size 16 anywhere near them! Hard to think of oneself as the victim of a sexist, capitalist plot, but here we are. Suckers on the escalators of life. No department was made for us. We can get the piercings, we can get the tattoos, but finding a sexy blouse to fit that doesn't cost twice as much as a size 9 is almost impossible.

It started out seeming like a conspiracy against me personally, but I've grown! And I now don't even believe it's a plot against large women. It's really a reflection of how the system (that applies to fashion, fabric manufacturers, department stores, and capitalism) has no respect for women of any size. That's why it costs more to clean our clothes; why our clothes and shoes wear out faster then men's; and why an extra two inches of fabric for a size 18 costs you as much as an extra outfit. Woman are cash cows, not real people. (Maybe I should have kept that jacket.)

With that political perspective, my anger turned away from myself and toward the systems that continue to treat women like cattle. It also turned to sharing information with other women when something great showed on the horizon—a store that did make clothes for me; a website that sold the right bra sizes or boots that will zip over a normal-size calf.

In many ways being larger was a huge benefit as I tried to figure out my presentational self. Being traumatized at a young age forced me to push boundaries to find my own way. Having department stores of the '60s, '70s, and '80s totally ignore 60 percent of the female population led me to think outside the shopping bag.

In 2006 my partner, Diane, had a dress made for me based on an authentic design from 1906 (everything but an unneeded bustle) to celebrate the centennial of the San Francisco earthquake. I've discovered that I lust after period clothes, corsets, and lace. It still costs more for me to get them in my size, but now I don't hesitate to wear them. I know they say much about who I am as a colored femme and as a feminist. Two days later, without a moment of hesitation, I was wearing a purple suede skirt and lime green flip-flops; the next weekend I went to an event wearing my Jackie O. midnight blue silk sheath with matching coat. It took thirty years to put these clothes in my closet and let go of the hurt little girl in the Chubettes section. Who knows what it'll be tomorrow? Maybe that layaway cow coat will turn up at a secondhand shop.

20

Pony

ELLEN FORNEY

Favorites

Has this hat in 6 colors

"ALL GIRLS, ALL ZEPPELIN" -- can't argue with that!

LEZ ZEP ALL GIR LL ZEPP

motorcycle jacket from extremely cool aunt

wallet carries one crumpled dollar bill + coffee card for that café where that cute barista works

FORD

So it's not a Mustang, at least it's a Ford.

Pony's brother wears a "DYKE" tag.

FFAG

Boxers or briefs... boxers or briefs... Both!

3 pairs in red, 3 pairs in blue, 3 pairs in green.

Dressed Up

Totally absolute favorite outfit.
Thrift store SCORE!

↑ was grandfather's fedora

vintage Betty Grable tie

ZEP

belt buckle circa 1970

← Fluevog wingtips

"John Bone'Em" (John Bonham)
Won first prize at King of Hearts
competition -- played air-drums to
a condensed version of "Moby Dick"!

Special Occasions

Utilikilt. (It's **not** a fucking skirt, it's a **kilt**! Fuck you, okay?!!)

Chinese fighter pilot's helmet (cherished gift)

for those intimate moments

workin' on the 'Stang

TEAM PONY DRESO

also has Spongebob slippers

NOW MAKE MAGNETS! IT WORKS! CARTOONIST-TESTED, NEIGHBOR-APPROVED!

Izod

SAMARA HALPERIN

NEW YORK CITY, 1980

The Izod Lacoste two-button short-sleeved piqué polo shirt. Without one, you were nothing in Mr. Yemer's fifth-grade class at the yeshiva. That little alligator held the keys to popularity and acceptance in its pointy white teeth. Unfortunately, my mom was a fashion designer who didn't believe in buying clothing just for the brand name. She cut the labels off every item of clothing she owned and taught my sisters and me how to use a permanent marker to black out the labels you couldn't cut off. My mom laughed at the way my classmates said "Ralph Lauren" with a French accent and told me his name was really Ralph Lifschitz, from Brooklyn, which I saved for ammunition at school.

Izod was different. It wasn't just a label, it was a smiling green alligator. If I had one I would be accepted, I would fit in, for once. Normalcy was within my reach, and I knew it would never be this easy again. There were very few fashion trends at the yeshiva because the girls had to wear a uniform of a skirt below the knee and a shirt that covered our shoulders—no T-shirts, tank tops, or pants allowed. On Fridays we had to wear a blue skirt and a white shirt in honor of Israel. The boys got to wear *kippot* (yarmulkes) in whatever material and style they wanted—suede, velvet, satin, brocade, hand-embroidered with their name in Hebrew, or checkered in the colors of their favorite sports team. A few of the boys wore the big, square silk *kippot* from Israel, but they got made fun of.

I was weird and never fit in, even in a uniform. My colors and patterns were bold and bright in a sea of beige and navy blue. There are nine entries in the back of my fifth-grade yearbook that say, "Dear Samara, You are weird. Have a good summer." I was a class clown and one of only two non-Orthodox kids in my class at an Orthodox Jewish yeshiva. My family didn't keep kosher, which automatically made me a pariah at school. My best friend, Shana, wasn't allowed to come over because we didn't have separate sets of dishes for dairy and meat, and her mother was worried she might forget and eat a non-kosher cookie off a non-kosher plate. She was right to worry, because Oreos filled with creamy, white lard were my grandpa's favorite meal.

To distract from my non-kosher status at school, I memorized and recited television commercials and challenged boys to eating contests. I earned respect by eating whole raw onions and drinking cups of white vinegar, stolen from home. I ate my way to victory, beating the reigning champion, Greggy Flicker, by eating thirty-five green grapes soaked in Tabasco sauce. Greggy puked up his barely chewed tuna fish sandwich after thirty-two grapes. I hated Greggy because he made fun of the way my eyebrows went up and down when I sang morning prayers and called me "Elevator Eyebrows," but he shouldn't have talked—his eyebrows were as big as the fuzzy black caterpillars I found clinging to leaves on Riverside Drive. Even though I got sent to the rabbi's office for bringing the non-kosher food that made Greggy puke to school, it was worth it.

Greggy had eight Izods, one for every day of the week (two white ones for Fridays). I wanted to cut the alligators off of his shirts and keep them in my "special box" with my googly-eyed puffy-sticker collection.

I saved up $28 from my feather barrette business and the $10 my grandparents had sent me for my birthday, from Brooklyn. I was ready to buy my Izod. While my mom and my sisters and I walked to the store, eating free slices of bologna that the butcher on the corner gave us, she asked me why I was going to spend all of my money on a shirt with a little alligator patch when I could get four identical shirts for the same price and sew on any patch I wanted. I didn't have any answers, other than that the alligator was really cute and everyone else in my class had one, which I couldn't say out loud. I had my pride. I had no choice but to agree that brand names were stupid and a waste of money, and instead of buying an Izod shirt for $35, I bought a rubber alligator at the toy store on the corner for thirty-five cents, and my mom taught me how to sew it on to a perfect, preppy, two-button short-sleeved polo shirt that I wore to school the very next day. And for the rest of the year Greggy Flicker called me "Alligator Girl," or "Gator" for short, which I secretly loved.

The Fly

JENNY SHIMIZU

I.

Two Fridays ago I met Martina Navratilova. She was wearing sweaterpants—pants made of a cashmere/wool blend with a 360-degree row of pleats that traveled down her leg. I couldn't take my eyes off of them. My mom used to have a skirt similar to Martina's sweaterpants, I think. After I shook Martina's hand and made some feeble comments to the King, I looked away and saw a poster of her. Unbelievably, she was wearing the same outfit in the poster as she was wearing that night. The sweaterpants. It was at this moment that I realized Martina had a "dress-up" outfit. I couldn't have loved her more. You see, I also am a creature of habit and I also have a "dress-up" outfit. Yes, my outfit is much different than Martina's, but we now had something more than just being gay in common.

I have always worn a uniform, ever since the day I watched *Billy Jack.* It's a variation on Levi's, a Levi's jean jacket, a T-shirt, and boots.

I also heard somewhere that Einstein used to wear the same outfit of dress shirt, black pants, and black jacket, and that cemented my decision to not expand on my tastes. I have many jean jackets, many pairs of jeans, many T-shirts, and many pairs of boots. I do admit that in my older age I have started wearing brogues and sneakers. I want to grow old gracefully and handsomely, and big boots are not as political as they used to be. In the late '80s and early '90s I dressed as a skinhead, with bomber jackets, Dr. Martens, Levi's, and a Comme des Garçons or Paul Smith long-sleeved T-shirt. I always loved throwing a bit of fashion in, very subtly. I learned about designers when I got a job at Ecru. It was a store on Melrose Avenue that specialized in haute couture. There I was taught all about European designers, fabrics, shoes, accessories, the rich, and how to sell to them. We carried folders that outlined every client and their fashion needs, and I excelled and I had a secret: I was a late '80s, Queer Nation, shaved-head dyke who loved cashmere, oiled dark leathers, and clean silhouettes. My journey into fashion had just begun and I didn't even know it.

II.

For two years I walked the runway for one of my favorite designers, Yohji Yamamoto. The first time I met Yohji was in Paris. It was my first Fashion Week and I was still in a state of shock that I was actually doing this. The house of Yohji was an old, beautiful Parisian building on the outside, and on the inside it became a modern fortress of minimalism and creativity and inspiration. Upon entering I was filled with awe and deep respect for this man. He had long black hair, a kung fu–style beard, and the most amazing deer eyes. Instantly I couldn't talk, because he didn't talk. He whispered to his assistants and they spoke Japanese quietly back to him. The assistant said, "Walk," and I began to walk, and I could barely look at Yohji, he held so much dignity. He was an artist, and he could bring a coliseum of sports fans to silence just by entering.

I got the call later that afternoon—I had booked the Yohji show, and I was so excited and proud. I developed a relationship with this silent master of quick smiles and side glances. Still, after two years I was unable to speak to the man. The last time I saw Yohji I was digging through a giant cardboard box. I was ravenous and I had found bento boxes Yohji had brought to the show for his staff. A voice I had never heard before said, "Are you hungry?" The master had finally spoken, and he spoke English and spoke it well. I had to laugh.

III.

I have a new Ducati and it is beautiful. It is black on black and makes me crazy. I have ridden Hondas, Triumphs, and Harleys my whole life, but this new Ducati is different. Maybe it's a part of my growing-older-handsomely campaign. The decision to buy this bike has been life changing. Having ridden cruisers all of my life, I was perfectly happy to be covered in oil after each ride. I was used to avoiding cops, because my rigid choppers had a number of "custom" touches. I've never had a mirror on any of my bikes, and sometimes I like to ink my own registration stickers. Now that I have a Ducati, I ride with a full-face helmet. I like to wear aerodynamic clothing—big boots get in the way of this beast's agility—and I am more fashionable than I've ever been on any bike. I have choices now, and it's broadening my world. The choice it offers is to change or not to change. Go with the flow and try a mandarin collar and new lightweight fabric, or stick with what I know: dirty jeans, T-shirts, and boots. Either way I'm still a biker, still a modern-day outlaw, still a free spirit. You will not find me in full red racing leathers, DUCATI written on my back. I want to incorporate fashion into my lifestyle, not become my lifestyle through fashion. To be comfortable in my own skin is the only trend.

Green with Envy

DEXTER FLOWERS

"You know what would look beautiful with your red hair?" some adult I don't even remember once said to me in sixth grade. "A green velvet dress. That's what you need." This person, who is totally blanked out from my memory, somehow started a real compulsive obsession. I think a part of me felt like I wasn't living my redheadedness to its fullest, and that if I found this perfect velveteen dress of deep forest green, things would be different for me—like I'd put it on and my hair would glow all fiery and golden, and forest animals would lift my dress as I walked, and fairies would illuminate the green until it shimmered like city lights on water.

I sat in school, daydreaming in my purple stretch pants and huge lavender sweater that went down to my knees. *Someday I'll have one*, I thought. "What I really want is a green velvet dress," I'd tell people all the time, as if by focusing on it constantly I'd channel my energy in a prosperous way. Cosmically speaking, green velvet did start flooding into my life, but the cosmos worked in mysterious ways. First came a forest-colored hat. One of those upturned ones with a huge flower like Blossom had on that TV show.

"It's so pretty with your red hair!" my mom gushed, helping me pay, like, $25 for the overpriced fashion faux pas. I lowered my standards. Green velvet was green velvet, and I squealed with delight at my ugly treasures. Hair scrunchies of the same material appeared for me. Pouches with dangling crystals that I wore like a necklace, slap bracelets—they were all the same. As if piling green velvet accessories over my Easter-colored stretch pant/sweater outfits would somehow equal the dress.

One day in seventh grade I went browsing in Target with my mother. "Oh, look at these, Rhiannon! These are *nice!*" my mom said, holding up a green velour shirt with matching stretch pants.

"I like them!" I said without hesitation, feeling their softness in my snatchy hands as I carried them to the dressing room with desperation, like this outfit was one everyone would want and was selling out fast. I was prepared to hiss at any frenzied shopping woman who might try to wrest them from my arms. I quickly put the leggings on, and the shirt. I looked in the mirror, my hair all messed up from pulling the shirt over my head, but all I could see were crimson locks over velvet clothes. I decided velour was like low-income velvet, so I refused to call it velour.

I modeled my "velvet" outfit for my mom in the fluorescent lights. "That is so beautiful on you!" my mother exclaimed. I didn't like the way the pants showed off my butt—just hanging out there—and my tummy pouf, but at least the top was loose enough to conceal my little boobies, and the material was what really mattered, anyhow. The woman working at the dressing room was wearing black-and-white spandex pedal pushers and a huge orange scrunchie.

"Oh my god, that outfit is darling! I'm going to try a set on. You have to get it!" she said with a big smile.

"Velour is such a nice material, too. Really comfy," my mom said, briefly touching her curly black hair in the mirror.

"Velvet, Mom," I said. "It's velvet."

I didn't come to Target much, but I usually had good experiences there. Later that year, after I'd saved some baby-sitting money, I picked out a couple cardigans and a T-shirt. At the register I realized I was short on cash. "Get rid of this one. You don't need it," my mom said, holding a navy-blue-and-white striped cardigan. My mother hated striped clothes.

"But I like that one," I pouted rebelliously. The woman working was probably about thirty-nine years old and had amazing crimped hair that was both bleached and red. She looked me in the eye.

"Oh, these have Xs on the tags, so they're on sale, sweetie." She winked at me, making up some imaginary discount.

"Um, I'm still not sure I have enough," I said, nervous that I'd still be too broke for everything.

"Oh, don't worry, I'm sure you have enough. That will be $15.48," the woman said, smiling intensely. I dug in my purse to find exactly $15.48 with no extra change—I swear. My arms went up in goose bumps as I thanked the lady, and she said, "Have a nice day."

"That woman's psychic!" my mom and I both agreed in the parking lot. I couldn't help but wonder how Target could be keeping such a magical creature caged in that stupid checkout stand. I never saw her working there again. I always hoped she hadn't gotten fired over that ugly cardigan.

The whole green set was a little pricey for my mom, so she suggested I pick between the shirt and the leggings. "Ugh! I can't decide. I *love* them both. They look so good together!" Less fabric meant less like the coveted dress, and besides, a perfectly matching outfit sounded like a perfect relationship to me, and I didn't want a lack of funds to destroy their harmony. My mom and I were okay. She was keeping me well fed, warm, and housed, but it was moments like these that were somewhat painful for her. The way clothing is valued and so easily bought by some makes not being able to buy one $30 outfit for your daughter feel shameful—especially with whiny, bratty girls all around us, their carts full of clothes, begging their parents for expensive shoes when all I wanted was one frumpy velvet set.

"You're right. They're so good together. Let's get them both," my mom said, hugging me.

"Are you sure?" I asked. Now that I'd gotten my way, I felt a little concerned.

"I'm sure," she said.

Back at home, Mom's dreaded boyfriend, Terry, greeted us. "How'd it go?" he asked, hugging my mom as I slid past with my Target bag and ran into my room.

"Rhiannon got the greatest stuff." I could hear bits and pieces beyond my door. I laid the clothes out on my bed like an imaginary person was in them and stared admiringly. "Come model your new clothes for us!" I heard my mom yell, like it would be an event to remember.

"Okay, hold on!" I said excitedly. Mom's boyfriend or no Mom's boyfriend, a fashion show after a trip to Target was my favorite part of the experience. I put the outfit on, ripping off the tags to make it more real. This outfit was all mine.

I walked into the living room and paraded myself all around in front of the big living room mirror. My mother reveled in her approval, complimenting me with a look on her face that had no financial regrets. Terry's eyes were huge and wide, the way they always got when he tried to seem thrilled. His mouth was kind of ajar and smiley-shaped, so that his beard almost touched his chest. "Those pants are beautiful!" he said. It seemed like he actually meant it, and maybe I'd misjudged his genuineness. "Velour is one of my favorite materials!" His red curls trembled near his ears. I couldn't help but express gratitude for his support of my new style.

"Thank you, I love them too!" I smiled a little at him. "But it's velvet." He didn't argue; it wasn't worth it.

Terry liked my stretch pants—a lot. Where at first I'd mistaken his interest as fatherly and supportive, I soon found it was much more. "I just really, really love those green pants," he beamed the next time I wore them before leaving for school. As it happened, he began talking about the pants daily for the next week. "Felicity, those pants you got Rhiannon are the perfect pants. I've always wanted a pair like that." His face would contort in the same way every time he mentioned them, like his eyes were going to pop out of his sockets, or like he was a hyperactive Pomeranian.

At school, the kids couldn't help but stare; the outfit made me look like an elf in the middle of puberty. No one said a word to me about it, but when I'd have to readjust the pants so they didn't show the full shape of my anatomy, I knew what they were thinking. Regardless, I continued to love the velvet set. Then I came home after school one day to find my mother happy and grinning. We sat down on the love seat and Terry walked into the living room like a vision from my most shocking nightmares. There he was in *my* green stretch pants. "Terry loved them so much that I surprised him with his own pair," my mother gushed. To my mom, buying yet another gift for someone she loved made her feel more abundant. As if it weren't traumatizing enough for me to be thirteen years old and walking the junior high halls with my ignorant fashion issues, my mother's boyfriend would be seen all over town in the same clothes. It made it painfully apparent how unhip what I was wearing happened to be.

In the summertime my eyes had been assaulted by his tight, tie-dyed biker shorts with the pronounced bulge that spandex gives men.

It had been mortifying to go places in public (as a normal, judgmental preteen), and I'd thought I was saved by the winter—too cold to break out his shorts—but I was wrong. Not only did he now own *my* pants, he wore them all the time. On a fancy night out with my mom, or to a drum circle, he put his fancy Moroccan-print shirt on and, usually, the leggings.

I didn't give up right away. I'd put the pants on and walk into the living room and he'd walk out from his bedroom and be wearing them. I'd rush to my room and change right away, cheeks flushed, I was so embarrassed. It was like having a twin, with a mom who gets you matching clothes. While I looked elfin, Terry looked more like Kermit the Frog. I now believe this is why my mother liked the green velvet so much. She was enchanted by the idea of our looking like fairy creatures from the forest, like a small gnome family. This was all too taxing on my self-confidence. I'd begun to despise the velour clothes, begun to see them for what they really were—spandex and not real velvet.

"I'm not wearing them if he is!" I'd say with residual anger if my mom ever suggested I wear them with an ensemble. I stuffed the velour garments into the dresser, swearing to never think of them again.

A year later my stepmom finally came up with a green dress for me. This dress wasn't the vision I'd had. It was crushed instead of silk velvet, a baby-doll style with long sleeves that was very tight under the arms. I'd gotten pickier since the whole Terry fiasco, like a person who knows the difference between good merlot and a jug of Carlo Rossi.

I never really wore the dress out until ninth grade, to my first Ani DiFranco concert. It was before she got all popular, so the audience was dreamy-eyed hippie girls who rubbed the softness of my crushed velvet, beaming at me as they gently pushed me to the front of the stage. I spent most of the show looking for my best friend, Violet, whom I was infatuated with. I didn't find her until the end of the set, when she softly bit my neck from behind, whispering that she'd gotten a little tipsy. I coveted her style; she was a fashionista molded from Courtney Love, Kim Gordon, and anything cool in my teenage eyes. I noticed she had many dark hickeys all over her neck, and I gulped back jealousy for whomever the boy had been, wishing she weren't drunk and that I could profess my deep, fourteen-year-old love for her. I stared down at the folds of my dress and thought, *The material's pretty, but this just isn't me.*

Soon after that, I finally found my heart's desire. I was looking through a vintage store called Raspberry Beret when I found it—a silk velvet, forest green dress. It had a great crinoline under it, so it poufed out. I eagerly tried this emerald jewel on to find that it barely zipped up. I couldn't breathe, and my breasts were matted down like dirty hair that's been under a baseball cap all day. It was $40 and I convinced myself that the whole "fitting" thing could be overlooked, because from the waist down it was a dream come true. I twirled around in front of my mirror at home, having visions of myself at an enchanted ball. I never wore it outside of the house again. My fantasy of it fitting could only last in my room, and so there it stayed . . . until Violet and I decided to get married. "Married" consisted of Violet telling all the slacker kids we hung out with at school that I would be her "wife."

We set a date for Friday and no one was invited. We told everyone it was an intimate thing for just the two of us, and my mom was going out with friends that night, so naturally I assumed this would be the night I would lose my virginity. In my room, the dress fit even less than it used to. I couldn't zip it past my waist, no matter how much I tried. I put on a white lace robe that my mother had lent me several weeks before so Violet wouldn't see my unzipped back. Violet came to my home wearing layers of sexy lingerie and ample rhinestone jewelry. I was her fashion-clueless friend, and somehow there we were, exchanging vows. I put her ring on her long finger and she tried to do the same to me, but hers was too small and it pinched me, my finger fat bulging painfully. We put the ring on my pinky. "Now for the kiss!" she said, and we shared lips and lots of saliva. My heart beat with anticipation as I carried Violet across the threshold. My dress split down the back, the zipper totally off track. The sound of velvet tearing was a sad sound for me as I dropped Violet on the hardwood. She wasn't too hurt as she collected herself and announced that she'd rented the movie *Trainspotting* for our "honeymoon." I lay with Violet on the white love seat, realizing things were not as they'd been imagined. Violet fell asleep in twenty minutes, and I, reclining and torn in unsexy green velvet, spent the rest of our honeymoon watching heroin addicts swim in a dirty toilet bowl.

The next year, something happened to Violet—she stopped wanting people to notice her. Button-up cardigans were replaced by a huge, unflattering red rain jacket she'd found in her dad's closet. Violet rubbed olive oil in her hair so it looked greasy and unkempt. She put hand soap under her eyes and let it dry and crack so that people would be so disgusted, they might not look at her altogether. I think she was sick of all the boys sizing her up, the word "slut" floating behind her back, the alcohol she'd drunk, and the pettiness she seemed to associate with people finding her attractive. But I never suspected how far my shining star of a best friend would fall. "Can I look for something of yours to put on?" Violet said, rummaging through my drawers like they were bargain bins.

"Sure, I don't care," I said lethargically, lying on my unmade bed.

"What's this?" Violet looked at me suspiciously, and my cheeks almost burned off me when I saw what she was holding. The. Green. Stretch. Pants.

"I don't ever, ever wear them. My mom—"

"Can I try them on?" Violet did not wait for a reply and stripped to her underwear, pulling the item that I'd hidden for years over her slender legs. She asked to borrow them and I said yes, full of regret now that the person I looked up to most had brought my most hideous pants back to life. It made me wish they were still mine. It's like when a baby won't eat her food and an adult starts picking off her plate and the baby gets hysterical, suddenly wanting the creamed corn all to herself—my fashion stolen, tragically, again.

Violet started wearing the pants almost every day. She'd light candles in her dark bedroom, spinning and dancing for hours in the stretch pants and a silk shirt, listening to The Cure. While spandex might make some people less noticeable in high school, the way the leggings hugged Violet's curves and accentuated her butt still made people stare. Combined with her dad's red coat, it was like Christmas every day. Devoted to the pants, Violet hadn't realized they weren't built for the amount of love and dedication she'd bestowed on their life. They started to get holes through the knees—like blue jeans, only not blue jeans at all. Violet remedied this with safety pins and continued wearing them to school every day. Eventually the material ripped through the pins, and the stitching started unraveling on the crotch. Violet wouldn't accept their rapid death, as if they were the Velveteen Rabbit. She sewed patches out of an old flannel shirt all over the rips.

Her mother didn't like it at all. She constantly tried to convince Violet to throw them out with the dinner leftovers. Scoffing at the open trash bag, Violet would storm off, her mom getting a view of the back of the pants, held together only by a loosely sewn patch over the butt crack. One day Violet called me, livid. "My mother threw the green stretch pants away! She fucking got in my room and washed them," she said. "Apparently they fell apart, and so she threw them away!"

"That sucks, sweetie," I tried to comfort her, though I was secretly glad to see them gone again.

"I can't believe she would throw them away! I could've fixed them. They always unravel a little when they get washed." Violet spoke in a sunken way, like an old man who is the only one who knows how to start his Thunderbird when others call it a piece of junk.

It was the fate of the pants to end this way. If they hadn't been thrown out they would have become a quilt of patches—everlasting evolution. My green velour was gone forever, while Terry's may be somewhere in his clean dresser, still folded, preserved, and in perfect shape.

Beats Me

EILEEN MYLES

W<small>HEN</small> I <small>READ</small> the novels of Leopold von Sacher-Masoch, the inventor of masochism, it seemed he was kind of a Pygmalion of pain. He wanted women who reminded him of statues, cold and cruel, and he liked them in big furs, I guess so that he would know they were protecting themselves from that same coldness that he found hot. There's an inside-out-ness to masochism that made tremendous sense to me. A masochist doesn't even like art, he claimed. It hurts the animal's eyes to see something that's not nature. So art is the first hurt and then you run with the story, I guess.

The masochist makes a story out of the world. And so it is with clothes. I remember at the height of my drug addiction—I mean at the height of the early, good part—I liked wearing clothes that could have been worn by a boy who died in 1910. That was my dream. My family seemed addicted to its own sadness, and though I left them because they were too sad for me, I carried a loyalty on my back—I bravely carried their stories out into the world. My father had a gang of brothers in Boston—well, this is much later than 1910, but they had kind of Dutch boy haircuts and wore suspenders and their shoes looked kind of high and lace-up, and when any piece of clothing coincided with this look of cute masculine loss I thought, *That's mine.* I wanted to be a statue of romantic loss. Before the world hurt me I would dress for the part. I'm thinking shirts buttoned up to the neck in an immigrant way. I'm thinking tweed worker caps like Mayakovsky would have worn in the teens and twenties of the last century. I'm thinking cigarettes and loose, hapless pants. That's one road into fashion I've covered. Yes, shirts being large. There is a really great picture of Willem de Kooning in a large cotton shirt, tucked in, smoking a cigarette. I think he had the sleeves rolled up above the elbow, but it was clear that the shirt was enormous (but nice cotton) and so it had kind of an old-world artist look. Slightly pathetic, but classy.

Occasionally I've bought new clothes—I do a lot, now—but used clothes, particularly in New York, used clothes bought right off a blanket on the sidewalk, have been my very best source of clothes. For instance, in about 1990 I found a pale blue agnès b. shirt for sale on Astor Place. It was really smooth cotton, small collar, kind of loose but elegant. It still had a paper dry cleaner's wrapper around the body of it, so I assumed it had just been stolen right out of someone's apartment. I suppose with it having been 1990 it could also have been the shirt of someone who had just died of AIDS, but it was a very expensive shirt, soft blue, and I wore it until it was tearing at the shoulders, stained, and torn on the back. It only looked better. I did buy a very expensive shirt ($100 in 1986) at a store in Paris called Hemispheres. I was breaking up with the girlfriend I was traveling with, so any excess felt powerful. It was gray-and-black striped, and it was kind of thin and almost see-through, that light, and it looked particularly good with a tan. Good shirts are really nice to touch, especially when they are old and they become a fetish for your girlfriend because they are on your body when you're holding her and she is sliding her fingers around your shirt. I understand this, it's important, and when she doesn't love you anymore she's sad because she still loves the shirt, because it reminds her of how she used to feel. Black shirts are amazing.

Here's something interesting. When you age you change colors. I mean your hair becomes lighter. For a while people don't know what it is. They go, Your hair's getting lighter. But what it does is change how you look in certain colors. For instance, light blue is a little weird unless it's exactly the right shade. Pale blue can look like an old-person color. Some fag will say, Oh, buy it, it looks good on you, and then you realize you look like a middle-aged golfer. Good what? Your hair keeps getting more white, so the colors that look good keep changing. It's weird. I have found a certain gray that's almost black that I think of as my color. You can see the white in my hair, but it sort of works. You want things to happen, not *stop* happening. White used to be bad, I used to wear white shirts all the time, then they looked bad, now they're back.

Suddenly I'm wearing ties. There are men who influence me enormously. Johnny Depp is one. I get such an immense crush on certain men, I have to settle myself down and say, *Stop—what is it that you want?* I never want to have sex with these "beautiful" men. I want to be them. I want their clothes. Johnny Depp and a whole range of handsome (mostly) young men in film are wearing black ties. You wear a black tie with a white shirt, or a pale blue shirt and the dark gray jacket, and you feel like a stud. You know what it is. I feel like I'm not trying to be young. This is a new fashion turn in my fifties. With a little seriousness I can be sharp. I need a new suit. Suits, yes. I had a wealthy girlfriend a few years back and she bought me a very expensive suit. Again, agnès b. We strode into SoHo and I slid it on. It was cotton but it was shiny like sharkskin. It was greenish with blue highlights. I was going to give a commencement address at a college graduation and I would have thrown a suit jacket on and black shoes and felt proud, but she wanted more. To tell you the truth we were going to a wedding in Richmond, Virginia, after the graduation, so I think she didn't want me to look poor. That's sad, and not in the good way. I thought of it *my* way at the time—like she simply wanted me to look good. That was generous of her, and it was. The suit's old now but it was gorgeous then. It was gorgeous for about three years. They told me in the store that Willem Dafoe had just bought the same suit and that felt great, and I'm actually the same color as him so it makes sense.

What I wanted to say about the suit is that the best play it ever got—well, two—was a memorial reading for Allen Ginsberg at John the Divine. Let me say in passing that no one expects a lesbian, particularly a poet known to be poor, to be wearing a hot, well-fitting suit. The well-fitting implying it's yours. But here's what was really fun: I wore sandals. Which means I rode the subway barefoot with a really good suit all the way up to 103rd Street. And to wear a really good suit with sandals suggests that you might have several good suits. Jean-Michel Basquiat famously used to paint in beautiful suits like mine. It's a very *I don't give a fuck* relation to style and it's very powerful. You can do it from on high or on low. It is very fun to do from on high. I'm going to scribble a bit in that area and then I am done.

When I worked at the Harvard Coop in high school I saw that the Harvard freshmen, the ones who had clearly gone to expensive prep schools, wore beautiful wool tweed topcoats and sweatshirts and jeans or chinos and bare feet in their loafers. It was a rich vulnerability. It was like, *I'm in a rush, I'm careless, but this is a beautiful coat.* So in my thrifting for many years it seemed to me that it didn't matter so much if the shirt or the jacket fit you as much as if it had a sincere look of quality. It had been in the family for a long time. Anyone's family. That you threw it on in your urgency.

For instance, I found a sweater on a rug outside the Second Avenue station about ten years ago. Very dark gray. It sounds like I like gray a lot, and I do. I've always liked gray. It's almost my favorite color. Anyway, almost black. And the label was old. This was a very old classic nice wool sweater. And it had major holes in it. And it had been mended. Many times. This sweater would break your heart. It was fairly small. Not tight, but not loose and floppy. And you could push the sleeves up over the elbows and the cuffs would get out of shape and look kind of pathetic. The waistband would get stretched out, too. It was like paper. The sweater had a look of tremendous sincerity. And this was in a black leather time. Black leather jackets and black leather pants. Though not together. And the sweater, because it was close to black but *not,* gave you a feeling of variation—even in the dark. And it was soft like leather was hard. It felt important to me to put these things together—to say that. Because a poet is not hard. A poet is soft like wool, kind of a lamb. Clothes give me an opportunity to say these things. Dressing is like art, like a drawing. It's like being your own avatar in this world. And I'm coming around to saying two more things and then I'm done. Though I care about clothes so much and I think about clothes so much. They're the day.

I think about those Harvard boys and how rich people can be a little poor—sockless in winter, they've mastered that look. And in my years of dressing and thinking about class I want to meet them musically. If they're coming down a little bit, well, I'm not exactly coming up, but I'm meeting them there. The undressing within dressing is a level you set and it's an opening you make into the world. I've always gotten along better with rich people than with the middle class. Because the middle class is simply worried.

Yet, I have had a middle-class income for about four years. It's the second thing I meant to say about the suit. It got me a job, because if a lesbian walks into a job interview in a good-looking suit, she gets hired. They assume you know a lot, and I do. In the time of the job I've spent a lot of money on clothes. I have a closet full of new shirts. And I don't want a job anymore, so I'm trying to not spend money on clothes, so I'm treating my own wardrobe like a thrift shop. Pull from here and there, making unique combinations. The look I'm trying to describe is awkward. I mean, there's the gray and the ties. I'm from the '70s, so I will always love minimal. Minimal is strong. But I'm thinking awkward, slightly dandified, eclectic—I think that's the look. And sleazy, a little bit sleazy. I'll always like that. So, like a silver tie with a denim shirt and a suit jacket. Like you're a country singer trying to be serious. Or, you know, one of those stretchy shirts with a collar; you know the short-sleeved ones, with a tie. I'm letting my hair grow long. I'm thinking composer, genius. Someone being a little "wild" but basically too into their work to think so much about clothes, just throwing whatever on. But animated. An awkward animated guy. And sincere in her thoughts, something like that.

High Gloss: My Lifelong Love Affair with Makeup

SILJA J. A. TALVI

By the time I pry open my eyes wide enough to be able to roll out of bed, it's usually early in the afternoon. To say that I'm not a morning person is an understatement; my brain doesn't clear up for work, conversation, or social engagements until 2:00 PM, and that's if I'm lucky. Afternoon is a better time for me to begin my waking rituals: black tea and a poached egg, feeding my cat, a glance at accumulated email, and, perhaps most important of all, my day's first application of lip gloss.

I don't bother with any other makeup unless I have to leave the house. On those days when I stay inside all day to work, I wrap my dreadlocks on top of my head, wrap myself in a robe, and keep my lips happy with L'Occitane shea butter or Dr. Bronner's & Sun Dog's Magic Orange Ginger Organic Lip Balm, as well as occasional reapplications of gloss. (Sometimes, if I'm feeling really inspired, I'll also put on a pair of heels while I write.)

The makeup I wear is an external thermometer of how I'm feeling, and how I feel like relating to the world around me on any given day. Days when I need an extra jolt of confidence and bravery find me tending toward purple pigments, and days when I need to be taken seriously doing an interview have me heading toward deep reddish-browns and gold colors to complement my skin tone. On those late nights when I head out on the town alone to work on my laptop at a bar (it's one of my ways of *really* getting things done on deadline), I usually show up with carefully groomed eyebrows and a don't-mess-with-me fierce femme look, for which black mascara and a smudge of dark eyeliner are musts.

I do not exaggerate when I say that I am an unapologetic makeup aficionado. Facial skincare runs a close second, because no amount of makeup will really work if it's painted over seriously distressed or disregarded skin.

All of this seems to have started as far back as elementary school, when I first began my eager experimentation with eye shadow. I had no idea what I was doing when I picked a horrendous powder blue to go with my dark hair and my hazel eyes, and was greeted by the genuinely puzzled look of my teacher upon arriving in my classroom. But by the time I reached junior high and dove headlong into the L.A. punk/hardcore scene, makeup wasn't just a passion, it was an integral part of how I chose to express my dissatisfaction with L.A.'s peculiar homogenization of women's physical attributes, clothing styles, hairstyles, and, yes, their boring ways of wearing their makeup.

L.A.'s conformist, materialistic popular culture is something that came to mind when I spotted a December 2006 cover of *Star* magazine, featuring photos of J.Lo and Katie Couric before and after their makeup had been applied. "Why Makeup Matters!" the headline screamed. "Shocking Photos Inside!" Inside the magazine, the two women were accompanied by the likes of Eva Longoria (who looked about ten years younger *without* her makeup), all ostensibly looking terrible without their faces painted. In the "after" photos, they were all pictured wearing very similar styles of straightened hair, black eyeliner, and nonthreatening, light-colored lipstick to match their demure smiles.

Yawn.

The *Star* beauty editor on the story had this to say to her readers: "After writing this piece, I'm never leaving my apartment without makeup again."

But my love affair with makeup has never been about conformity or a desire to blend in with any kind of mainstream trend. On the contrary, when it came to my sources of makeup inspiration, I studied the looks of older female punks with spider tattoos, multicolored mohawks, black lipstick, and drawn-out-to-their-ears eyeliner; *cholas* (Chicana gangsters) for their perfectly exaggerated, darkened lips and eyebrows; and early 1980s Hollywood Boulevard streetwalkers for their daring, in-your-face war paint. These were women who had nothing to *do* with gender or social conformity, and one of the most obvious ways to demonstrate that fact was achieved by the way that they decorated their bodies and faces. In a sense their makeup styles, like mine, served the simultaneous purpose of being a warning signal to anyone who might want to mess with these women, as well as a kind of homing signal for those who had a better sense of what these women were about—and what their terms of engagement were likely to be.

I've long since left Los Angeles behind for the decidedly non-makeup-focused Pacific Northwest. Just as I did in L.A., I do in Seattle: I'm not really interested in the prevailing look around these parts, which has everything to do with practicality. I respect the look for what it is, but that doesn't mean it does anything for my fascination with aesthetic possibilities. (The city's only lesbian bar, for instance, is the kind of place where makeup is a straight-up rarity and a near guarantee that no one will try to pick up on me.)

Here in the land of fleece and no nonsense, the top of my bedroom dresser is both a testament and a shrine to my artistic relationship with makeup. My obsession centers on daring shades of lip color, and then fans out to my flings with highly pigmented eye shadow, complementary lip and eye liners, various shades of mascara, pressed and loose powder, and all manner of shimmering, accenting special skin effects. Concealer and moisturizer are musts; tinted SPF 15 moisturizer is usually a better choice for an average day than foundation; and the skin must be able, always, to *breathe* at night with a thorough cleansing.

I'm the kind of woman who studies seasonal makeup lines to see what's new, high quality, and utterly worthwhile—Urban Decay, Smashbox, Aveda, Chanel, Clarins, Estée Lauder, Cargo, and M.A.C. are usually at the top of the list—and who gets excited about Sephora catalogs the way other people fixate on pornographic material.

I'm also the kind of woman who has perfected the art of obtaining as many cosmetics and skincare samples as is humanly possible so that my obsession doesn't drain my wallet. I can say, with conviction, that I think that certain drugstore products are just as good as the spendy ones, especially when we're talking about Revlon's Skinlights, its fabulous skin illuminator; Dickinson's witch hazel astringent; Burt's Bees lip liner; any of Aveeno's facial cleansers; and Jergens Natural Glow Daily Moisturizer. In fact, most department store and high-end makeup is terribly overpriced, even when the quality isn't anything to get excited about: Guerlain, Dior, Hard Candy, Too Faced, DuWop, Benefit, and Stila are among them, although their loyalists would completely disagree.

Did I mention that I *love* makeup?

It's also true that some people just have no *inkling* of how to wear their makeup—oh, the horror of seeing someone who still combines a hideous light pink lipstick and pink blush with bright blue eyeliner! Far more dangerous is that most women have no idea how much toxic crap is crammed into far too many tubes and jars of makeup and skin-care, something that has had me leaning more and more toward Flower Fusion lipsticks from Origins, Zia pressed face powder, and Urban Decay's range of vegan products.

But makeup is *not* for everyone, and women and men alike should be able to wear what they want on their faces, if they feel so inclined. In the San Francisco County jails, for instance, the administration has even recognized the right of self-expression to the degree that male prisoners and transgendered people are allowed to order cosmetics from the commissary if they want to. (It may seem trivial, but a little piece of respect for self-expression in an otherwise bad time in people's lives is actually a big deal for many prisoners who are otherwise reduced to numbers and identical, jail-issue clothing.)

Most important, I'm a firm believer in the fact that makeup isn't any more of an intrinsic threat to feminism than having a great, kinky sex life ever was. A woman has to have the *attitude* to match the makeup she wants to wear, and that kind of an attitude, coming from a place of internal strength, is a good thing indeed. In the same way that a $300 Coach purse is not going to make you look desirable unless you already *feel* desirable, a $25.50 Yves Saint Laurent Golden Gloss is not going to make you more confident if you don't know how to *feel* confident. The cosmetics industry would like you to think otherwise, of course, but that's about as genuine as an airbrushed *tuchus* on a *Sports Illustrated* swimsuit model.

When I'm in public, I think of makeup the way I think of wearing sunglasses: If done right, they can both be stylish, while serving a dual purpose as an emotional buffer zone that I use to protect myself from folks who might otherwise try to test my boundaries. In fact, well-done and highly expressive makeup tends to be *intimidating* to many men, a phenomenon that I've tested out in my own, unscientific way in cities like L.A., San Francisco, Seattle, and New York by gauging how many times I get approached with or without makeup when I'm in public. From my experience, a woman who looks like she's rockin' a distinct, individual style in her makeup and/or clothing seems to come across as too challenging and self-determined to constitute easy prey. But that's just my going theory. If anyone's got research funding for me on this one, I'm game.

It's especially important for me to emphasize that I don't always wear makeup (although it's rare that I leave the house without something on my lips), and that I don't wear it because I'm trying to get attention from men or women (although I certainly know how to play up my makeup if romance is on the evening's agenda). I don't wear makeup the way that I do because I need or care about male "approval" of my femininity, although I do admit that I genuinely appreciate and compliment other women's style choices and often get that kind of sentiment in return.

Back in 1988, however, when I headed to the undergraduate, all-female Mills College in Oakland, California, it didn't take long for my peers to start asking me why I bothered to wear lipstick every day, since men weren't even sitting in our classrooms. Who was I trying to impress, anyway? In this environment my very commitment to feminism was actually questioned from time to time, although I was the cochair of Mills's only feminist student group (membership usually hovered between three and six women).

Very few women there seemed to *get* that I really wore lipstick because I loved to wear it, and I always felt that it complemented my survivor strength and my unique style. Although I was far less of a heel-wearing femme in those days, I still wore lipstick in 1991, when I taught hundreds of other students about civil disobedience strategies, on the first night of what was to turn out to be a headline-grabbing, two-week college strike against coeducation. I also wore lipstick when I talked to the press about why they kept showing footage of women crying rather than holding strong, and I wore lipstick on the last day, when we celebrated our victory in front of hundreds of flashing camera bulbs and microphones.

In my grown-woman life, my love of makeup has seriously taken the role of an artistic pursuit and a celebration of my femininity and fierceness, right next to dancing and writing, which used to be the only one of the three that I did for a living.

That is, until one particularly nasty winter in Seattle when the writing portion of my brain stopped working. I didn't just block, I hemorrhaged. I knew the only way to jump-start my creative juices again was to do something *completely* different. Nearly overnight, I became a well-paid, independently contracted makeup artist, working for a few of the top lines at the downtown Seattle Nordstrom, the mother ship of all Nordstroms nationwide.

All it took was the recommendation of a makeup line manager at the store. I had worked on putting her look together as a volunteer makeup artist on an all-day film shoot relating to the myriad reasons why people choose a vegetarian diet, and she immediately wanted to know whether I was available for freelance work at the store.

I started at $18 an hour, which felt like a fortune by typical freelance-writing standards. With no actual training to speak of, I was on the floor almost immediately, assuming the role of one of those enthusiastic makeup artists equipped with an apron full of amazingly lush cosmetics brushes.

The other women and men working the floor were an ethnically diverse bunch, nearly all of whom shared at least a little bit of my fervor for makeup. Many of them, like me, were tattooed and artistically inclined, although it was notable that almost all of those folks worked at M.A.C., as opposed to Clinique or Chanel. Some believed in their products, and others didn't. What I quickly learned to frown upon, however, was the terrible problem that many of my erstwhile peers had with a kind of makeup-inspired superiority complex, and especially the catty ways they would talk about customers and each other's looks. Makeup is superficial, but that doesn't mean that the people who sell or wear it should be.

My most significant insights into women's relationships to their appearances came when I left the posh digs of the downtown store for the makeup counters located farther north. Customers there had less money to spend and were genuinely more thankful for the attention we were able to give them. The women there often approached the counters with a look of insecurity, something that quickly yielded to vulnerability and gratitude when I started to talk to them about how they felt about how they looked.

Out came women's stories about their struggles with weight, self-hatred, and a belief that if they didn't meet a narrow definition of beauty, they were just plain ugly. Although it would hardly have been acceptable to my managers if they had known, I talked to these women about the ways in which the industry actually plays *up* those kinds of insecurities, and I always emphasized that makeup could be a great way to accentuate one's own natural beauty.

I wasn't on commission, and I didn't care if I spent an hour empathizing with a woman while I applied the kind of makeup she had never even dared to wear before. I introduced greens and golds to women who existed only in the realm of beiges and pinks and shared every little bit of cost-cutting cosmetic wisdom I could think of with each person who expressed even the slightest bit of interest. Many of these sessions would end with warm embraces and many of the women in tears, thanking me for giving them a different way of looking at themselves. I felt more like a counselor or a healer than a makeup artist, and that's about the time that the writing part of my brain kicked in again.

I knew I was about to get back to my primary occupation, but I decided to give it a few more weeks. Back again at the flagship store, the wealthy women were wearing on my nerves, and the bratty teens with credit cards were driving me to the point of wanting to snap on them for their palpable senses of entitlement.

My passion for makeup was being eroded by every single one of these exchanges, though that erosion was tempered by my realization that several cross-dressing men started to show up at my counter, right as the store was about to close. Just as I had done with the women who expressed their insecurities, I welcomed these men to tell me what it was they were looking for, and what it was they were worried about.

One man in particular became a favorite customer of mine, because it took a bit of work to get him to even accept a makeover from me in the first place. His look, until then, had emulated a style not far from my elementary school experiments. He had figured out how to wear bras, dresses, and pumps for his feminine evening excursions (by day, he dressed in a suit and assumed a masculine role), but he had no idea what to do with his face.

We worked together over the course of a few weeks, until he got comfortable with an entirely different kind of look. I wasn't selling him much of anything, but I was getting enormous satisfaction from helping him to integrate and embody the person he wanted to be.

Those triumphs notwithstanding, and just five months into the gig, I was ready to get out. I couldn't stand the way we had to try to lure people to our counters, and the daily lack of any intellectual conversation or stimulation was starting to hurt my head.

The day before I quit, I had the experience that did it for good.

I was working alone at the Tarte counter, wearing my purple shirt with the brand's name on it (as required by the company), when a fifty-something woman came waltzing in, her husband and dozens of shopping bags in tow. She had the look of a woman dripping with money, and an attitude to match.

She snapped her fingers but never met my gaze. She thrust a very well-used lipstick in my face and demanded a replacement.

The lipstick wasn't one from our brand, so I tried to tell her precisely that.

It didn't matter. She wanted what she wanted, and was clearly accustomed to people doing exactly what needed to be done to make her life as comfortable as possible.

We went back and forth like this for a while.

"That lipstick isn't one of ours, but I'd be happy to recommend a similar shade. Would you like to try one of these?"

"I want *this* one replaced."

"I understand that, ma'am, but I can't give you that one, since it's not from this line. I'd be happy to walk you over to the counter that sells that brand."

"I want *this* one. Now. Don't you understand?"

"Yes, I do, but I can't replace your lipstick, since this brand is Tarte, not Clinique."

Finally, something seemed to break through, and she looked at me, directly, for the first time.

"Did you say that Tarte is the name of the makeup right here?" she asked, pointing at the display in front of her.

"Yes," I replied tersely, wondering how much longer all of this would go on.

"Oh," she said, wrinkling her brow. "I thought that was *your* name."

It was just the kind of moment I needed to make a graceful exit. Writing deadlines and lip gloss application quickly resumed their normal place in my life; my loving appreciation for makeup, thankfully, resumed shortly thereafter.

Joni on My Chest

TARA JEPSEN

I'M NOT A great dresser but I'm not horrible, either. I admire true talent, like that of San Francisco writer and DJ Chelsea Starr, and Gwen Stefani. The truly fashion innovative seem to always make their own clothes. Currently my favorite shirt in the whole world is a Joni Mitchell crop-top from her 1979 tour. It's a light beige softie with Joni's name written in blue cursive above a drawing of a guitar and two lady legs in heels. There's some abstract detailing in red, yellow, and blue. A friend of my ex-girlfriend's friend was getting rid of it and knew I loved Joni after I waxed rhapsodic over the Mitchell oeuvre at a dinner party. I probably referred to the Joni Mitchell–athons I'd been having with Jody the Ex and a couple of fag friends—rich affairs with candles aflame and light appetizers. The wine is implied.

I don't know why this clown of a former owner cut a perfectly incredible T-shirt into a crop-top. I lack a basic understanding of why a person would wear such a style; random, considering the bizarre styles I choose to employ. I won't wear crop-tops because I don't want to showcase my body that way. I kept the Joni Mitchell crop-top even though I didn't think I would ever wear it. It was just too good to get rid of. I knew I would be so mad if I saw someone else wearing it. Four years after scoring the shirt I realized I could wear it over another, longer shirt, and I sat at the dawn of a new era. Sometimes I am stunned and disturbed at how long it takes my brain to become innovative in a challenging situation.

I remember how in high school I always wore the most giant T-shirts of your life. A constant tenting of my body, like I had termites and was fogging my insides. That was my fashion: anything in an extra large. I could have shared upper-body wear with my beer-swilling football player cousins of Hungarian and German descent. Having terrifically large bosoms made me want my body to disappear, and the second-best option to erasure was amorphousness. Some faves were: an XL Greenpeace T-shirt, an XL Cocteau Twins T-shirt, an XL pink-and-purple Benetton sweater. On my bottom half I sported colorful, baggy hippie pants from Guatemala via an import store in downtown Green Bay, Wisconsin. Another option was baggy black cotton pants with anything, though mainly an XL navy blue T-shirt. I thought that was one of my sharper ensembles. The fact of large, clunky shoes being popular was quite handy, so that my small feet would not be swallowed entirely by my billowing pant legs. This was before those impossibly overflared raver pants came along, though I never would have worn them. They just looked too stupid. Having tiny feet with big pants and their corresponding wide pant legs is not cute by any stretch—it looks like you could tip over, like you're wearing ballet slippers, or like your legs are pegs with dinner rolls stuck on the ends.

When I got to college I wore Levi's as large as possible. I had a stack of them in my dresser. Without a belt they would fall off my body. This was a particularly bizarre look because of my little legs and the really long fly. It appeared I had a huge older brother who was my sole clothing supplier. I was safely under wraps. I rotated through a selection of large T-shirts, just like in high school. I actually remember the first time I bought a non-T-shirt shirt. It was a ribbed girl-shirt in black, bought large enough to hang loosely on my frame. I thought it was almost trampy, which I now know was by Victorian standards. I agonized over whether I would be able to wear it and not feel extremely self-conscious, as though my boobs were flying around the room in everyone's face; like I was posing for a beaver shot in the middle of downtown.

So, regarding my boobs of the time: They were extremely large. On a visit home to Wisconsin (I was living in Santa Cruz, California), I saw a girl named Debbie whom I had befriended in my senior year of high school. We bonded heavily over how much we hated having a large rack. Beyond feeling physically encumbered, we both hated the spell our boobs cast over some men. The drowsy eyes locked on our chests, admiring and awaiting movement. The wide eyes and big ham hands tied in knots behind their backs.

When I saw Debbie this time around she had become unburdened. She wore a tiny red long-sleeved shirt with black capris. She looked great, happy, and free. She told me about her bilateral breast reduction and sang its praises. It took about five seconds for me to become completely convinced I, too, needed this surgery.

On December 15, 1992, my surgery dreams came true. I flew home to Green Bay, Wisconsin, and got my very own bilateral breast reduction at St. Vincent's Hospital. When I asked the doctor to take everything, he insisted he would "leave you with a nice breast to get a good husband." I bit my tongue, not wanting him to cancel the surgery because of my impudence. My breasts were reduced. My fashion was forever changed.

✺

Every woman I've ever slept with—it's the modern age, people, I lost count long ago—has stared at the scars from my surgery. Fascinated, never horrified—lucky me. I think the surgeon did a good job; he might not think so, owing to my lack of husband. No longer do I look down at my naked chest while lying in bed and feel profound revulsion and despair.

Invariably my date asks how large my boobs were before the surgery. Here is where the disappointment comes in: I have no idea. Once they exceeded 36C, I stopped buying new bras and developed a trick: the act of yanking my bras around to avoid displaying boob overflow. Boob overflow: when your breasts are too big for your bra, so there is a dent where the bra ends and the uncontained remainder of your breast starts. It's not sexy. It can look like a whole other unit. Maybe they were double Ds. That's my guess. I'm sure if I acted more authoritative when I told my consorts this size, it would add considerable thrill to their fantasy. Being uncertain is so rarely titillating. Wait, that's not true at all.

My whole wardrobe changed when I got a breast reduction. My shirts got smaller and smaller over the subsequent years. I became athletic because I knew a sports bra could actually immobilize my chest. I became interested in putting together "looks," rather than just pairing one enormous shirt with one pair of ballooning pants. I have long, keloid anchor scars from the reduction. This means there is a long scar like a smile underneath each breast and a scar from the smile up to the areola. Sorry to be so yucky. My best joke regarding these scars was telling a girl I started dating that I had been a man. She had such a great attitude. She just said okay, momentarily got a distant look in her eyes while she adjusted, and dove into having sex with me. I told her I was kidding. She liked me either way.

I consider dressing to look (my own version of) nice an act of self-love. I think my look could be labeled East Coast Horse-Riding

Enthusiast Meets Color Spaz Meets Former Modern Rock Fan. I became infinitely more comfortable in my skin with the removal of the largeness of my bosom. I can't imagine wrestling with that thing into old age. I had no desire to come to peace with the stares and discomfort and ill-fitting clothing. In the moments when I consider sex work, I realize I would have a better career with my original rack and its absence of scars, but that's the only time I'm at all conflicted. Plus, it seems easily solvable by sticking to scenes with a lot of whipped cream.

For all my love of shirts with huge ruffles and high collars, of cashmere sweaters with puffy sleeves and anything tight with a nautical theme, I am, for now, most in love with the Joni shirt. I like the line from my shoulders to my chest to my waist. I like the colors. I like the era it refers to and the virtuosity of the artist. I like that it doesn't make me feel like a boob.

Lipstock

KIM GORDON

RECENTLY I READ one of those *New York Times* articles espousing the idea that fashion isn't dictated from above by the elite few fashion editors, but rather comes from the street as a trend. The jury is still out about the recent non-underwear-wearing, snatch-baring shots of Britney Spears, Lindsay Lohan, and Paris Hilton. One fashion aficionado was very quick to gasp that the recent flashings of celebrities at the paparazzi were clearly not fashion: . . . *This is not a fashion trend.*

Fashion designers always talk about the back-and-forth of street to fashion and vice versa. Apparently a clitoris cannot be chic, much less deemed even approachably attractive. Unless, of course, you are a stripper or a porn star and you've had some work done. Out of context it seems unacceptable as an aesthetic experience.

Britney, Lindsay, and Paris are not the first celebrities to expose their vaginas (or at least just their vulvas) in public, but they are certainly the most photographed. And to do so at a time when they are at their peak public profiles, with the gossip rags and the Internet, with all their notoriety, it does seem undeniably deliberate. A deliberate fashion statement of girls simply hanging out together, joining forces of mischief and self-destruction to some new level of mythical proportion. Caught up in the moment of dressing with a little deconstruction of their own.

Are they bored? I like to think of it as an assault. Aggressive fashion for the occasion of the paparazzi. Here's something you can shoot but can't print. It becomes myth. Even for those who saw the shots on the Internet, it became, *Did you see the photos?*

Lindsay, since being nicknamed "fire crotch" by Hollywood gadabout Brandon Davis, is the most controversial for having exposed a clit so large and droopy as to be deemed shocking in its ugliness, or, one could also say, its *realness*. No Victoria Secret airbrushing or product placement here. The revulsion is just the thing to drive a girl into the ready knife of a plastic surgeon. These girls bring to mind Judy Chicago's famous piece *The Dinner Party,* done at the height of '70s feminist art. Each plate was a rendering, in fact a celebration, of different artists' vaginas. Britney was deemed prickly for her unkempt week's growth. Not quite the clean-shorn pussy of porn, or the innocent look of a prepubescent girl such as that which Paris sports.

When was the last time a fashion audience was so disturbed? It's not really fashion's vocation. But it is what distinguishes fashion from art, a modern relationship that makes art seem more relevant and gives fashion that much more depth. Exposing one's genitalia, as a new twist on going-out attire, is a real leveler. Nothing, except the groundbreaking and unappealing aspects of '70s feminist art, can compare.

Is it the ultimate expression or delusion of free will? It opens up many possibilities for all of us fashion voyeurs who also like to take in the celebrity landscape. How could any fashion designer create the wishful longing of a twenty-two-year-old with two children under the age of three, and whose career peaked at seventeen ("Oops! . . . I Did It

Again"), for a more innocent time when maybe a little girl could forget her underwear? Or deem it unnecessary (Marilyn Monroe deemed it unhealthy)? A kind of yearning for a girlhood day when one could be sensual without being considered sexual (oh, yeah, underwear is a drag, so inhibiting). A regression to a freer time—a freer time that Lindsay or Britney may have never had. Or any of us, really.

But these are sophisticated Hollywood girls, large celebrities with tiny imaginations. The biggest influence on Hollywood culture is strippers. Pole-dancing classes, breast enhancement, lip enhancement. Serious actresses cling to red carpet fashion essentials. *I might be showing cleavage but I'm doing it tastefully.* But the actresses who stray too far from the traditional sexy silhouette and embrace a more cerebral designer, say, Prada or Lanvin, that doesn't bare their sexuality in the most obvious way, are not the red carpet favorites. Madonna has actually made couture sexuality nerdy.

So does that mean that dressing like a porn actress or stripper and showing your clitoris to the world is the ultimate fashion statement? It is in Los Angeles, where clothes are always about the body. California has influenced street and regular fashion more and more with its seasonless dressing. And now the body-conscious thing has translated into Pussycat Dolls attire, strippers cum pop stars. One of my best friends, Julie Cafritz, who used to be in the band Pussy Galore, really nailed it when she proclaimed that, although Lindsay's peekaboo with the paparazzi has happened in both New York and London, "these people never leave California . . . if you know what I mean."

Early Lessons

KAT MARIE YOAS

SOMEHOW BIG, CURLY hair is bad.

There are other things that are bad, signs of being easy or fast, trashy. Like curly hair and eye makeup. Mom has soft, curly hair that falls around her face in blond ringlets. She wears blush and it makes her look hard, tough somehow. And this is ruddy red blush, a slash of color on each cheek. They are called the apples. The apples of your cheek.

Kristi Lynn tells me these things, about apples and boys and stuff. She's pretty bad, I guess. But she is my friend and I'm in love with her. Wears her older brother's plain white T-shirts and jeans. She already wears a bra like my mom. I don't, but I have "birthing hips." She goes, "Niiiice. Well, you'll get yours someday, maybe." She's talking about my boobs. She swears a lot, too. Every time I hang out with her I make a list of things to ask my mom when I go back home. So I don't sound dumb.

We go to Kristi's house, Mom and me, because Kristi's grandma sells discontinued Mary Kay and Avon from there. Pretty good deal.

I put on pink eye shadow and scram with some lipstick that tastes like glue or something bad, but it's red and I like that. Kristi wears brown eyeliner, but on her lips, around them, and natural light pink peeks through. It isn't even, the line, but I don't say. What do I know about makeup anyhow?

So Kristi's tough like all the other girls in my neighborhood. I'm not really so much, but I get on because we're all in the same boat. Broke or whatever, my dad fixes cars. At school they'd call him a grease monkey, but they never would here, in the neighborhood. You know what I mean?

I'm just weird or something, different every place. I'm the only kid in the neighborhood with a dress like this, all *Little House on the Prairie*. My Mennonite cousins made it. It's secondhand, but what isn't? This dress is beautiful. I only like to wear dresses, it's like I'm always ready to go to church or someplace good. My friends never wear dresses, at school or in the neighborhood, so I feel different in the good way. Seen, and seen as good. Safe, like this was God's dress and now it's mine.

This neighborhood is full of trouble, sweat stains, and diesel fumes. Almost everyone is named Mary and the cops are here every night. Girls here are always looking for trouble, that's what they say. Not even just the cops, but the grownups, the grandmas. We'll just be dancing or playing, and it's always, "You girls are gonna get in trouble someday." My eyes always close, like I'm waiting for it, this trouble. Pink eye shadow flash, dart-away-quick girl.

What kind of trouble? I ask Kristi this, she just looks around, like, *Duh—this is it.*

Trouble and no one to help.

As far as trouble, I have it in my mind to be real good. Extra good, so no one will be mean or give me the trouble they think I'm after. That is why I only wear dresses, so everyone can see on the outside how sweet I am on the inside. I dream up people who notice my specialness while playing dress-up with my mom's clothes, inventing whole new lives. One of my most-used lives is this: I'm me but sick, so sick and weak that people come to sit by my bed just to listen to me breathe and give me presents. Like closets full of Mennonite dresses and cowgirl outfits—fringe and spurs and everything. I wake up from my sickness glowing and loved. There are other dreams, about real people even. I think about being this girl, I don't remember her name, some pig-nosed thing who wouldn't talk to me. She wore dance and ballet shoes to school all the time, every color of the rainbow. She even had gold ones. When she wore them gold things to school, I never wanted anything so much as those stupid shoes. I really thought they were something. Like you could walk through anything. I told my mom about that, those shoes, and she just snuffed and went, "I'd like to see her walk on rocks with those shoes." My mom is tough about some things, even with kids. Always taking things I want and making them into jokes, so the not having them doesn't seem so bad.

I get older. We move to the trailer park. I start to get my mom's curly hair. How your hair can change all of a sudden is beyond me. Teachers get mean, say I'm too loud, my hair in the way of the other kids' view, that I'm trouble. Everyone knows where I live, where I come from. I don't need to have curly hair, too. I just want to blend or be invisible, but also really, really great, you know?

So I start straightening my hair. Teachers smile at me in the halls. *Hello, Kathleen.* I think I look more serious. I stand in front of my mirror and grab tiny sections of hair with one hand, my generic iron in the other. *Sizzle crackle.* Just like the other kids. *Sizzle crackle.* No trouble here. *Sizzle crackle.*

Clean face, no pimples, honor roll. *Sizzle crackle.* Maybe someday a closet of clothes from the mall, quiet colors, a boyfriend who plays sports. *Sizzle crackle.* I could spiral out of the trailer park, away from being a girl looking for trouble, go away. *Sizzle crackle.* Go to college, go anywhere. *Sizzle crackle.* Keep blending. *Sizzle crackle.* Get out all the kinks and stay away from Mary Kay. *Sizzle crackle.* Done.

I'm totally looking like a diet version of what I think I should be. Like a knockoff middle-class girl. But no one says anything to me about it, if they notice. There was this big meeting where they wanted to kick the trailer park kids out of the high school because we don't pay the same taxes, so we don't deserve the school that's across the street from us. This teacher comes up to me, and I like him and he likes me, and starts talking about the meeting. He goes, "Oh, we decided it was a dumb idea to make a separate high school for them." "Oh yeah," I say, real casual, like I don't care what happens, like I am not one of "them." Then he says, "It's not like any of them come to school anyway. Ha ha."

Ha. I hate that teacher now. I stop going to his class most days, just roam the halls and no one says shit to me. Not even him, and I more than pass the course.

Feeling invisible is funny. Like, I get to see all the undersides, the private jokes, the stuff that people say when they don't think a bad-news kid is looking. I felt all undercover at first. And then I would feel sick, because I don't like muted colors and I don't want to be quiet all the time. A little explosion goes off in my chest every time someone says something stupid, like I get afraid that I might blend so well, I'll fade right away.

I straighten my head before bed even, sometimes. *Sizzle crackle.* I stand in the bathroom with my boom box blaring and stare into the mirror hard. *Sizzle crackle.*

But there are always these underneath layers I can't get straight, no matter how I try. There are waves, and more waves peek out. I keep going over each tiny section, faster and faster. I get burn marks like hickeys down my neck. *Sizzle crackle.* Skin burning, and the damn thing breaks down on me. The iron breaks. I get to thinking I am going to have to drop right out of school.

My mom's mom dropped out of junior high because they were going to make her wear a swimsuit and go in the pool. Gym class. No joke. She cleaned rich ladies' houses up until she nearly couldn't walk with all her babies hanging off her. She was hidden in their shiny windows, the dust-free collectibles lined up real careful. She always had small hands.

Invisible.

Trouble.

If I've got to choose between the two, trouble.

I go to school, my head up like I mean to have my hair flying every place. *You look wild.* I have to say, all the comments make me walk a little swishier. My hair is so big it scares me a little.

I'm tall, and maybe even a little tough somehow. I feel a little power each time someone has to peek to look around me and my hair. You know?

Betsey Girls Saved My Life

KATE BORNSTEIN

TOMMY WELLS HAUNTED my erotic dreams all through grade school. He was a tough guy, short for a boy, and he lived on the wrong side of the tracks in Asbury Park, New Jersey. He was the closest thing to James Dean I'd ever seen in person. He wore sweatshirts and dungarees to school. They weren't called jeans in 1960. If you used a time machine to transport Tommy Wells as I knew him to, say, the Castro in San Francisco? He'd look like any baby butch dyke I've ever fallen for; of course I wanted to fuck him. And since I really couldn't do that, I wanted to *be* him. But I was a pudgy little Jewish boy who lived on the *right* side of the tracks. My parents were doctor Dad and schoolteacher Mom. They bought me all my clothes in the Husky department of Fisch's Department Store, which, interestingly enough, was on the *wrong* side of the tracks; but Fisch's had the deepest discounts—Mr. Fisch being a patient of my father's—so Fisch's Department Store is where Daddy and Mommy dressed me for grade school success as heir apparent to my father's medical practice. I wore khakis or wool serge slacks and button-down shirts to school. I was a tubby little boy dressed to look like Dad. But in 1960, I didn't want to be a boy. I wanted to be a girl. And if I *had* to be a boy, then I wanted to be the boy of my dreams: I wanted to wear a sweatshirt and dungarees to school.

It took about a month to convince my parents to buy me the coveted garments, and it took another month to convince them that *everyone* was wearing dungarees and sweatshirts to school, so why shouldn't *I?* So it came to be that one early fall day in 1960, I set off for eighth grade wearing brandy-new, never-been-washed dark dungarees and an over-large dove-gray sweatshirt. It was thrilling, and it lasted all of ten minutes into first period English. The teacher sent me to the principal's office to discuss my fashion faux pas. I was a good boy, the principal informed me, and good boys didn't wear such clothes to school.

"But Tommy Wells does," I blurted out.

"Tom Wells is not a good boy," said the principal, "Now go home and change your clothes."

My dungarees and sweatshirt were confiscated and donated, probably to someone who lived on the wrong side of the tracks. I was sent to an all-boys prep school. We all wore wool poplin, five-pocket, flat-front pants in charcoal-gray heather with a black blazer emblazoned with the red school crest (Washington crossing the Delaware—who knows why?), a white shirt, and a black tie. I learned how to not eat, and by senior year my newfound anorexia had turned me from husky to lanky, so I made that school outfit look *good*.

LATE 1960s—COLLEGE.

I grew my hair long, I smoked a lot of grass, and I studied and practiced theater. As artsy types, we theater people were expected to be either flamboyant or grungy. I chose the former. I wore flowered shirts, suede vests, and striped purple bell-bottoms over groovy Frye boots. When I looked in the mirror, I could almost see girl. It scared me so bad, I grew a mustache. But bless those bell-bottoms; they kept me out of Vietnam.

I was studying postgraduate acting at Brandeis University outside Boston when my draft notice came. My acting teachers helped me devise a subtle act of madness. The morning of my draft physical, I shaved off my mustache and all of my body hair. Hippie-boy me, I wore my hair down to my shoulders, and I brushed it shiny. I put on my purple bells and my brightest paisley shirt. At eight in the morning, I was standing in the locker room of a local high school gym with about a hundred other young men. We'd all been told to strip down to our skivvies and line up on the basketball court in alphabetical order. I stripped down like everyone else, and took my place in line between Borden and Borowitz.

"You there, naked boy!" a red-faced sergeant screamed at me. I smiled dreamily, the way I'd been coached to. According to my master plan, I wasn't wearing any underwear.

"Get your skivvies on, boy!"

"I don't wear underwear," I explained patiently in a soft voice. "It chafes."

It took at least five or six minutes for the United States Army to decide what to do with the dilemma I posed in my nudity. It was decided I would walk through my physical wearing my unisex striped purple bells, thus earning me both baleful glares and lingering glances from soldiers and draftees alike. They were all wearing olive drab or BVD white. I strolled from station to station, where I was poked, prodded, quizzed, measured, and queried. At the last stop, I asked the psychiatrist if I could maintain a vegan diet in the army. I'd already told him about the dreams I'd had all my life—the ones where I'm turned into a girl. The doctor glanced down at my unisex purple striped bell-bottoms. I'm pretty sure it was a wistful look he gave those girlie jeans hugging my lanky boy hips. Then he looked me in the eye and said, "Son, the Army doesn't want you." He gave me a psychiatric draft deferment, designation 1-Y.

I asked for his name, my father sent him a box of cigars, and I got back to studying acting. But I didn't last in graduate school beyond my first year. I was too restless. In the summer of 1970, I left grad school and drove west in my VW camper on a quest to find myself. I was skinny. I looked good. Move over, *Easy Rider*.

I visited the Amish as a working houseguest for about a week, wondering if I could live with a god that wanted me to dress like them all the time. That's what it came down to, even if I wouldn't have admitted it then. I remained equally fashion conscious through the B'Hai, the Kabbalists, and several genuine salt-of-the-earth hippie communes. The B'Hai were too Sears Roebuck. The Kabbalists were somehow even more dowdy. The communes tempted me. I traded one of my flowered shirts—the purple one with green-and-white blossoms—for a sweet embroidered peasant blouse that smelled faintly of sex. Unfortunately, I had to leave after only a few days. In my life, indoor plumbing is one of the few things that has nearly always trumped fashion.

Next up was the Church of Scientology, Denver, Colorado. The sign on the door actually read, ABANDON YOUR TEDIOUS SEARCH! THE ANSWERS HAVE BEEN FOUND! Fucking hell! Great! So I walked into the next twelve years of my life.

The woman sitting behind the desk at reception had radiantly luxurious, chestnut hair swinging down below her shoulders. She turned her headlights on me, and I melted. (Lust is another one of those things that trumps fashion sense.) One year later, I was serving aboard the twin screw motor yacht *Apollo*, flagship of the Sea Organization. The S.O. was the elite management arm of the Church of Scientology. We were reincarnated loyal officers of the Galactic Federation, serving on starships. Here on Earth, we lived and worked aboard *ocean*-going ships. L. Ron Hubbard lived and worked on the flagship. So did I. That's why I didn't mind wearing various naval uniforms for the next twelve years of my life. (Daddy has always trumped fashion sense, lust, *and* indoor plumbing. Tell me what to wear, Daddy, and I'll wear it.)

As a basic seaman, I wore U.S. Navy overalls as I swabbed the decks and patched up rust on the ship's hull. We were called "swampers," and we looked it. Later, as first mate and lieutenant, I wore navy or black polyester gabardine flared pants, a white shirt with epaulets, and a gold lanyard around my right shoulder that dipped rakishly into my left shirt pocket. I pushed the dress code as far as I could: I tried all blue, I tried adding touches of piracy, like a bit of lace at my wrists. This was the '70s, so I almost got away with that. It was 1980 when I finally ended up in European sales for the Church of Scientology International, and I demanded and received the right to wear civvies, the better to "identify" with the folks I was selling. I styled in leather and satin and denim. And then I left Scientology.

That story would completely derail the lovely tour I'm giving you through the many fashions of my life. Suffice it to say that after twelve years of communal, nearly monastic life in naval uniforms, I was suddenly out in the real world with no more Daddy. What would I *wear?*

1980

I was thirty-two years old and I wanted to be supermodel Cheryl Tiegs, so I spent my Jesus year diving headlong into my anorexia. I fell easily into a modified preppy look. No one was using the word "unisex" anymore, but that's what it was.

I worked at Satellite Business Systems, an IBM subsidiary in Philadelphia, selling long-distance service. SBS was the cutting edge. The company dress code was more relaxed than at IBM's headquarters. There was a gay man working in the office—he was out of the closet, bless his soul—which was quite a rare thing to be in those days. Alan knew how to stretch the corporate dress code, and I followed his lead. We wore the snappiest of sports jackets and the coolest of shirts with even cooler ties.

And then my father died of a massive stroke. A year later I had my sex change operation. I spent two more years in Philly, now as a baby dyke in her late thirties. I learned how to walk the edge of the unspoken politically correct dress code of Philadelphia's lesbian community. This meant lots of jeans and plaid shirts. I drew a line at the Birkenstocks. I was partial to jumpsuits, Frye boots, and scarves in a variety of pre-goth skull prints. At night, in the bars, I'd dress like a Madonna wannabe. I don't think I ever really pulled it off, but I began to learn how I could make girlie-girl work for me.

In the late 1980s, I moved from Philly to San Francisco to work as assistant to the lovely Susie Bright at *On Our Backs* magazine, with offices in the Castro. Here I discovered S&M, and suddenly I was wearing leather and an honest-to-goddess collar. I left *On Our Backs* because I needed more money for the rent, so I got a day job selling season subscriptions for the San Francisco Symphony. I spent evenings in rehearsals or hanging out with the lesbian theater crowd or the BDSM wonderground. That's when I started to develop a style that would let me walk in the Castro as comfortably as I might walk into a business office. I wanted to be pretty. I wanted to be an S&M delight. I wore leather and denim and silks and scarves and jeans and skirts and hats. Lots of hats. (It's *still* my weakness, searching for the perfect hat.) I added granny dresses and big funny boots and more hats: floppy hats, top hats, derbies, and cowboy hats, leather caps and hemp caps and silk-scarf hats. I wasn't quite Annie Hall, Liza Dolittle, or Liza with a "Z." I was just doing my best to make sure I didn't cross the line into complete clown.

In 1995 I moved to Seattle to become the owned and collared slave of a dyke couple. They were femme and butch, Mommy and Daddy, and I wanted to be attractive for both of them. The S&M dyke community dressed for their own sexual delight. There were butches who knew they were drop-dead handsome and femmes who knew they were complete knockouts. These were *my* people. This is when I discovered Betsey girls. Betsey girls are the retail clerks in the Mecca of girlie fashion, Betsey Johnson's clothing stores. Betsey's clothes are not cheap, but for me, shopping at Betsey Johnson is a state of grace. Betsey girls are killer femme fatale bad girls of any and all sexual orientations. They're sassy, sexual, sweet, and cute. Betsey girls are the thoroughly modern Millies of the Roaring Twenties who bobbed their hair and shortened their skirts. Betsey girls are the pinups that men painted on the sides of their planes in World War II. Betsey girls frolicked in *Playboy* magazine, as painted by Alberto Vargas. Betsey girls are kind. They want you to have fun. They want you to look good. They throw parties for themselves with themes like "Don't hate me because I'm beautiful." The year I was invited to one of those parties, I knew I'd made it.

And then Mom died. She coulda been a Betsey girl. She was all girlie-girl, a real flapper, a thoroughly modern Mildred. She prided herself on being a lady. Since her death, *lady* is what I've been trying to embody, no matter what I'm wearing. I'm fifty-nine years old now. Today I shop at Diesel, where I get my slinky sweatshirts and the boxy jeans that look almost like 1950s dungarees. I travel to college campuses all around the country—speaking about sex and gender—and I can finally wear what I want to school. I'm the bad girl and the nice lady I've always wanted to grow up to be. And somewhere between Tommy Wells and Betsey Johnson, I managed to find myself a style that lets me express all the many-gendered, many-aged ladies I've become. Imagine that.

Oh My God—Shoes!

CINDY M. EMCH

In April 2003 I had a transformative experience. I had finished doing my taxes and realized that the $300 I had saved to pay what I owed the government was actually mine, free and clear. It was 6:00 PM. I lived in the Upper Haight district of San Francisco. Home of tourists, coffee houses, old hippies, street punks, and some of the finest shoe shopping in all of the Bay Area. The shoe stores closed at 7:00 PM. I barely locked my door as I ran down my four flights of rickety Victorian stairs and speed-walked to the closest shoe shop. Not one pair caught my eye. The first five stores were a complete bust. At 6:45 PM I walked into the last store. When I saw them it was like first love. Like tasting fresh vanilla ice cream on a hot and sweaty day. I took a breath and felt the purest, cleanest air filling my lungs. My vision sharpened and every point and nerve on my skin started singing. It was a moment of truth.

In the glass case was a pair of orange platform bug shoes. When I say "bug," I mean they had antennae that bobbed back and forth and a hard plastic stinger that shot out from the back of the shoe. They were ridiculous. I had never seen anything like them. Were they gorgeous or ugly? I couldn't tell—they were just too fascinating. I needed them to be mine. They looked heavy and large and all-powerful, and yet silly and flighty with their bug ephemera. They meant business without taking themselves seriously. They were intense but liked to giggle. They were "The Shoes."

When I put my foot into them, laced them up, and wound the Velcro straps over the laces, I found home. These imported shoes—far too impractical to have been made in the States—were my newest crush. I asked the shoe guy how much they were. This is when I knew I was in deep. Those shoes cost all of the savings I had. I am a check-to-check-living, nonprofit-working sort of gal. I hadn't had $300 that wasn't assigned to groceries or rent in my life. Technically, considering my debts, I didn't have it now. But it was in my account. This was almost as much money as I had spent on a car a few years before. When I signed that slip of paper and bought those shoes, I sealed my fate once and for all. I had worshipped at the church of shoes for most of my life, but at that moment it was like I took my vows. I became a priest of Bootism, intent to spread the gospel of fabulous fashionista footwear to all who would listen.

I love a lot of things in this life: pop culture, Lake Superior, jazz, rhubarb, a wide variety of objects large and small. Mostly, though, I love shoes. Shoes are transformative. Shoes are religion. Shoes make the woman. Shoes make the man. Shoes make motherfucking everybody. Even people who hate shopping can appreciate a good pair of shoes.

I didn't start out this way, though. I started with dresses. I was always the sort of little girl who loved to climb trees and get dirty. I was the ultimate tomboy femme with ribbons askew, torn-up knees, grass-stained elbows, barefoot in a red velvet dress. I had an arsenal of frilly, glittery church dresses. My mother—the good, responsible Midwestern gym teacher that she was—tried to put me in overalls, jeans, shorts, but it just didn't take. I hated pants and refused to really wear them until winter hit and dresses were no longer an option. It shouldn't have surprised me that later in life people would always parse me as femme regardless of my girl/boy/andro affectations of the moment. If I could tackle and bring down a twelve-year-old boy in a football game when I was five and wearing my yellow Easter dress, it seemed pretty set that femmeness would be an inseparable part of my identity.

I was also a skinny kid and always sick despite my outdoor carousing. When I had my tonsils removed at age seven, my entire body chemistry changed. Overnight my health improved drastically. Just as quickly, I gained weight. It was okay at first, but eventually it became a problem. I started hearing more about my weight and my size than I heard about my grades and my bug collection. As I entered my prepubescent years I had to start wearing pants because the girl dresses that would fit made me look too old. Cemented in mall culture in the '80s, there weren't a lot of options for a quirky fashion sense, anyway—and being on the plus side of "normal" was an additional challenge.

The definition of what makes a body attractive isn't just something that is sold on TV and in the movies. Sure, Madonna and MTV could show me the prevailing notion of what was sexy. But that was less personal than going into Express and trying on cute trendy skirt after cute trendy skirt and having only the oversize sweaters fit, and snugly. Or running through fashion trends over the years and watching every aesthetic that felt like "me" shrink out of my size. I never thought the pop culture presentation of skinny was my only choice, or even demoralizing. However, it did make me want more than the available options. My eyes sparkled and shined over a variety of clothing styles that I knew would flip and swing and hang on me just right, if only the designers could envision their creation in a size larger than 10.

It was around this time that any pleasure I had taken in shopping for clothing went on hiatus. Because I was twelve years old and a size 14, most trendy tween stores saw me as a pariah. Fashionable salespeople in a variety of preppy couture would roll their eyes when I asked if they had something in a size extra large. A horrified exclamation of breath and a certain disdain that I would later define as "queeny bitchy" would pour off of them. Then, one day, a girl in the perfect plaid skirt, crisp white oxford, and navy sweater tied over her shoulders said to me, "Sweetheart, maybe you should try the plus-size store."

I knew about "that store." It was off in the farthest, cheapest corner of the mall, where everything felt dimly lit and kind of dusty. There was a mall hierarchy, and this was at the bottom of it. In the days before food courts, the greasiest diner of the mall sat knowingly across from that store. Its sign always flickered kind of weakly, as if to help the fat women hide their shame at shopping there in the land of sexless clothing with appliquéd sequined kittens. As if to say maybe the store itself was a little bit ashamed. I always thought it was fucked up to put a diner across from the fat-lady store. It seemed to imply they couldn't go five minutes without eating. It was so rude. At twelve, the idea of going into the land of caftans, muumuus, and kittens was too much to bear. There would be no red velvet dresses there. No new wave skirts, neon tights, or strategically slutty, off-the-shoulder shirts. I would be old and fat and my clothes would trumpet this to the world.

At that moment, I knew. I wasn't finding what I needed in any sort of clothing. I took all of my energy and love for hip and cute fashion and dresses and poured it right into shoes. I turned on my heel, left the sales-girl and her pile of "to be foldeds," and headed straight for the "alternative" shoe store. The one with the shinier leather, the higher heels, and the clunky shoes that I would later know to be creepers. Here I found my people. The hunt for basic clothes—forget fashion—had turned into a traumatizing ordeal, but at the shoe store none of the workers wore pastels, and sure as shit no one folded sweaters over their shoulders. There was no judgment here about my shoe size—in fact, there was an appreciation from the workers for the shoe styles I was drawn to. The gothy new wave employees were obviously tired of the endless brown leather penny loafers that walked in and out of the store, mocking their patent black platforms and Mary Janes. I walked in and was like the weirdo, artsy kid sister they had always wanted. And . . . I had a mother with a credit card. Soon I was a regular and learned what good customer service, without judgment and assholery, could feel like.

The shoe store. The blessed church of fat fashion teens. Here anything was possible. All I had to do was tell them my size and it always fit. My regular, non-chubby foot sliding into a perfectly shaped, rounded-toe, faux-leather masterpiece gave me power. Knowing any shoe in the entire store might fit me gave me confidence. I saw the endless possibilities. My regular jeans could turn into hip, intentional fashion before my eyes. A plain black skirt could become goth couture with shiny, buckled Mary Janes. Pale, dimpled, fleshy legs turn into strong, badass gams with a pair of boots that let people know that if they touch you, they're more likely to get a foot in the chest than the weak, helpless giggle of the Pillsbury Doughboy. Stacked heels transform big calves into luscious and curvy R. Crumb–worthy porn. Put simply, you can find any random clothes to cover yourself, but your shoes will always save you.

Once I was firmly in high school and the '80s were retreating into a neon- and safety pin–flavored haze, the fashion uniform changed a little. The commodification of punk and new wave, with a splash of grunge thrown in, meant that I could walk the walk of my chosen lifestyle without the same sort of clothing pain. Shapeless jeans and concert T-shirts and I was golden. Still, I could always rely on the shoes to transcend the just-average. Tall and stompy boots thrifted from military surplus shops. Perfectly gothy spooky strappy Fluevog shoes. I could find ways to work the sexy of my extra-curvy body. The stripey tights and short mod skirts of my friends weren't options for me, but I could work that patent leather or those Chuck Taylors like nobody's business. I made a science of how to turn adrogynous alt-boy drag into sassy femme armor, and I did it mostly with my shoes.

I wasn't completely conscious about the link between my weight and my love of shoes. Shoes were my option, my haven; they were safe and I knew the territory. They might have leather that bites, plastic that can make your feet sweat in thirty-degree weather, soles that always leak; every pair has its own quirks, like a lover. Every pair takes time to know, to embrace, to work into your daily life. As an adult, I had more than thirty pairs of shoes at one point. I belong to three different online communities to talk about the merits of different lines of shoes. What styles fit how. What sizes to buy when ordering online. And here is where I had the revelation, where I saw how shoes can liberate our thinking about sizes in general. How shoes are the key to a normal and healthy way of looking at our entire bodies, not just the feet.

When I joined the shoe communities online, I also joined a fat fashion community. I had been recently fluctuating in my size and wanted a place to talk about it, to get tips and tricks and ideas. I like my curves when they're both larger and smaller, and I have figured out ways to dress them up regardless of what size I am walking in. I saw an amazing thing—no matter how many issues people had around their clothing size, when you mentioned shoes all the rules and worry and size issues fell away. No one cared if they had to try on a 9 instead of an 8.5; they just blamed the manufacturer. Things vary. No big deal. How revolutionary.

Of course, clothing designs can vary depending on cut and style. But trying on a size 20 when you are usually a 16 can result in crying jags, breakdowns, and depressions that last for days. It's an assassination of self-image.

Trying on a different shoe size carries none of that. There are, of course, exceptions—I certainly know people who struggle with shoes and sizing and not fitting the "normal" mold. But for so many of us plus-size women, before we find a place of loving ourselves at any size, there comes a loving of ourselves in some fabulous shoes, shoes that love us in our 8s, 9s and 10s and help to show us how fierce and gorgeous we are from the ground up.

This realization brought me to a new place in my fashion journey. There are hipper places for plus-size clothing now. Fat- and size-acceptance activism have changed how I think about and look at my body. With definitions like "inbetweenies" (sizes 12–16), and stores like Torrid and Old Navy and dozens of online options catering to larger girls and women, trendy isn't just a dream to get frustrated and crazy contorting ourselves into. The stores for the size-12-plus set aren't even shoved into the dark and dusty corner of the mall anymore. At the mall closest to my house, the Torrid is right smack in the center—though there is still a cookie shop right next door. Fat is still shown as shameful in the majority of American pop culture, but the stores are catching on, and there is less daily shame in just trying to find a pair of jeans.

Fashion has gotten a little easier, and it's pretty simple to find a red velvet dress now. Still, if I am having a really hard day, I head for the shoes. They are the source of my self-love. They are my liberation. In the end, it's not the clothes. It's the shoes. Shoes make motherfucking everybody.

My Grandma's Attic: Dressing Up and Acting Out

DEBBIE RASMUSSEN

WHEN I WAS LITTLE, my grandparents' attic was one of my favorite places to be. I loved climbing the narrow, rickety steps, breathing in the smells of musty old linens and damp cardboard boxes, and peering into the street through the tiny, wooden-frame window. I loved feeling like a giant amid the low, slanted ceilings. But most of all, I loved the trunks full of my grandma's old clothes. Stepping into her shiny white plastic platform boots, dipping my hand through her jangly metal bracelets, slipping into the dress covered with marshmallows.

I was eight the first time I pulled the marshmallow dress from the trunk. It was a simple cotton dress; my grandma had glued the marshmallows on. They were as hard as rocks, but still firmly affixed, perfectly spaced, and seemingly as white as the day they came off the factory line. She'd also made a matching purse. Her trunk was full of things like this—there was a flapper dress she'd fashioned from the Sunday comics, a suit made from a giant cardboard box with a tie drawn on in Magic

Marker, "space-shuttle" gear made from bubble wrap and duct tape, and a giant clown suit she sometimes wore around the neighborhood for no other reason than to make my sister and me laugh. The trunk items, of course, weren't her everyday wear. But even on a regular day, she usually stood out, whatever she was wearing usually patterned, brightly colored, playful, and perfectly complementing my grandpa (since she often picked out his clothes, too). She loved every detail of dressing herself, and she instilled in me what she considered the important rules of fashion: Don't dress like everyone else; dress to make yourself happy; and once in a while enter your own fantastical world where it's perfectly normal to wear plastic and newspaper.

I learned from an early age to appreciate loud prints, original hand-made clothing, and costume as fashion, and developed an equally strong aversion to the mass-produced goods at department stores. I spent many childhood days fashioning my own creations under her direction—a skirt made into a beehive, complete with beaded bees attached by coil springs, a pair of pants covered with little plastic rabbits and trees, and a long tube dress covered with fuzz to resemble a caterpillar. When I wasn't dressed as part of another world, I wore a sometimes-dizzying array of mismatched colors, prints, and textures.

That's not to suggest that I shared my grandma's everyday fashion sense, or even her priorities, when it came to dressing myself. We've always been on different sides of the fashion-versus-function divide— she's quick to trade comfort (and at times safety) for style, while I've put a premium on clothes that allow for easy movement. It wasn't until last year, at age eighty-nine, after falling for the seventh time in as many weeks, that she finally agreed to forego shoes with heels; meanwhile, she'd been subtly suggesting for years that I trade in my "orthopedic-looking" shoes for a "more feminine" pair.

As I grew out of childhood, I went through a political awakening that my grandma had never experienced, and she stood by, bewildered, as my fashion stylings became more and more confrontational—as when, at age seventeen, I constructed an apron made of "dead" rubber chickens to drill home the point that "meat is murder" (plastering the words across my bedroom wall in red paper intended to look like dripping blood wasn't enough). Our fashion gap widened throughout my twenties as I self-consciously expressed various political identities in ways that took me away from our shared sense of playful fashion and toward outwardly telegraphing my internal drama and intensity. For instance, when I learned—and freaked out—about the inevitable environmental collapse, I turned to hemp, neutral colors, and earnestly pleading T-shirts.

When I discovered feminism and dyke culture, I swore off makeup, skirts, and dresses, and wore an array of "smash the patriarchy" T-shirts. I went through various manifestations of punk: The crustypunk days were characterized by infrequent showers and lots of metal studs. During a brief gutterpunk phase, I momentarily considered (and thankfully decided against) getting a facial tattoo. The cyberpunk/robot chic interlude was filled with metallics—everything had to fit snugly and clasp diagonally. Interspersed in there somewhere were raver and goth phases, in which I sported brightly colored hair extensions pushed back with goggles, with an array of mismatched petticoats and gloomy skirts accompanied by bondage collars. And like the best anarcha-feminist, I went through a long period of combat boots paired with ripped skirts, refashioned T-shirts, utility belts, and Leatherman tools.

Though my grandma and I remained close through all of these phases, there was definitely something missing. We no longer spent time together fashioning imaginative creations, and she was clearly disappointed to see my bright colors and intricate patterns replaced by a lot of angst, black, and metal. Looking back, I'm embarrassed that I seemed so incapable of applying my previous fashion imagination to how I expressed newfound identities, but I was so concerned with being seen as part of whatever identity I was moving through that I think I was afraid to tweak the styles.

By the time I turned thirty, I'd begun to settle down. I took a breath and realized how unhappy I'd become trying to cram myself into the styles dictated by the identities that I aligned myself with. I often felt like I was replicating the sheeplike style conventions of the mainstream. I missed applying my imagination to how I dressed. I missed the bright colors and stripes, the humor. It's not a stretch to say I felt visually deprived. Ready to return to my old ways, I selected remnants from my style identities that resonated with me, and I ditched the rest. I held on to the lip piercing, a handful of petticoats, the combat boots, and some random hair extensions that I occasionally affix to my hair with hot glue or clips. But I shed the metal studs, the crustiness, the angst.

For the past few years, my style has essentially been a mashup of all that's come before, with a slight undercurrent that could probably best be described as part clown, part pixie. I've also returned to my fondness for layers; it's become an amusing daily task to arrange colors, patterns, and textures into some combination that's visually stimulating. On an average day, I wear about fourteen items of clothing, including, most often, a pair of striped knee-highs, leg warmers fashioned from the sleeves of old sweaters, a skirt over a pair of pants, a long-sleeved shirt underneath a short-sleeved one, knitted arm warmers, a striped scarf, a brightly colored knit hat, and, depending on the temperature, a pair of fingerless gloves and a hoodie or sweater or two. I have a particular affinity for things that fasten, clasp, or button. For the most part, I no longer wear things emblazoned with political messages. It's not that I don't want to telegraph my politics; it's more that the desperate need to prove something to the world around me dissipated, along with my pathological need to be understood. Like my grandma, I'm more comfortable in the world of bright colors, stripes, and textures; people can affix their own meanings to the way I present myself. And happily, I've learned that more often than not, people tend to assume that I'm just trying to add a little pleasure to the world.

That's not to say that I don't still struggle with fashion—it's just that many of my questions have evolved: How do I dress in a way that represents my various subcultures and values in a way that feels natural, rather than forced or hackneyed? How do I continue to work out my inner confusion around issues of, say, gender, through constructing an intentional exterior? But back in the foreground is the idea of dressing myself as my grandma always has—as a simple and easy way of making myself happy, as a way of combating the uniformity and assimilation in the world around me. It's my own form of DIY therapy—carefully selecting colors, patterns, and textures and combining them in an effort to find the perfect sensory experience.

Now ninety, my grandma hasn't constructed a cardboard suit, applied clown makeup, or adorned herself with marshmallows in more than fifteen years. But she still carefully selects and combines her clothes every day in a way that adds vibrancy and stimulation to her environment. Whenever I visit the housing co-op where she lives, I can spot her from far away. She's the one wearing the bright red floral-print dress, or the perfectly constructed black-and-white suit, a coordinating fabric rose affixed to her lapel, with a bright yellow scarf tied neatly around her neck. And she's the one who always looks like she's having fun.

Milla and Me

MARY CHRISTMAS

THERE AREN'T MANY ways that a twelve-year-old girl who is nearly six feet tall can feel normal. In 1988, my mom and I lived in Manhattan, so the logical solution to this height deformity, it was decided, would be a career in fashion modeling. I had already made the plans in my head. My mother worked in the fashion business, designing costume jewelry that was sold in department stores and boutiques. Her job necessitated that she bring home a lot of magazines. In came *Vogue, Elle, Mirabella,* and even the occasional *Cosmo.* Mostly, she read the fashion bibles to keep up on trends, but sometimes her jewelry would be featured in a spread and she would have the page cut out and mounted on a cardboard display. Since I already hid in my room reading all the time anyway, I took to hoarding these magazines and flipping through them for hours after school.

They were on every page: the models, my people. The girls, mostly in their teens, were like me in that they were completely out of proportion to other female humans. At school, tougher kids would come up behind me with a tap on the shoulder, asking, "Hey, are you anorexic or something?" Most of the girls in my classes were robust and curvy; Puerto Rican, black, and Jewish kids represented the majority ethnic groups of the city. I tended to be about a foot taller than my friends, and my height only contributed to my ability to stand out in a crowd as a socially awkward, sickly-thin weakling. But in the evenings I read teasers in which up-and-coming young models were quoted as feeling like ugly weirdos, too—and look at them now! While everyone else in the world was probably laughing and saying, "Yeah, right" in the direction of tall, skinny, rich complainers, I was perfecting my dream of becoming one of them. After all, I was sick of hearing "Do you play basketball?" Physically incapable of any form of exercise, my fear of being accidentally nudged by some big jock girl overrode any possibility of participation in team sports. It was clear that if I were going to do anything about being a giant, it would have to be a gentle activity that didn't involve people hurtling objects through the air. Either way, I had been born with weird genes that tended to make people rich, and I was determined to milk it for all it was worth.

My mom's rampant partying in the gay scene gave us a leg up. Rubbing elbows with people like RuPaul at the Pyramid Club wasn't just good for her career; now it was good for mine too. She knew designers and makeup artists, but more important, she knew a bunch of femme boys and fag hags who were as obsessed with fashion models as I was.

After taking some arty black and white Polaroids on our roof (the New Yorker's version of a back yard), we begin the death march. Starting from the top, we were turned down by the big guys—Elite and Ford—for having too little experience and too "commercial" a look. After an encounter with one of those shady pseudo-agencies that pressures you to give them money, my mom and I finally scored. Next Models was a strong and well-respected new agency, founded by an experienced rep in exile from one of the majors. It was small enough to provide guidance and attention, and just big enough to ensure that I would be able to work on weekends and after school. In the lofty, minimalist office, surrounded by huge windows and stylish people with high cheekbones, I felt important. Suddenly, I was way more than just a junior high school student. Who cared about my inability to do division? Before getting signed by Next, my biggest worry was avoiding girl fights on the sidewalk outside school, in which someone's earlobe was inevitably torn when the loser's chunky gold doorknockers were ripped off her head; now I was a model. Twelve years old with a long road ahead, yes, but with an important career and a purpose in life that would raise me high above the shredded earlobes and maddening math equations of the adolescent world.

The first step on the mission was to build a "book." A model's portfolio gets shipped around the city back and forth all day long, traveling in some bike messenger's shoulder bag between the offices of ad agencies, fashion editors, and photographers. Without a book, I wouldn't really exist. Next, I had a list of photographers who were building their careers by shooting new models for the mere cost of film and processing. It would take some investment, but not much, and the agency promised that after two or three shoots, I would be working right away.

I started to drift off in class even more than usual, fantasizing about the apartment I'd soon have to rent in Paris and about getting legally emancipated as child stars so often do. I'd soon be talking to *Elle* magazine about how hard it is to juggle a successful modeling career with a normal life—"I never sleep," I'd say, while sipping on Evian in my makeup chair. "I'm always on a plane, so I just get catnaps whenever I can." I practiced feeling like no one took me seriously as an actress. After school, I rehearsed my new modeling skills. With *Vogue Italia* spread over the bathroom sink, I mocked Christy Turlington's puffy lips and Cindy Crawford's raised-brow, lip-curled snarl. I became a model impersonator over a few short months, with the ability to name each model as I imitated her signature stance/face/hand position. I knew the photographers,

I knew which models worked most for which magazines, and I knew what lucrative catalog and advertising contracts were bestowed upon which of "the girls." My mom found all of this obsession amusing, and she would coach me along by yelling out a supermodel's name and watching as I flung my body parts into my version of "Cindy."

The weekends had me trekking to appointments with photographers. The basic formula for what the agency called "test shoots" was this: young male photographer, hip female stylist with rack of clothes, and usually gay hair and makeup artist, all of whom were at least ten years my senior and who loved to coo over my age. "She's so young," they'd say, as if I weren't in the room. "Have you seen that skin? Not a mark on it." After my first couple of shoots, I felt the weird sensation that I wasn't a part of the shoot. I might have been a sweater that the stylist grabbed off her rack, touching the fabric and holding it up to the light, asking, "What do you think about the cut?" I was told to turn left, move slightly toward the right, turn my head down, smile, stop smiling, "Give me more in the eyes," open my lips just the tiniest bit. And then, when I got into whatever weird position they wanted, the group of them would stand there and rip it to shreds. "Her hair's all wrong." "The eyebrows need to be darker." "Can we pin that shirt in the back?" Meanwhile, there was the constant discomfort of the superpowered fans blowing air so hard it made eyes water, and the extreme lighting, reminiscent of a tanning bed except without the protective goggles. It was like the scene in *Zoolander* where Ben Stiller's male-model character is being shouted at by a photographer, "You're a monkey, Derek! Dance, monkey, dance!" while the crew throws bananas at his head. I began to see why models complained endlessly in those magazine interviews, the ones in which the writer always emphasizes that the idea of models' having anything to complain about is a joke. Still, I was willing to submit to the dominatrix demands of the image-makers if it meant a successful career lay ahead.

At thirteen, I started getting work. Magazines that targeted young girls, like *Sassy* and *YM* and *Seventeen*, started using me for editorials, and I got some catalog jobs in between. Unlike test shoots, there were other models at these jobs, girls my age who were also just starting out. And paid shoots had perks apart from the money, like catering and interesting locations. I started to rack up a list of modeling clichés, like the Japanese catalog shoot at which I couldn't understand anything the crew was telling me to do, and the summer clothes fashion shoot that took place on a frozen beach in dead winter. At that beach, as I smiled crazily and leapt into the air about a hundred exhausting times like a ballerina doing *tour jetés*, I felt a deep sense of pride. Humiliation aside, I was a real professional now. Doing ridiculous things in freezing weather in a bikini was a model's life.

At Simon Baruch (Junior High School #104), some of my classmates began to talk to me. In a school where I didn't know anyone or have friends, I now had the respect of strangers, and that was even better than having friends. I didn't want real friends, just books to read and an exciting modeling career. But being recognized as someone important, someone different, felt good. I imagined that teachers might be letting me slack off, that later they would beam at my mom and say, "Oh, well, it's okay. School's not as important when you're a child star."

It was all going along as planned. I was just getting started and sure to go far. For guidance, I prayed at the altars of some established teen models that were my own age but had already struck some kind of stardom lottery. Their names were Milla Jovovich and Niki Taylor, and, at thirteen or fourteen, each of them had already secured big contracts like Cover Girl, and each was already posing for magazine covers, something usually reserved for older models. In fact, Milla had been one of the youngest models ever to do so, gracing the cover of *Lei* (an

Italian fashion magazine) when she was just eleven years old. Because she was my age and modeling at the same time, I followed Milla's career incessantly. She was Russian, and projected a maturity that was unheard of in eleven-year-olds (and, looking back, a Lolita-esque erotic appeal rooted in pedophilia). She claimed to be a reader of Dostoyevsky and even had a reputation for a sort of cockiness and antifashion attitude that made her that much more of a cool rebel in my eyes. *Sassy* magazine wrote mean things about her, saying she was full of herself, that she was a pseudo-intellectual. I just thought it was amazing that a girl my own age could have such an effect on people. The fashion world was alternately fascinated and annoyed by her.

I was in awe, while realizing that she was just a kid like me; it worried me that adults—in fact, a whole industry—would be catty to such a young girl. I started to feel like maybe being famous wasn't a good idea after all. Sure, it made you rich, but it also made you a target. How did Milla feel when she went home at night? I wondered. Where did she go? Did she live with her parents and have to do the dishes? Did she have any friends? Or was she a young loner like me, who went to work every morning feeling alienated in the presence of bitchy fashion queens who talked shit about her behind her back? I vowed that someday, when I got my big break, Milla and I would be friends.

My big break possibility was seriously dented when my family decided to leave New York and move back to Chicago, the city where I was born. It was 1990 and I was fourteen. I fought and cried and refused to speak to my mom for a while. There were a million reasons why I didn't want to leave, and there were a million reasons why Mom decided that we had to, but at the time, I felt like my life was ruined forever. But there was a saving grace: Arlene Wilson Management, a Chicago agency that signed me up and sent me off to work immediately.

The Windy City, home to the famously mohawked Mr. T, is known more for its corridor of cattle butchers than for its place in the fashion world. Because I had a book full of magazine tear sheets, I got some of the best work the city had to offer, which by my teenage New Yorker's standards were the tackiest and most embarrassing jobs I'd ever had. There was an ad I did for Marshall Fields, my hair curled up like a 1950s Jane Russell, with copy that read, HOLIDAY PERM SALE! ALL PERMS 30% OFF! Several times, I was rented off to the Style section of the *Chicago Tribune* to pose with such high-fashion props as a baseball mitt and love beads.

But the best tear sheet I got in Chicago was a photo spread accompanying an article about grunge fashion. The article named sources of fashion inspiration like Primus and Pearl Jam, while in the pictures a scruffy-haired male model flexed his muscles and made bad-boy faces as I, dressed similarly in flannel shirt and Doc Martens, looked up at him adoringly. I guess you were supposed to think he was my boyfriend. In real life, I hated boys and was just a few short years away from figuring out that I was a dyke. Luckily, the article mentioned bands that had women in them, like Babes In Toyland and L7. I reached a breaking point after that shoot. Why was I stuck here, pretending to adore some stupid boy for a meaningless newspaper that no one even read, much less counted on for their style news? If I wasn't going to be a real model, then I might as well be in one of those grunge bands or do something else worthwhile with my life.

I started listening to the bands listed in the article. Slowly, I became as obsessed with music as I had been with models. I wore my Walkman everywhere, listening to cassettes of the Pixies, Pearl Jam, L7, and Metallica. I had always liked hip-hop, too, the music that kids in New York schools listen to, and now I got deeper into it, discovering A Tribe Called Quest and De La Soul. Then I met a girl named Dea and developed a huge crush on her. We soon became best friends, and I followed her every move. She was goth, with dyed black hair shaved off on one side, superpale skin, and blue eyes. She was kind of a weirdo, and I would sit rapt at the foot of her bed as she described her psychic visions and explained that she didn't have to do acid because she was born with dilated pupils and always saw trails. Dea and I would sit in class, sewing spiderwebs into our palms with needles and black thread. She got me into industrial music and noisy stuff like Throbbing Gristle and the Legendary Pink Dots. We were fifteen, so we couldn't go to shows, but there was an all-ages club called Medusa's that catered to little vampires like us.

There were worlds beyond fashion modeling, beyond the blandness of high school in Chicago. Inspired by Dea and the Morrissey-loving kids I started meeting at Medusa's, I transformed. I had a friend shave my hair into a chickenhawk, and we dyed it bright red, inspiring comments like "Hey, Rooster" at school. I cut slashes into my arms, wanting to feel sensations I'd never felt before. I tried acid and other drugs, and spent every non-school moment hanging out near the corner of Belmont and Clark, a hot spot for punk and goth teens and the antiracist skinheads who ruled the alleys of the neighborhood. It was clear that there was more to be learned out in the world, exploring all of these new subcultures that were unveiling themselves to me, than by sitting in a room full of half-asleep kids pretending to memorize facts about geology. School became less and less a part of my new life. Most of the time, I stayed up as late as possible drinking Cisco and Boone's Farm with my punk friends and went to school in a morning daze after no sleep. There was no schedule to anything anymore, just the mania of roaming in packs, ingesting whatever substances we needed in order to keep the energy going until everyone started to crash, at which point I usually caught the El home and fell into a coma until my mom discovered me.

At some point during this lifestyle makeover I had to show up at Arlene Wilson to explain myself. I had just sort of fallen off the radar, no longer contacting the agent to get the week's schedule of open calls and appointments. With a mixture of reluctance and bemusement, I walked into the office and sat in the client chair before my agent's desk. She looked at me, dressed up like Daryl Hannah's punk hookerbot from *Blade Runner*, hair shaved off in random chunks and colored some mushy blend of green, blue, pink, or whatever Manic Panic shade had been left over that week, and fresh razor scars, including the name "Miriam" carved in huge letters into one of my calves. There was a long moment of silence as she solemnly inspected me from head to toe. Her expression was that of a politician who had just been informed that a neighboring country was declaring war on her own—serious and burdened, but resigned to fight. She murmured a couple things about maybe being able to cut all my hair off and cover the cuts. Then, without mincing words, she asked if I wanted to quit. I said yes. We shook hands, and I left the office.

Where modeling had offered a stepladder out of poverty and mediocrity, punk gave me a kind of strength that I had never found anywhere else. As a fashion model I would have joined a wealthy, elite class. But it took about five minutes in the fashion world to see that I hated the idea of a wealthy, elite class, and that I hated the feeling of being the public face of that lifestyle. I also hated being gawked at and depersonalized. Sure, as a punk, I was gawked at, yelled at, harassed, and threatened, but instead of pretending to represent a world I wasn't really part of, I gained an identity that felt like home. As I grew older, that identity deepened as I continued to play in bands, publish zines, and work on feminist projects.

Sometimes I look at the magazines still. I read about teen stars who grew into millionaires, the Lindsay Lohans and Jessica Simpsons of the world, and wonder what I might have become. If I had continued to live in the shadow of Milla Jovovich, would I be starring in action flicks and designing my own line of handbags? I think about how most of the time I can't pay the $560 rent on my house and worry that I made the wrong choice. It would be nice to have Milla's money. But if it meant that I never would have gotten to hitchhike around the country going to protests, hop freight trains, or play in noisy no-wave bands, the chips would still fall in punk's direction. No contest. Sometimes I even forget modeling ever happened.

Being a lesbian, I have a lot of pop culture–obsessed queer friends who watch *America's Next Top Model*. I can't really take it, myself. I get so angry at Tyra Banks and her court of abusive fashion whores; watching them take out their issues on a crop of sensitive, naive young women makes me ill. I yell at the TV screen in the direction of the wannabe models, demanding to know why they put up with the games and bitchy comments. I know that if it were me up there, I would tell Tyra to suck it. Then I remember: That's pretty much what happened.

And there are no real regrets. No matter how often I get tired of being poor, or wish I could get my hands on some Balenciaga, I'm glad I walked out on modeling before it walked all over me.

Prêt-à-Porter

MEGHAN WARD

IT'S MY THIRD show season. My first season I booked one show—I forget what it was—and my second I booked four, so I'm on an upward trajectory. When I call my parents, my dad answers and asks what I'm up to. I tell him I'm in the middle of show castings.

"So that means you'll be modeling the spring collections," he says with an air of pride.

"That's right."

My mom and dad, who buy their clothes from Petite Sophisticate and Sears, respectively, are now in tune with international fashion trends. My dad hands my mom the phone.

"Will you be going on to the London shows next?" she asks. "Or skipping London and going to Milan?"

"Probably Milan," I tell her. My mom has been watching *Style with Elsa Klensch* on CNN. I've seen Elsa, in her thin red lips and thick brown bangs, sitting in the front row of the audience at shows, and my mother has seen me on *Style with Elsa Klensch*—one three-second clip of me walking down the runway in the Hermès show. In the video I'm looking down, not straight ahead, because no one has explained to me yet that the cameras I'm supposed to look at are up *there*, out of sight, not down *there*, where photographers mob the stage around our feet.

"And will you be doing the Tokyo or New York collections this fall?" my mother asks. "I hear polka dots are in."

I hate polka dots. "Tokyo. I'm going to Tokyo," I tell her. I can't wait to go to Tokyo. *Tokyo!* Land of sushi, Godzilla, and samurai! I'll buy a kimono! Drink some sake! Meet a sumo wrestler! They have three alphabets, each with its own script, and I want to learn all three. Marilyn, my agent, doesn't want me to go. She says Tokyo is for second-rate models, and that I should be going to New York instead. But I have no interest in New York, because it's in the United States. The only reason I'm modeling is to (a) see the world and (b) make some money. I want to be one of those lingerie models who goes to Tokyo empty handed and comes back two months later with $60,000 cash stuffed in her boots. With $60,000 I could put a down payment on a three-unit Victorian in San Francisco and rent two of the apartments out while I live in the third and use the rent to pay the mortgage and my tuition at UC Berkeley. Even if I buy just one unit I could get a three-bedroom apartment and rent two of the rooms out while I live in the third. That's what I'm going to do. And I'll learn Japanese in the process. And French, German, Spanish, and Italian. I'll be one of those cosmopolitan diplomats who winters in New Zealand and summers in Provence. I'll decorate each room in my house like a different country—African masks in one room, hand-painted Japanese screens in another, and Indian bedspreads and pillows in a third. I'll collect objects from all over the world—kilims from Turkey, boomerangs from Australia, marionettes from Prague. I can't wait!

It's show casting week, and I'm being sent to see all the prêt-à-porter designers. The haute couture shows took place in July, and I look far too young to do those, so no Chanel or Yves Saint Laurent for me. But I'm perfect for prêt-a-porter—young, modern, and androgynous looking, 5'11" and 122 pounds (I've lost three pounds since I started working out). Etienne, the show booker at my agency, sends me on castings every day. I've been to see the French: Hermès, Gaultier, Claude Montana, Sonia Rykiel. I've been to see the Japanese: Kenzo, Comme des Garçons, Issey Miyake, Yohji Yamamoto. I've been to see the British, Germans, and Italians: Betsey Johnson, Helmut Lang, Enrico Coveri.

Hermès, known for its silk scarves and leather handbags, has me walk up and down the room in a short-sleeved blouse, cotton pedal pushers, and flats. I book the show. At Claude Montana, I'm asked to try on a blue leather jumpsuit. I am instructed to look strong, walk strong, so I try, like a gladiator, but Claude looks bored. I don't book the show. At Enrico Coveri, the clothes are bright and colorful, like Enrico himself. He's a big man, jovial and sweaty. He asks me to walk in a multicolored dress and I do. He hugs me and tells me he loves me, right there onstage. I book the show. At Helmut Lang the clothes are gray, black, and green, camo colors, and again I walk strong, tough. I am perfect for this show and I know it, but Helmut barely notices me. I don't book the show. At Comme des Garçons the clothes are black and white, *only* black and white. I wonder if it's a religious thing, and whether Rei Kawakubo is Buddhist. I meet Rei and she is short, with an angular black bob and ruler-straight bangs. Her asymmetrical skirt hangs down to her ankle on one side, and she doesn't smile or speak any English. She looks at me and nods. I book the show.

At Sonia Rykiel the clothes are conservative and made of lightweight, natural fabrics, the kind my sister buys from Ann Taylor. I try to walk sexy in the high heels they ask me to wear. I cross one foot in front of the other and swing my hips, but I lose my balance and wobble. I don't book the show. At Issey Miyake the clothes are orange, pink, yellow, green. They are made out of an intensely wrinkled synthetic fabric that is Issey Miyake's signature style. They are even sold that way—twisted and knotted into tight little bundles to keep their pleated shape. The material feels crisp against my skin. I love the clothes, and I walk like I'm on the street, no heels and no hips, and I smile, a coy, impish smile. I book the show. I book nine shows in all: Issey, Yohji, Comme des Garçons, Kenzo, Hermès, Cerruti, Michel Klein, Enrico Coveri, and Popy Moreni.

My first show is for Kenzo. Backstage racks of clothes line one side, while rows of hair and makeup tables line the other. Because Meghan Douglas is a rising star, and we have booked many of the same shows, the sign on her rack reads MEGHAN D., the sign on mine, MEGHAN W., and that is how our names are called when it's time for us to line up. At the hair station I see Christian and I am relieved because Christian is the best, the very best, of the hairdressers who do fashion shows. When Christian is on duty, I ask for a trim. He's busy now, but I motion to him, and he puts a hand in the air with his fingers spread: five. Come back in five. He's working on another model's hair, so we're communicating through our reflections in the mirror. Five minutes later, I sit down in Christian's chair. Without a word he begins to cut, the shiny points of the professional hairstyling scissors cold against my temples.

"I heard a complaint about you," he says in his Dutch accent. *A complaint about me?* I'm flattered that I'm well known enough to be complained about. "I heard you are difficult with hairdressers, very difficult."

"Oh." I bow my head.

"Lift your head," Christian says, placing his index finger under my chin. "And uncross your legs. Is it true?"

"What?"

"That you're difficult."

It was true, but I hadn't realized I was so difficult that news had spread among the hairdresser elite. "It's just that I don't have much hair," I tried to explain. "So if it gets messed up, *I'm* messed up." It was true. I was terrified of new hairdressers, and when my hairdresser at Bruno moved to New York I sat white knuckled in the swivel chair while his replacement cut my hair. And I hated it. It was too short around the ears and too square on top. It made me look like a boy.

Finally, Christian smiled. "How's that?"

"Perfect. Thank you," I said, getting up from the chair.

"Hold on. I may as well style you now, while you're sitting here." He lifts a can of Phyto Plage—they love to put Phyto Plage in my hair—squirts a long stream of the sage-smelling oil into the palm of his hand, massages it into my scalp, then slicks it back with a comb—like a boy's. I sigh.

"Thanks," I say, forcing a smile.

"You're never happy."

"That's not true! I just don't always like to look like a boy."

"Androgyny is in. You got those *Glamour* and *Marie Claire* jobs because you look like a boy. You probably got booked for this show because you look like a boy. Don't fight it."

"Okay."

"Don't be difficult."

"I won't." I get up from the chair and walk over to the row of makeup tables, where one row of models is getting makeup done while another row waits in line. In front, on the left, is Christy Turlington. She is stunning, even in person. I stare at her reflection, hoping she won't notice me, wondering if she's had a nose job like I have. Her face is just too perfect, too chiseled, unnatural. She has a calm about her, though, that the other supermodels don't. Between the show coordinator, Yoshi's, barked orders to hairdressers, makeup artists, and hairstylists, I catch pieces of her conversation with supermodel Yasmeen Ghauri. Yasmeen's waist is so tiny in proportion to her broad shoulders that rumor has it she's had two ribs removed to look thinner.

"How are you handling this season?" Yasmeen asks Christy.

"Handling it," Christy responds, as though she can't wait to go home. I try to imagine how hectic her life must be—being chauffeured in a limo from one show to the next, doing two or three shows in one day, having her hair and makeup undone and redone that many times as well. Just when I am starting to feel sorry for Christy and her hectic schedule, I remember that I heard that Versace offered her $40,000 not to do any other shows but his in Milan. $40,000 for one show. I was making $600 for this show. I wonder how much she is making. Probably $5,000. Maybe $10,000. I don't feel sorry for her anymore.

Meghan Douglas sits down next to me. "We need to talk."

"About what?"

"Your name."

"What about my name?"

"You need to change it."

"I do?"

"Look, you're doing all the shows, which means you're going to be a star. It's just too confusing with two Meghans. All this Meghan D., Meghan W. stuff—it's a total pain, and I'm already known by my name. So you need to change yours."

"Change my name? To a completely different name?"

"Yes."

"Like what?"

"I don't know," she shrugs. "Whatever you want." She doesn't say it in an unfriendly way. It's more like she is giving me professional advice, advice that will simplify both of our lives. It's like she is asking me for a favor. Meghan Douglas isn't a supermodel, not yet, but she is a rising star, unlike me. I know I'm not, because in order to be a star you have to want to be a star, and I don't. I really don't care that much about modeling. I just want to see the world, learn some languages, fall in love, and make enough money to go back to school after a few more months. While some of these girls have always dreamed of being models, I am simply biding my time while I earn my California residency so I can attend UC Berkeley.

I take a sip of Evian and scan the room. I know most of the models by name, especially the famous ones: Yasmine Le Bon, Karen Mulder, Yasmeen Ghauri, Beverly Peele, Christy Turlington, Tatiana Patitz, Kirsten Owen, Emma S., and the list goes on. There are twenty girls in all, pretty standard for a show, and although several—Kirsten, Emma, Beverly—are models I've worked with before, none of them are my friends. I retrieve my spiral notebook and pen from my backpack and retreat to the corner of the tent. A model next to me is listening to headphones. Another is meditating in a corner by herself, and another is imitating catalog positions, throwing her head back and smiling a wide-mouthed smile, like she's hysterical with laughter. Two other models giggle. All of them, like me, are smoking cigarettes.

I don't know what to write in my notebook, so I scribble "I don't know what to write" in cursive a few times, then look up. A model compliments Karen Mulder on her Gucci shoes, and Karen says she got them when she did a shoot for *Elle*. I didn't know clients gave clothes away for free, and I'm envious that I'm not good enough, beautiful enough, or well known enough to get free shoes. I bought mine at the local shoe store for $60. They're flat, with thick rubber soles, so I can walk around all day on castings without hurting my feet. But Karen doesn't have to do castings. None of the supermodels do. Their agents messenger their books to clients because they're too busy working all the time.

"Does anyone know algebra?" Beverly asks. She is six feet tall, probably one hundred twenty pounds, and fourteen years old. Unlike me, Beverly does the haute couture shows, Chanel included. With makeup she can pass for twenty-five, but I still look my age—nineteen. Her mother attends most of the shows and sits with her backstage. I'm surprised at how the other models fawn over Beverly's mom. I'm always embarrassed to introduce my mom to my friends because, in her pink knit stirrup pants and her white Keds, she's not exactly a fashion plate. But no one is shunning Beverly's mom. They think she's cute in her sweatshirt and jeans, like a model's giant teddy bear. I wonder if they all miss their moms as much as I do.

"I do!" I call to Beverly, and carry my notebook to where she's sitting. I dropped out of calculus halfway through senior year because I could no longer concentrate on logarithms and limits. I wanted to find myself and explore the world, and Sister Sharon hadn't convinced me that the quadratic formula was on the path to enlightenment.

"How do you multiply 5^6 x 5^7?" Beverly asks, hoping one of the several models who jumped to her aid will know the answer. The other models shrug.

"You add the 6 and 7," I tell her. "So it's 5^{13}, which you can do on your calculator."

"Thanks, Meghan!" Beverly is my friend now. "How about this one—how do you factor (x^2-y^2)?"

"It's (x+y) times (x-y), because when you FOIL (x+y)(x-y), the xy and yx cancel each other out. Like this . . . " I feel so smart helping Beverly with her homework, even though this is eighth-grade-level math. I didn't feel smart back home when I dropped out of calculus with a C. Maybe I could make a career out of this—tutoring models backstage.

No. Most models have either finished high school or have dropped out for good. The only other model I know who is Beverly's age is Kimora, who's with my agency. Kimora is fourteen, too, and she's on her own in Paris with no one to supervise her, and she stays out late, sometimes all night.

"It's time!" Yoshi shouts. "Change into your first outfits!" I turn to see Linda Evangelista racing in, with full makeup and hair, from another show. Christian is flattening her hair and combing it to one side, and Thierry is standing by with a box of tissues and a lipstick brush. I look at my watch: four fifteen. The show was supposed to start at four, which means that they held it for Linda, and which means that hundreds of people—from movie stars to magazine editors—are shifting in their seats waiting for the show to begin.

A waiter carrying a silver platter offers me a glass of champagne. I take it, sipping it, then the music starts. It's George Michael's "Freedom," which is ironic because most of the models in the video are right here in this room. I watch Linda as she lip-synchs the words, dancing, joking around, while Christy smiles silently, apparently amused by Linda's antics. The energy backstage is palpable. The show is about to begin, and I yawn. I yawn and yawn and yawn, like I always do when I'm nervous.

"Don't look so excited," Christian says as he checks my hair one last time. He thinks I'm bored, and I don't correct his misconception.

Kenzo walks down the line, examining each of our outfits to make sure we look perfect before we go onstage. Then the show begins. Linda and Christy go on first, and the audience roars with applause. Then Beverly and Yasmeen, Kirsten, Karen, Tatiana, and . . . me! Yoshi is wearing a headset, shouting orders before the models go onstage. He says something to Tatiana and me, but I can't hear him because the music is too loud and Tatiana is standing between us.

Then he shouts, "Go! Go go go!" I take a deep breath, hold my chin high, and step out onto the runway. Beneath the bright lights, I saunter past the editors of *Vogue, Elle,* and *Marie Claire,* before celebrities like Robert De Niro and Isabella Rossellini, to the foot of the runway, where shutters release like locusts attacking a fresh harvest. My blazer glides seamlessly off my shoulders and down my arms behind my back. With the middle and index fingers of my right hand, I catch it and flip it over my right shoulder. With my left hand on my hip and my left foot thrust to the side, I take a small step forward, spin 180 degrees to the left, pose once more, spin another 180 degrees, pose again, then turn and walk back to the top of the stage, where Tatiana and I turn, pose, and exit off opposite sides.

Backstage, Tatiana yells at me, "You walked off the wrong side!" and I realize that that is what Yoshi must have said: "Both exit right."

"That was the way we rehearsed it," I reply meekly, wondering what difference it makes as long as we don't bump into each other. But Tatiana is already at her rack, throwing her clothes at her dresser, so I race back to my rack, too, where I undress, throwing my clothes on the ground, not at my dresser.

"Meghan! Meghan!" Yoshi is yelling, but I'm wearing nothing but a skirt.

"Vite!" I urge Elise. *"Vite!"* and another dresser comes to her aid. While one ties my shoes and the other buttons my shirt, I pull the sleeves of another jacket up over my arms.

"Meghan!" Yoshi yells. "Meghan!!"

Thierry chases me with a makeup brush while I run toward the stage. Christian quickly resculpts my bangs, while Kenzo yells, "Jacket off! Jacket take off!" He means onstage, at the end of the runway, and I nod. Yoshi pushes me onto the runway, this time alone. When I walk, I realize my shoes are too big, and it's too late to do anything about it. I try to act natural, like I'm not stumbling drunk down the runway, but it's impossible with three-inch heels flopping off my feet. I finally bend down and take my shoes off, then saunter down the runway barefoot, swinging my shoes in one hand as if I meant to do that. That's another lesson I've learned from modeling: Never show you messed up. Always make it look like you meant to do that.

Style Your Own Damn Self

JENNIFER BLOWDRYER

I HAD THIS EVE, as in *All About Eve,* a blond bombshell from Cullman, Alabama, and in endearing moments she'd tell the truth. *All About Eve* is an old movie starring Bette Davis. This younger actress, Eve Harrington, starts coming around, kissing Bette Davis's ass, helping her out, but gradually tries to take over her identity, power, and stardom. Although my power and stardom are of the most tenuous nature, I've had a few of these little Eves, and Claudette was the most amazing one.

She started out by bleaching my hair and working for my friend, and then moved on to my couch, my life, my men, my friends, my shows. Fantastic. Beautiful. She was a driven survivor with many of the qualities of a creep, and used fashion in a uniquely effective way. Claudette transformed herself into a comic book vision of platinum beauty, amping up the Southern accent, the heels, the pouting lips, and shellacking on a patina of gloss that left no hint of the shit background she'd escaped in Cullman, where she had a small daughter to rescue from an idiotic, molestation-prone family.

In Cullman she'd worked on the fantasy retro pinup look, which won her some contest at a putatively upscale sex magazine. Claudette flew to New York City to pick up her prize and never looked back—at least not until she'd snared a bigwig at a comic book empire to finance both her daughter's airfare and her own lavish lifestyle. My couch was a midpoint while she worked that undertargeted market: the comic book geek with money.

Claudette was portrayed in an issue of *Spiderman,* hobnobbed with the almost prescient higher-ups at Troma Entertainment, and snagged that big fish, one she clung to with a passion. Let me just say, in this book on fashion, that fashion is not small. It was her whole mechanism, and it just might have saved her daughter from having an uncle shove a finger up her butt while she lay in a small bed in the South, ineffectively covered by sheets from the local superstore. We were in the bathroom at the Marvel Comics party, Claudette and I looking in the mirror. She was looking glossy; I was a bit too haggard for mingling at a corporate affair in a beautiful Manhattan building. My poverty was showing.

"When you get older, you have to look nice," she commented, hastily adding, "Oh, you're not that age yet; you can still pull it off! But when you're older . . ."

Good point. I looked in the dim mirror and tried valiantly to smooth down my problem hair, Sephardic Jewish frizz and curl, which doesn't hold itself down properly because of my Anglo half, giving it more of a frisée salad appearance when unattended. You know, that hectic-looking lettuce that always sounds good but looks unwieldy, with even the most expensive vinaigrette dressing refusing to coat it properly, never really worth the $8.95.

What Claudette was saying was, *Get on top of that hair situation.* Claudette was beautiful and dangerous, so I took her pronouncement seriously. I don't know what the hell ever happened to old Claudette after that night—eventually something really bad, I think. That night, though, in the corporate bathroom, she was 100 percent correct.

Grooming has always confounded me, and now that I'm middle aged, if I don't smooth down my hair with enough products, the stealth security guard at the Key Food in Woodside, Queens, some retired gentleman with a penchant for low-level skullduggery, will follow me with a lead as short as three and a half feet as I pick up and examine the goods.

But let me start at the beginning. In first grade, at about five or six, I had two dresses to wear. This did not yet make me unhappy. I remember one of the dresses, a muted gray plaid number with a white collar.

"That's a nice dress. Is that the only one you have?" asked an older girl on the school bus, meaning it kindly but giving me one of those tiny social revelations that occasionally enter the life of the societally clueless. Its meaning: "Are you In, or are you ... Out?"

By the third grade, something had gone wrong, or wronger, in my family home. Out I trotted to Hamilton Elementary, with weird purple pants my sister had outgrown and rat's-nest hair. I liked the hand-me-down pants—one pair had wide, orangey stripes—and besides, they belonged to my big sister. Years later I saw a teacher's comment on my report card. She wanted to know why she had to untangle my snarled hair every day.

I had begun to look weird, not pulled together enough, even for a small child. The other kids started calling me a witch, based on my messy appearance. Encouraged, I went to a sleepover at Debbie Viera's and cast a spell on a teacher we didn't like and somebody's brother. Soon the teacher became sick, and the brother died. Watches stopped running when strapped to my pale wrist, silver necklaces turned black the same day I put them on, and I hissed curse words during the Pledge of Allegiance. I had gotten a little power, but not the good kind. I spooked the other kids with my large vocabulary, curse words, snaggly hair, hand-me-downs, and even perhaps my witchcraft.

By about fifth grade I exerted a little more power over my wardrobe, and oh, how I enjoyed it. I adopted a nylon green patterned top with flowing sleeves and a deep neckline. Though I didn't have any cleavage just yet, I was looking forward to it. I piled on as much turquoise as I could appropriate, taking a little something from my sister's private stash, and my pre-product hair spazzed out furiously.

By sixth grade I'd added some thin-ribbed dark blue cords that outlined my plump vagina. What was I thinking? Fashion has always been more like a pull than a thought. How else could I have worn, even for a year, what we used to call Earth Shoes, wide as a boat and confusingly angled up toward the front? Did anybody else have these Earth Shoes? They must have, though I've never seen photographic evidence in these days of endless trend recycling. Perhaps even the unimaginative have a vestige of taste that forbids a public re-airing of the Earth Shoe.

The other night I saw these unfortunate "Crocs" on a woman and, despite her lengthy explanation of their qualities as a good river shoe, I couldn't envision the river in question. They're a really hard sell, or should be: wide, plastic, like clogs but not clogs, spasmodic holes dotting the top. I guess the Earth Shoe will always be with us in some form or another. I thought of them when I saw the new flower-patterned Birkenstocks in the window of Shoe Pavilion, though they don't seem to be catching on.

By ninth grade, my mother and I had left Rhode Island and moved to Berkeley, California, and inappropriate I remained, cast into Berkeley High at the height of African American social studies and whites with backpacks. I remember sitting in a confusing and ill-informed social studies class, vaguely listening to a teacher who was later busted for the negligible crime of selling cocaine to students, and just staring at Yolanda, the bombshell who sat right in front of me. Her toes—goodness, her toes!—beautifully polished, with sandals that were not wide and floppy, her hair pulled back just so, and dark smooth skin with understated makeup, Yolanda was so perfect.

Though petty in other areas, I've always been more fan than foe of my superiors, which frees up a lot of emotional energy. I gazed at Yolanda every day, from the back; I did not think I could become her. Manicures just don't stick on my kind of hands; the next day my cuticles sprout back, the polish peels, those rough edges get jagged all over again.

There was another girl in that social studies class who sat more to my right, Cherie; she spotted an ad for gold jewelry in the magazine I read during class. How could she order *that*, she wanted to know, and I felt such a warm thrill to be a conduit between her and this large gold jewelry, clearly better than small jewelry of any kind. I felt just the same about turquoise jewelry. I could stare for hours at catalogs of necklaces and belt buckles featuring giant slabs of Russian turquoise, a deep, speckled green with a zigzag silver vein running through it; robin's-egg-blue turquoise with a silvery dent at the edge, right near the Native American–style braiding. Unaffordable, beautiful. Cherie, however, went and got some of that big gold jewelry from the magazine. Fashion high-five!

Then my big sister's *Creem* magazine came into my hands, and there was word fashion, wild-ass Lester Bangs and Legs McNeil talking about Johnny Rotten with the beady eyes and acne pits. Sid Vicious said that sex was just two and a half minutes of squishing noise, and I knew that was a grandly reductive statement to make on the world stage of a music magazine. Lester Bangs's words were a story I wanted to jump into so badly that I scribbled ANARCHY on a white T-shirt, ran into another life, and stayed there. Dirk Dirksen's club, the Mabuhay Gardens in North Beach, San Francisco, was my endgame. I was at the beginning of the misfit leap, from wanting to belong but not knowing how, to not giving a fuck and flaunting my difference. Try it.

After a lot of effort my hair got more unnatural. I had it died Liberace silver and cut into a mini bouffant, and ran around in my ANARCHY T-shirt, along with a black slip and ill-fitting shoes purchased at the tiny thrift store right near Berkeley High. This disgusted the other students, all of them: those engaged in African American pride, the brainiacs from decent homes, even the burnouts, who shared a tiny patch of brownish lawn with the Dungeons & Dragoners. Ah, the life of a social exile.

When hardcore punk came in, around 1980, I switched from handcuffs to used prom dresses. Punk rock had turned into an organized sport somehow, with a uniform that included pricey Doc Martens. In 1985, when I moved to New York to go to Columbia University, I was wearing rhinestones, Thrift Town's finest vintage gear, and elf boots. Elf boots? In the low-key earth tones of the upper-class East Coast, I was hopelessly tacky, brassy, sloppy, not real. But this is not an essay of victimhood, dear reader, despite how it began, for I have now assembled the ultimate wardrobe of hope and time, one so confusingly vast that I hesitate to describe it except in the sketchiest of terms.

Some days I like to misappropriate black culture, *Ab Fab*–style, with a velvety non-jogging suit, or perhaps my pearl- and gold-decorated top from Rocawear. Right now I favor the brand Baby Phat. Oh, it is odd, and I have a great time with it. The obsession of the hip-hop brands, the little cat etched in rhinestones or gold, the way they fit a curvy gal, like she shouldn't go hating herself, it all makes me so happy. Baby Phat's founder, a beautiful gold digger called Kimora Lee Simmons, wrote an entire book on her personal style, *Fabulosity*. Get it.

A friend dropped a bunch of beautiful feminine clothes on me when she changed her style and size, and they're mostly from Torrid, a sister company of Hot Topic that provides cute dresses for us plumpers. My friend is now too small for her Torrid wardrobe, but I just go on ahead eating those fries, smokin' in pink sweaters and flouncy dresses, cherries and crinoline in cutely suburban patterns. My large collection of clothing defies the colorless imagination.

You might find me imparting wisdom at a literary reading, wearing a too-tight T-shirt bearing some elite gearhead logo, perhaps sporting a thick silver chain necklace. If it's chilly out, this will all be topped off with a black velour cowboy shirt with leopardette darts on top, from Cargo Cult in Chicago. Excellent store. I have a lot of stuff from independent designers who love me, like TuraLura of Brooklyn. Once I went to London and Lydia Lunch told me to go to a shop in Kensington Market and mention her name. I did, and got a rubber dress at a terrific price. During my commercially beautiful years, I was frequently photographed wearing it at my own fabulous event, a performance series called Smut Fest.

Before my current triumphant style culmination, I had some years, some bad ones, where I'd be walking around Central Park West in gray corduroy flairs and busted flip-flops. Claudette was right about the grooming—cab drivers would ask me if I had money before I could hop in, and a diner in Hell's Kitchen wouldn't even let me in. (Yes, a diner.) I couldn't brush my hair at all, and I got told to move along a whole lot, by police, security, proprietors. If you're too sloppy, you can go tumbling down the stairs, and I did, for a while. That's another kind of fashion, and I will know it forever.

Art in the Heart. Dirt in the Skirt.

RHIANNON ARGO

I FOUND OUT who my barely ex-girlfriend was fucking because I saw this girl wearing her favorite T-shirt in the park. The thing was, it was *my* favorite T-shirt when we were together, so much so that there was a time when I would wear it every day. I was attached to how it was so soft and thin, with the name of the Midwest state she was from lettered across the front, and how it always smelled like her, the real good softness of her.

When she came by my house post-breakup to do the divvying up of belongings, I made sure to have her clothes folded in neat piles waiting for her, except that T-shirt, which I had stuffed deep into the chaotic mess of my dresser. I was hoping she would be so distracted by the nice way I had folded up all her other clothes that she would just politely take her goods and go. It seemed only fair that I should get to keep a memento from my visit to her heartside attraction.

But no, she wanted the shirt back. I tried to offer up all kinds of really good trades—"You can have my Swedish jeans that you love." I was willing to give them to her even though they had my traveling memories worn into the knees. I had traded them for my nuclear reactor hoody that I had gotten on Take Your Daughter to Work Day when I was a kid. I'd gotten to hang around a huge reactor that split atoms, and the sweatshirt was proof of this, but I'd passed it along to a Swedish guy I met in France for the jeans off his floor. They were called Elvis Jeans and you had to go all the way to Sweden to get them, and even if you did go all the way to Sweden, they still wouldn't be the same because you would have to break them in for, like, a year because they were superstiff and too dark at first. The Swedish boy had worn and faded them out just right, in the ass, and the wallet part, and the knees. They looked real good on my ex-girlfriend, better than on me. She would always wear them when she played shows and channeled a bit of Elvis.

So why wouldn't she swap them for the T-shirt? "No, no, I've had that shirt forever," she said. "I got it from someone special."

Special. I thought about that word for a bit while I sat in the park and looked down at the new girl wearing the coveted T-shirt with the lettering stretched out wide across her tits. That was what I called a *special* little trick on my ex's part. I mean, the only way I couldn't have noticed this flaunted property transference was if by some chance the pigeons in the park had all of a sudden contracted some wild and rabid disease and pecked my eyes till I was blind.

Really, what could have easily prevented this situation was every fashionista's essential tool—a good, sharp pair of scissors. No, no, not so I could have cut my heart out, but so I could have snip-snipped and insta-personalized that T-shirt back when I had had the chance. The marvelous thing about scissors is that they can make anything yours, and I'm not talking about shoplifting. I'm talking about reappropriating clothing with a few concise cuts. The real way to never have to give back that boy's T-shirt you love is to completely femme-inize it. Cut the neck off in a scoop if you want it to hang off your shoulders when you're dancing hard; cut in a straight-down V-slice if you want it to be a titty shirt; cut the back into ladder slices and tie knots with each if you want it tighter; cut the sleeves off if you want it tougher; cut across the center if you want a crop-top; or cut it into shreds if you just need to work out some anger.

Snip, snip.

Now whoever liked that shirt as a boy's shirt won't ever ask for it back.

You can start a revolution in any closet with a good pair of scissors. That is why it's always good to keep a pair with you, in your bag or purse. Then you could pretty much wake up anywhere and potentially make yourself a new shirt for the day from any too-big or boxy T-shirt that is lying around at whoever's house. You could even make a dress out of a pillowcase if you wanted something sexier. When I was fourteen I saw this in *Sassy* magazine, and I ended up cutting holes in almost all the pillowcases in my house. That really pissed my mom off, but since she was pretty crafty herself she just sewed my snips up and turned the paisley and checkered-print dresses back into pillowcases.

My mom taught me how to sew and refashion old clothes. When I was little, she turned curtains into shirts, scraps into Halloween costumes, and balls of yarn into warm things. Growing up poor gave me the knack for DIY style that's instilled in kids who learn quick how to make something out of nothing. I got some new clothes when my school gave my family a $50 coupon to Ross as part of a low-income program, but mostly what I made do with were giveaways—sewn-up hand-me-downs, last-ditch clothes, holey homemade clothes, or finds from my mom's thrift store excursions that tended to be extra unique because she had a sense of humor that the kids at school destroyed me for.

The ironic thing is that these kids, who made so much fun of me during my entire school existence, are the ones now sporting the "fake thrifted" look, the vintage dresses sans the authentic smell of Grandma's attic. The other day I cruised through a trendy department store and there were all these shiny, vintage-style thrift dresses, exact replicas of the ones with the $2 price tags at the Salvation Army, but the difference was that these ones were probably made in a sweatshop or something and they smelled all factory-clean. The suburban girls on day shopping trips to the city loved them and were scooping them up regardless of the pricey tags.

That's one of the most hilarious things about current fashion trends—that people like to pretend clothes are used, rugged, cut up, or vintage. A lot of trendy people like to be clean but "pretend" to be dirty. Recently I saw a shirt—like this band one I've had for five years that I got at a last-end thrift dig, perfectly comfy, all black, soft, worn out, and stained—for sale for, like, $60. A closer look reveals that the shirt is really brand spanking new; it's just *dyed* to look dirty and rubbed out by some machine to look worn. WTF? It's okay to look dirty, but only if you paid up the ass for it, and only if you don't actually own up to your own funk. What's so "bohemian" about $5 thrift store cowboy boots bought used on eBay for a hundred bucks?

The only awesome thing about this expensive trend are the rare times real artists get to cash in, like when my friend Sarah makes her rent sitting in her living room all day, sewing up used, oversize clothes. She sews jagged lines on inside-out shirts and cuts them up. She bleaches splotchy splotches on skirts and spray paints and screen-prints dresses until, in the end, they look like they've been caught in the tires of a semi truck and dragged around for twelve hours. She then sells this stuff to fancy shops where girls pay a hundred bucks for a shirt or whatever. People pay a lot for clothes that look crafty, or thrifted, or dirty.

Growing up poor makes it hard to be such a poseur. While the other kids jumped on every new trend—like brand-new skate shoes that never got scuffed, a new goth look from the mall, or a rap shirt because of whatever song on the radio—poor kids got ultracreative with whatever was around. Fashion has also got to have function, because you end up wearing your life on your sleeve, all the rawness of it. You gotta be able to wipe your hands on your clothes. I hate when I see a girl looking superhot in some heels, and then she walks away and she's limping and still trying to work it. Impractical girl clothes ruin all that hotness for me. You gotta be able to run in your heels, even jump a fence if necessary. You gotta be able to sit anywhere in your skirt, on street curbs or on the train platform, or to roll around in the park dirt.

My best friend, Tiger, calls this "Art in the heart. Dirt in the skirt." It's how she likes her girls. It's about working your style hard and owning it. Riding your bike in a miniskirt, wearing your big hair real real big, your stilettos real real high, your fat with your tummy-baring shirts, your gold chains, your sweatbands, your hot neon nail polish, and your flagging bandannas. You just gotta own it and let your life sweat, fuck, and bleed all over it.

I like to let the city dress me up in its love. I know it's a good day when I leave my house and by the time I come back I'm wearing a completely different and more bizarre outfit. All I need for this ultracheap city makeover is those aforementioned scissors, maybe a sewing kit, and definitely a really big bag or purse. The purse is for stowing your finds and carrying around backup accessories, and the scissors and thread are so you never have to care if something is not your size. Free clothing is by far the best retail therapy—all that trashy indulgence without the guilt! It's also a zillion times more fun than shoplifting. Who wants to bother with shoplifting when it's so exhausting to even have to *enter* a corporate store or mall and pretend to shop? Why bother? There's free stuff all around.

A good time for street bargain hunting is Sunday afternoons. This tends to be when people give up on their garage sales and start giving things away or leaving them out for free. One time I found a red vintage slip dress and perfectly matching heels on the street curb with a cute, child-size suit vest lying next to them. It was like they were waiting for me. I hopped off my bike, threw the clothes in the wash, and wore the outfit out that very night dancing at a club. Everyone said it was hot, and I said, "Thanks, I found it in the gutter this morning."

Once, there was a question of where you draw the line. This was when I found a wig in the middle of the street late one night, lying next to a tossed-aside mountain bike. The whole scene got this fantasy started in my head, like, what if the bike thief was wearing the wig and was getting chased by the cops and had to throw the bike and wig down and switch into incognito man-drag to run off? I left the bike because I already had one, but I really wanted the wig. It was so pretty, all long and blond, and I was drunk, so I took it upstairs and washed it with shampoo while leaning over the bathtub.

It wasn't until I had put the sloppy wet wig in my lap and started to brush it out that I thought, *What the fuck am I doing?* I don't know why brushing it out felt weird, when washing it like real hair in the tub hadn't fazed me. Maybe I was starting to sober up. Either way, I had already started the process of making the wig my own, so I had a hard time leaving the poor thing wet and half brushed out. I hung it on the windowsill to dry, and in the morning my roommate was like, "What the fuck is that? What, you found that on the street? Throw it out, throw it out, throw it out!"

I called Tiger. "Do you think I should throw the pretty wig out? I mean, where do you draw the line?"

"Yeah, I guess you have to," she said. "It's not like you used bug shampoo on it or anything." It was sad, but if Tiger, my partner in street-fashion crime, was saying that, then this find truly was scroungy. I didn't throw it out, though. I threw it back in the street, because maybe there was someone who'd wanna wear it out that night.

Besides the street, most of my favorite clothes come to me from giveaway piles, friends, ex-lovers, or the free bin at the strip club I work at. Frequent clothing swapping with friends is essential to keeping your wardrobe exciting. It's also always fun to stop by someone's house if they are moving, because they probably will be getting rid of a lot of clothes. That's one way I might come home wearing a new outfit, like when I stopped by Lacey's house and she was cleaning out the back room because her roommate had left town suddenly. I helped her out, and later we cut some stretchy striped tube tops into skirts.

That was also the day I found this boy's hoody with a Camp Trans drawing on it. I could see the traveling tales thick in the seams. I imagine that the just-skipped-town high-femme roommate probably threw the hoody onto the dirty ground to sit and sleep on, and maybe she even got fucked in the woods on it. I took it home and reworked it for the next few days. I sewed a new patch over the old drawing, from these scraps of fabric I snipped off an old skirt. I also gutted the hoody by cutting slices up all the seams and sewing it real tight on all sides, so it fit like a sausage casing, which also lengthened the sleeves, which I turned into really useful multipurpose gloves.

Someday I might run into the girl who used to own that hoody. I bet her smile will be full of nostalgia, like I'm wearing her memory and waving it like a sweet flag that keeps it alive. Maybe one day it will be passed on to another girl's scissors, or dug from a bag of clothes on the street, or die a shredded death as a small casualty of a love affair. But for now it's mine, a new hoody for me that's ready to huddle through the night and collect new stories like dirt.

Acknowledgments

THANKS TO Jill Rothenberg for instigating this project and to Brooke Warner for shepherdessing it through till the end; and thanks to everyone at Seal for their overall awesomeness. The editor also wishes to express deep gratitude to all who have served as inspirations and guides as she has struggled through time to learn to dress herself outrageously but not like a complete clown: Kathleen Black, Tara Perkins, Alexis Persyko, Jessica Lanyadoo, Clint Catalyst, Heather Haynes, Sash Sunday, Laurenn McCubbin, and Shar Rednour, to name but a teensy few. A special thank-you to Rocco Kayiatos for the Hipposchemes and Diane von Furstenberg dresses, the lady-purse, and the love.

About the Contributors

RHIANNON ARGO is a writer whose stories have been published in the *Lowdown Highway* anthology, *Baby Remember My Name,* and in her own handmade chapbooks. In 2007 she took her tales on the road with the new wave of Sister Spit. She spends most of her free time trying to make a novel out of fifteen cents. She really loves when tenny shoes (and many other articles of clothing) have secret hidden pockets that she can stuff with impromptu napkin poems.

ADELE BERTEI is a storyteller who continues to work in many mediums. She resides in Los Angeles and is currently near completion on her first book, a memoir.

JENNIFER BLOWDRYER, slave name Jennifer Waters, is fry-coastal, commuting between NYC and the Bay Area. Her most recent book is *Good Advice for Young Trendy People of All Ages,* and she dreams of being a college lecturer without having to change a thing about her naturally flashy appearance. She is an availabilist who can be contacted at www.jenniferblowdryer.com.

KATE BORNSTEIN is a fashion-conscious author, playwright, and performance artist whose latest, most fashionable book is *Hello, Cruel World: 101 Alternatives to Suicide for Teens, Freaks, and Other Outlaws.* Other published works that remain in fashion after many years include the books *Gender Outlaw: On Men, Women and the Rest of Us* and *My Gender Workbook.* Kate's books are taught in more than 120 of the most fashionable colleges and universities around the world, and ze has performed hir work live on college campuses and in theaters and performance spaces of high fashion across North America, Europe, and Australia.

MARY CHRISTMAS is a freelance writer in Portland, Oregon. Her friends are pretty entertained by her illustrious past as a *Sassy* magazine model and by her completely implausible claims of being "soft butch." Mary lives in a tiny, weird cottage with wood paneling all over the inside, where she plays drums and spends an unhealthy amount of time reading books about yoga, Buddhism, and gay sex.

SHERILYN CONNELLY is a San Francisco–based writer. She's read at shows such as "K'vetsh," "The Unhappy Hour," "Siren," Ladyfest Bay Area, the TGSF Cotillion, "TransForming Community," and the UC Berkeley production of *The Vagina Monologues.* Her words can be found on paper in *I Do, I Don't: Queers on Marriage, Good Advice for Young Trendy People of All Ages, Girlfriends, Morbid Curiosity,* and *Instant City.*

DIANE DI PRIMA lives and works in San Francisco, where she teaches privately. She has published forty-three books of poetry and prose, among them *Loba,* books I and II; *Recollections of My Life as a Woman;* and *Pieces of a Song.* A new, expanded edition of her *Revolutionary Letters* is available from Last Gasp. Diane received the 2006 Fred Cody Award for lifetime achievement and community service from the Northern California Book Reviewers.

CINDY EMCH is a poet, performer, curator, and all-around community-building hellraiser. She splits her roots between the deep woods of the peninsulas of upper Michigan and the farm towns of lower Michigan. She has called San Francisco home since 1998. She founded the Queer Open Mic at the Three Dollar Bill Café (San Francisco) in 2003. She has published five chapbooks, has written for the Hillgirlz.com blog and a variety of film and pop culture mags, and has been published in *Lodestar Quarterly*.

DEXTER FLOWERS is a Portland writer. She spends most of her time digging up awkward stories from her childhood, reveling in fantastical eccentricities and sentimental moments, and running away with the circus. Dexter has a zine titled *maybe it was something you ate*. Dexter is currently in the process of writing two books: one about growing up with a single mom who was a feminist witch on food stamps, and another a fictional book about teenagers growing up in a group home. Dexter uses dark humor, as well as compassion, to lead readers through surprising and sometimes difficult circumstances.

ELLEN FORNEY has been a freelance cartoonist and illustrator since 1992 and a comics professor at Cornish College of the Arts since 2002. Her most recent book, *I Love Led Zeppelin,* is a collection of her comics from newspapers such as *LA Weekly* and *The Stranger,* magazines such as *BUST* and *Oxford American,* and various comic anthologies. She is currently working on a novel with Sherman Alexie for Little, Brown, and on a book collection of her weekly comic, "Lustlab Ad of the Week," with Fantagraphics.

LAURA FRASER is the author of the best-selling travel memoir *An Italian Affair.* She is a longtime freelance writer from San Francisco who has written for lots of magazines, including *MORE, O, The Oprah Magazine,* the *New York Times, Glamour, Self,* and *Vogue.* Though she writes for fashion magazines, she has never actually written about fashion before. She recently purchased a new pair of cowboy boots, with inlaid turquoise, and believes they will never go out of style.

Nicole J. Georges is an illustrator, educator, zinester, and pet-portrait artist living in Portland, Oregon. Voted Miss Specs Appeal 2006 by *Hey Four Eyes!* magazine, Georges is best known for her work in the autobiographical comic zine *Invincible Summer.* Nicole teaches children the power of self-publishing through the Independent Publishing Resource Center and can be found absentmindedly walking the perimeter of her home with two dogs and three pet chickens in hot pursuit.

Jewelle Gomez (www.jewellegomez.com) has published seven books, including *43 Septembers,* a collection of personal essays. She's a lesbian/ feminist activist who wants everyone to be angry and do something about the thousands of poor and colored people in New Orleans who still have no electricity or water after Katrina!

Kim Gordon is a founding member of the rock band Sonic Youth. Her visual and installation art has been shown all over the planet. She created and designed clothing for the brand X-girl. She wrote, directed, and appeared in the film/live music event Perfect partner, and appeared in Gus Van Sant's *Last Days,* as well as the season six finale of *Gilmore Girls.*

Samara Halperin is a filmmaker and writer whose movies have been making audiences laugh, cry, and scream in screenings from Australia to Saskatchewan since 1989. Samara loves sneakers, palm trees, and pencil tops shaped like fruit people; Samara hates eggs, opossums, and the religious Right (although she does like the Pope's red Prada slippers).

Samara's ultimate fashion icons: Ralph Furley on *Three's Company*, Little Edie Bouvier-Beale, and Quentin Crisp. Samara's writing has appeared in *Cometbus* and *Lowdown Highway*. She has been a featured writer at the RADAR reading series, "K'vetsh" queer open mic, the Porchlight storytelling series, the "Pages from the Past" reading series, the San Francisco Street Theater Festival, and "Homo A Go Go."

TARA JEPSEN is a writer and performer from San Francisco. She has been hosting the award-winning queer open mic "K'vetsh" for more than six years. Her most recent film, *Diving for Pearls*, won the Most Innovative Short award at the Seattle Lesbian and Gay Film Festival. She has been featured at the Porchlight storytelling series, at the RADAR reading series at the San Francisco Public Library, and at Litquake. Her story "Swimming with the Dolphins" was published in the anthology *Pills, Thrills, Chills, and Heartache*. She is at work on a novel entitled *Like a Dog*.

BETH LISICK is the author of three books. *Monkey Girl* is partly poetry, *This Too Can Be Yours* is mostly fiction, and *Everybody into the Pool* is a collection of personal essays and stories. Beth has a comedy duo with Tara Jepsen, in which much of the comedy derives from looking pretty terrible and/or being naked. She never knew why fashion made her so anxious until she tried writing the piece that appears in this book.

FELICIA LUNA LEMUS is the author of the novels *Like Son* and *Trace Elements of Random Tea Parties*. She lives in the East Village in Manhattan.

ALI LIEBEGOTT has published two books: *The Beautifully Worthless* and *The IHOP Papers*. *The Beautifully Worthless* won a Lambda Literary Award in Debut Fiction. Currently she's finishing an illustrated novel, called *The*

Crumb People, about a post-9/11 obsessive duck-feeder. Even though she has a big heart, she hasn't found a way to embrace people who litter.

SANDRA TSING LOH is a writer/performer whose solo shows include *Mother on Fire, Sugar Plum Fairy, I Worry, Aliens in America*, and *Bad Sex with Bud Kemp.* Sandra's books include *A Year in Van Nuys, Aliens in America, Depth Takes a Holiday: Essays from Lesser Los Angeles*, and a novel, *If You Lived Here, You'd Be Home By Now*, which was named by the *Los Angeles Times* as one of the one hundred best fiction books of 1998. Her story "My Father's Chinese Wives" received a 1997 Pushcart Prize and was featured in the 1999 Norton Anthology of Short Fiction. She and her husband, Mike Miller, composed the music for Jessica Yu's documentary short *Breathing Lessons*, which won an Oscar in 1998. Her 1989 solo piano CD is *Pianovision*, songs from which still surface occasionally here and there as "buttons" on public radio. She has been a regular commentator on NPR's *Morning Edition* and on Ira Glass's *This American Life.* Currently, KPCC (89.3 FM in Los Angeles) broadcasts her daily segment, "The Loh Down on Science," and her weekly segment, "The Loh Life." American Public Media's "Marketplace" broadcasts her monthy segment, "The Loh Down." She is currently a contributing editor for *The Atlantic Monthly* and was a 2006 finalist for the National Magazine Award.

EILEEN MYLES is one of the best-known unofficial poets in America. Read her weekly blog on art at http://openfordesign.msn.com. In 1992 Eileen conducted an openly female write-in campaign to be president of the United States. She's toured all over the world and with Sister Spit in 1997 and now 2007 again. *Sorry, Tree* (poems) was released in April 2007 from Wave Books. Eileen lives in So Cal and New York and teaches mainly at the University of California, San Diego.

PARISA PARNIAN is an Iranian American fashion designer, performance artist, and social catalyst whose work concentrates on the concept of being an outlaw in society, whether that be defined by one's sexuality, gender, religious affiliations, or nationality. Whether on a stage performing her one-woman show, *Dirty Phoenix and the Asses of Evil Show*, or presenting her latest line of subversive style through her indie fashion label, RIGGED OUT/FITTERS, Parisa's aim is to challenge and question society's concepts of beauty, desirability, normalcy, and safety. You can check out her designs or contact her at www.riggedoutfit.com.

DEBBIE RASMUSSEN grew up in Minneapolis, a city that still claims her heart. She's been active in queer, labor, anarchist, and animal rights movements almost all her life. She's the publisher of *Bitch: Feminist Response to Pop Culture*, although she's kept the name of the magazine a secret from her grandma.

Herstorian TRINA ROBBINS writes about women: women who draw comics, women who kill, women from Ireland, women who happen to be goddesses. She lives in a moldering 102-year-old house with her cats, shoes, books, and dust bunnies. She is the thrift shop queen of San Francisco.

JENNY SHIMIZU is a model/mechanic with an endless supply of possibilities. She is currently training for "motogiro" and is always looking for love.

JILL SOLOWAY was co–executive producer and writer on *Six Feet Under* for four years. Since then, she has written the film *Tricycle*, which she will direct, and adapted the book *Pledged* for the big screen. She has written two books: a memoir, *Tiny Ladies in Shiny Pants*, and a novella, *Jodi K*. Before all that, Jill cocreated the theatrical phenom *The Real Live Brady*

Bunch and the still-running "Sit 'n' Spin," a night of music and essays at the Comedy Central Stage.

CHELSEA STARR lives in San Francisco, where she writes stories, makes clothes, and throws a superfun queer dance party called "Hot Pants."

LAURIE STONE is author of the novel *Starting with Serge*, the memoir collection *Close to the Bone*, and *Laughing in the Dark*, a collection of her writing on comic performance. A longtime writer for *The Village Voice*, she has been theater critic for *The Nation*, critic-at-large on National Public Radio's *Fresh Air*, a member of The Bat Theater Company, and a regular writer for *Ms.*, *New York Woman*, and *Viva*. She has published numerous memoir essays in such publications as *Ms.*, *TriQuarterly*, *The Threepenny Review*, *Speakeasy*, and *Creative Nonfiction*. Her short fiction and nonfiction appears in the anthologies *Full Frontal Fiction; Money, Honey;* and *The Other Woman;* and her reviews can be seen in the *Los Angeles Times, The Washington Post*, the *Chicago Tribune*, and *Newsday*.

SILJA J. A. TALVI is an investigative journalist, essayist, and senior editor for *In These Times*. Her book *Women Behind Bars* will be released by Seal Press in fall 2007. Talvi's work has appeared in more than seventy-five newspapers and magazines nationwide, ranging from *High Times* to *The Nation*, as well as several book anthologies, including *Body Outlaws; The W Effect: Bush's War on Women; Prison Nation;* and *Prison Profiteers*. In 2006, Talvi was awarded a national New American Ethnic Media Award for immigration-related reporting, as well as her second consecutive national PASS Award from the National Council on Crime and Delinquency for excellence in criminal justice magazine reporting. She is also the recipient of twelve regional Pacific Northwest SPJ Awards for excellence in journalism. She still applies lipstick or lip gloss every morning, even if she's just hanging out with her cat on her living room couch.

FRANCES VARIAN is a writer and performance artist based in San Francisco. Her work has been featured in *Without a Net: The Female Experience of Growing Up Working Class*, *Vox Populi*, and *Lodestar Quarterly*. Her essay "Getting Out" will appear in the forthcoming *Women: Images & Realities, A Multicultural Anthology*, fourth edition. During the 2004 Bumbershoot Arts Festival, she debuted a feature-length poem dedicated to the victims of Gary Ridgway, the Green River Killer, which she choreographed to the opera *Carmen*. She has been reading and performing in bars, bookshops, theaters, parks, and schools along the West Coast since 1998.

MEGHAN WARD is a freelance writer and editor at work on her first book, a memoir titled *Paris on Less Than $10,000 a Day*. Meghan worked as a high-fashion model in Europe and Japan from 1988 to 1994, before returning to the United States to attend UCLA and pursue a career as a journalist. She has written hundreds of news and feature articles for various publications, including the *San Francisco Examiner* and *The Oakland Tribune*, and she holds an MFA in creative writing from Mills College. She lives in Berkeley, California, with her husband and two cats.

CINTRA WILSON, culture critic for Salon.com, is the author of *A Massive Swelling: Celebrity Re-Examined as a Grotesque Crippling Disease* and the novel *Colors Insulting to Nature*. She publishes a daily blog at www.cintrawilson.com, where viewers may also download the video and audio podcasts of her regular column, "The Dregulator: Bi-Monthly Lowlights of the Yellow Press."

COOKIE WOOLNER is the former editor of the seminal riot grrrl–era zine *Girl Fiend*, the former drummer for the infamous girl band Subtonix, and one half of the burlesque duo The Chainsaw Chubbettes. She is now climbing the ivory tower, where she researches and writes about weird and wonderful ladies of the stage, and she is a fierce advocate for freaky fat chicks everywhere and always.

MARY WORONOV is a painter (her first love) and the author of six books: *Wake for the Angels,* short stories illustrating her paintings; *Swimming Underground,* a fictional memoir of her time at The Factory; *Eye Witness to Warhol,* essays on questions she is tired of answering; the novels *Snake* and *Niagara;* and her new book of short stories, *Blind Love.* Living in L.A., she also has written and directed three half-hour TV shows for *Women's Stories of Passion* on Showtime. From 1980 to 2003, she acted in more than seventy-three Hollywood films, acquiring the dubious title of cult queen thanks to films like *Chelsea Girls, Eating Raoul, Rock 'n' Roll High School,* and Warner Bros.' *Looney Tunes.* She now teaches graduate fiction at Otis College of Art + Design.

KAT MARIE YOAS is a twenty-three-year-old queer working-class warrior/ performer/writer/lady about town. Kat performs spoken word and stories by herself and improv comedy with a gang of ladies. When she is not skipping stones, making videos with her love, or dancing with pals, you can also find Kat articulating her intense love of pizza—through impromptu monologues or more conventional means (eating). Kat has copies available of her story/chapbook entitled "Perfect Endings: Fresh Stories and Rotten Characters." You should write her for a copy: kat.marie.yoas@gmail.com.

© LYDIA DANILLER

About the Editor

MICHELLE TEA is the author of several books, including the Lambda-winning *Valencia* and the illustrated *Rent Girl*. Her novel, *Rose of No Man's Land,* was declared "impossible to put down" by *People* magazine. Her writing has been published in *The Believer, The Best American Erotica, The Best American Nonrequired Reading,* and *The Outlaw Bible of American Literature.* She was voted Best Local Writer of 2006 by both *SF Weekly* and *The San Francisco Bay Guardian.* Tea is a founder of the all-girl performance happening Sister Spit, and artistic director of Radar Productions, a nonprofit that stages underground, queercentric literary events in the Bay Area and beyond.

Selected Titles from Seal Press

For more than thirty years, Seal Press has published groundbreaking books. By women. For women. Visit our website at www.sealpress.com.

Single State of the Union: Single Women Speak Out on Life, Love, and the Pursuit of Happiness edited by Diane Mapes. $14.95, 1-58005-202-9. Written by an impressive roster of single (and some formerly single) women, this collection portrays single women as individuals whose lives extend well beyond Match.com and Manolo Blahniks.

We Don't Need Another Wave: Dispatches from the Next Generation of Feminists edited by Melody Berger. $15.95, 1-58005-182-0. In the tradition of *Listen Up*, the under-thirty generation of young feminists speaks out.

The Chelsea Whistle by Michelle Tea. $14.95, 1-58005-073-5. In this gritty, confessional memoir, Michelle Tea takes the reader back to the city of her childhood: Chelsea, Massachusetts—Boston's ugly, scrappy little sister and a place where time and hope are spent on things not getting any worse.

Valencia by Michelle Tea. $14.95, 1-58005-035-2. A fast-paced account of one girl's search for love and high times in the dyke world of San Francisco. By turns poetic and frantic, Valencia is a visceral ride through the queer girl underground of the Mission district.

Word Warriors: 25 Women Leaders in the Spoken Word Revolution edited by Alix Olson, foreword by Eve Ensler. $15.95, 1-58005-221-5. This groundbreaking collection of poems and essays, the first all-women spoken word anthology, features the most influential female spoken word artists in the movement.

Rock Your Stars: Your Astrological Guide to Getting It All by Holiday Mathis. $14.95, 1-58005-217-7. In the lively and intelligent *Rock Your Stars*, syndicated columnist and "rock 'n' roll astrologer" Holiday Mathis offers a modern manual to making every life decision, whether it's what to wear, who to love, which career ladder to climb, what color to paint the bedroom, or how to find the right exercise plan—all by using astrology as a practical guide.